REAL WORLD
PRINT
PRODUCTION

CLAUDIA McCUE

PEACHPIT PRESS
BERKELEY, CALIFORNIA

REAL WORLD PRINT PRODUCTION
Claudia McCue

Peachpit Press
1249 Eighth Street
Berkeley, CA 94710
510/524-2178
800/283-9444
510/524-2221 (fax)

Find us on the Web at: www.peachpit.com
To report errors, please send a note to errata@peachpit.com

Peachpit Press is a division of Pearson Education

Editor: Nancy Raiken
Project Editor: Becky Morgan
Production Editor: Lisa Brazieal
Technical Editor: Premedia Systems
Proofreader: Haig MacGregor
Compositor: WolfsonDesign
Indexer: Colleen Dunham Indexing
Cover design: Aren Howell

ISBN 0-321-41018-1

9 8 7 6 5 4 3 2 1

Printed and bound in the United States of America

For my mother, who taught me to love words.
And for my North Star.

CONTENTS AT A GLANCE

Preface..**xvii**

Chapter One: Life Cycle of a Print Job..**1**

Chapter Two: Ink On Paper..**27**

Chapter Three: Binding and Finishing..**51**

Chapter Four: Preparing Raster Images..**77**

Chapter Five: Vector Graphics...**97**

Chapter Six: Fonts..**107**

Chapter Seven: Cross-Platform Issues...**119**

Chapter Eight: Job Submission...**125**

Chapter Nine: Photoshop Production Tips..................................**143**

Chapter Ten: Illustrator Production Tips....................................**165**

Chapter Eleven: FreeHand Production Tips................................**189**

Chapter Twelve: InDesign Production Tips.................................**217**

Chapter Thirteen: QuarkXPress Production Tips.......................**263**

Chapter Fourteen: Acrobat Production Tips...............................**287**

Appendix: Print Production Resources..**319**

Index..**335**

TABLE OF CONTENTS

Preface ....**xvii**

Chapter One: Life Cycle of a Print Job 1

The Olden Days 1

Brave New World: Desktop Publishing 3

Job Submission 4

Scenic Tour of a Typical Printing Plant 4

    Sales 6

    Customer Service 6

    Planning, Estimating, and Scheduling 6

    Preflight 7

    Prepress 8

        Production 8

        Scanning 9

        Image Work 9

        Raster Image Processor (RIP) 9

        Trapping 11

        Imposition 11

        Proofing 11

        Corrections 12

    Creating Plates 12

    Pressroom 13

    Finishing 14

        Trimming 14

        Folding 14

        Stitching 14

        Die Cutting 15

        Binding 15

        Gluing 15

    Fulfillment and Shipping 16

    Glossary of Printing Terms 17

Chapter Two: Ink On Paper **27**

  Fundamentals of Black-and-White Printing...27

  Fundamentals of Color Printing 30

    Limitations of CMYK 33

    Spot Colors 34

    Approximating Spot Colors with Process 35

  Press Issues 36

    Registration 36

    Trapping 37

    Large Ink Coverage Areas 38

      Rich Black 39

      Problem Inks 40

      Specialty Inks 41

      Custom Mixed Inks 41

      Coatings and Varnishes 42

  Digital Printing 43

    Digital Printing Advantages 43

      Short Runs 43

      Variable Data 44

    Digital Printing Issues 44

      Registration 45

      Spot Colors on Toner-Based Digital Presses 45

      Paper Requirements and Limitations...46

      Cracking and Flaking 46

      Resolution and Screen Ruling 46

  Your Monitor is Not Made of Paper...47

    A Quick Overview of Color Management...47

    Control Your Environment 48

    Realistic Expectations...49

    Contract Proofs 50

Chapter Three: Binding and Finishing...**51**

  One Size Does Not Fit All 51

    Rule Number One: Build to the Correct Trim Size 52

    Rule Number Two: Provide Bleed 54

    Rule Number Three: Stay Away From the Edge...................................55

    Rule Number Four: Follow the Print Specifications.............................55

  Folding: High-Speed Origami 56

Imposition 58
  Basic Imposition 59
  Multipage Imposition 60
Binding Methods 65
  Saddle Stitching 65
  Perfect Binding and Case Binding 65
  Comb Binding 67
  Coil Binding 68
  Other Binding Methods 68
Moving Beyond Two Dimensions 69
  Die Cutting 71
  Embossing 73
  Foil Stamping 75

Chapter Four: Preparing Raster Images **77**
Ancient Times: B.P. (Before Pixels) 77
Now: A.P. (All Pixels, All the Time) 78
  Scanners 78
  Digital Cameras 79
  Imaging Software 79
Resolution and Image Fidelity 80
  Scaling Up 81
  Scaling Down 82
  Planning Ahead 82
  Digital Photographs 84
  Cropping and Transforming Images 84
    Cropping 84
    Rotating Images 85
    Where to Transform: Image Editor versus Page Layout Application 86
Appropriate Image Formats for Print 86
  TIFF 87
  Photoshop EPS 87
  Photoshop Native (PSD) 88
  Photoshop PDF 88
  Moving to Native PSD and PDF 89
  Special Case: Screen Captures 90
    Converting Screen Captures to CMYK 92
  RGB versus CMYK 94
  Inappropriate Image Formats for print 95

Chapter Five: Vector Graphics..**97**

   Vector File Formats 97

      Encapsulated PostScript (EPS) 97

      Native File Formats..99

      PDF 100

      Vector Formats Not Appropriate for Print 100

         Microsoft Windows Metafile Format (WMF)............100

         Enhanced Metafile Format (EMF) 101

         Raster Formats 101

   Handling Text 101

      Embedding Fonts 101

      Outlining Text 102

   Incorporating Images into Vector Files 103

   Avoiding Unnecessary Complexity..104

      Simplify Your Paths..104

      Recommended Approaches to Document Construction ..105

         One Piece Per Page..105

         It's a Drawing Program..106

         Creating Multiple Pages in Illustrator......................106

         Creating Multiple Pages in FreeHand 106

Chapter Six: Fonts..**107**

   Font Flavors..107

      PostScript (Type 1) Fonts..107

      TrueType Fonts..108

      OpenType Fonts 109

      Macintosh OS X System Fonts..111

      Windows System Fonts..112

      Multiple Master Fonts 112

      Substituting One Font Species For Another 113

   Activating Fonts in the Operating System............................113

      Apple Font Book 113

      Windows Control Panel..114

   Font Management Programs 114

      Automatic Font Activation..115

      Font Conflicts..115

Font Licensing Issues 116
    End User License Agreements (EULAs) 116
    Embedding Fonts in PDFs 117
    Converting Text To Outlines 118
    Sending Fonts to the Print Service Provider 118

Chapter Seven: Cross-Platform Issues **119**
Crossing The Great Divide 119
File Naming 120
    Let's Have a Lot of Brevity 120
    Filenames Don't Need Punctuation. Period. 121
    Watch Your Language 122
    Include File Extensions 122
Fonts 123
Graphics Formats 124

Chapter Eight: Job Submission **125**
Preparations During the Design Process 125
Talking with the Printer 126
Planning for Print 128
    Checking Raster Images 129
    Checking Vector Artwork 130
    Checking Page Layout Files 131
Sending Job Files 132
    Submitting PDF Files 133
    Submitting Application Files 133
        Platform Issues 135
        Sending Files 135
Preparing for Proofing Cycles 136
    Checking Image Proofs 136
    Checking Page Proofs 138
    Checking Corrections 139
    Checking Imposed Bluelines 139
    Signing Off on Proofs 140
Attending a Press Check 140

Chapter Nine: Photoshop Production Tips 143

Off to a Good Start 143
Know the Fate of the Image 143
Image Resolution...145
Color Space..145
Converting RGB to CMYK 146
Working in Layers 146
Don't Erase that Pixel! 147
Color Corrections with a Safety Net 148
Should You Flatten a Layered File? 148
Transparency..149
Silhouettes and Masking...150
Creating a Path: Right and Wrong 151
Path Flatness Settings 152
Paths that Aren't Clipping Paths...153
Alternative Silhouetting Methods 154
Beyond CMYK..156
Creating Duotones 156
Adding Spot Color to a CMYK Image 158
Beyond Pixels 159
Vector Elements...159
Saving as a Photoshop PDF 161
Saving for Other Applications...163

Chapter Ten: Illustrator Production Tips 165

Why Versions Matter..165
Saving For Earlier Versions...170
Quirks in Save Dialogs 170
Document Color Mode 171
Simplifying Complex Artwork...172
Using Filters and Effects...174
Filter versus Effect: Vector Shapes 174
Filter versus Effect: Generating Pixels 175
Using Filter > Stylize > Drop Shadow 175
Using Effect > Stylize > Drop Shadow 177
Document Raster Effects Settings..178

Creating 3D Artwork...179

Transparency...180

Flattening Transparency...181

Linked and Embedded Images...184

Blended Objects..185

Changes in Pantone Recipes..186

Saving for Other Applications...187

Chapter Eleven: FreeHand Production Tips...**189**

Fonts and Graphics...189

    Keeping It All Together...190

        Font Handling...190

        Images: Link or Embed?...191

        Modifying Linked Images...192

        Importing Images..193

        Importing Multiple Images Simultaneously..193

        Suitable Image Formats..194

        Special Handling: DCS Images..194

        Scaling Imported Images..194

        Importing or Opening Adobe PDF Files..195

Special Effects..195

    Live Vector Effects..196

    Live Raster Effects..196

    Lens Effects...198

    Special Fills and Strokes...199

        Gradient Fills..199

        Pattern Fills..199

        PostScript Fills...200

        Textured Fills..202

        Tiled Fills...202

        Custom Fills...204

        Custom Halftone Settings..204

    Extrude, Smudge, and Shadow..205

Simplifying complex artwork...206

    Clean House..206

    Smooth and Simplify..206

    Trim Off the Fat...207

Exporting Freehand Files..207

Exporting Raster Formats 208

Exporting Vector Formats 208

Providing Correct Bleed for Export..210

Exporting Documents Containing Multiple Pages...................................211

Exporting PDF Files..212

Exporting Directly to PDF 212

Print to Adobe PDF 213

Chapter Twelve: InDesign Production Tips..**217**

Graphics..217

Placing Graphics..217

There's *Good* Drag and Drop... 218

... and There's *Bad* Drag and Drop 219

Copy and Paste 221

Embedding and Unembedding Graphics..221

Updating Missing or Modified Graphics 222

Finding Missing Graphics..223

Updating Modified Graphics..224

Replacing Current Graphics...224

Editing Graphics..224

Transforming Graphics 225

Using Native Files 227

Photoshop Native Files (PSD) 227

Drop That Shadow..227

InDesign CS2: Object Layer Options...229

Illustrator Native Files (AI) 230

PDF Files as Artwork 231

Swatches...231

Stubborn Swatches..233

What to Do About All Those Extra Swatches 233

Ink Manager..235

Colorizing Images 237

Converting Legacy QuarkXPress and PageMaker Files 238
  Preparing for Conversion 238
  What to Expect..239
    PageMaker Conversion Issues...240
    QuarkXPress Conversion Issues 241
    Cleaning Up 242
    When *Not* to Convert Legacy Files...242
General Document Issues 243
  IDLK Files...243
  Automatic Recovery 243
  Going Back in Time 244
  Reducing File Size 244
  Let It Bleed 244
  One Size Fits All: Layout Adjustment 246
  Checking Out of the Library..246
Transparency...247
  Transparency Flattening 247
    Put Text on Top 248
    Choose the Appropriate Transparency Blend Space 248
    Choose the Appropriate Transparency Flattener Preset..249
    Invoking Transparency Flattener Presets 252
    Special Case: Spot Color Content...252
    Spot Colors and Transparency: Overprinting at the Print Service Provider 254
    Drop Shadows: The Sun Never Moves 255
Finding & Fixing Problems 256
  Forensic Tools..256
  Info Palette...258
  Preflight and Package 259
PDF Creation Methods 260
PDF Creation Settings...261

Chapter Thirteen: QuarkXPress Production Tips 263

Versions 263
  Saving QuarkXPress 6.5 Files to Earlier Versions 264
    Synchronized Text 264
    Projects: Convert to Individual Documents...................................264
    Font Issues 265
    Photoshop Native Files..265
    QuarkVista™ Picture Effects 266
General QuarkXPress Cautions 267
  Beware the B*I*O*S*..267
  Graphics 269
    No Pasting from the Clipboard...269
    Clipping Paths...270
    Portable Document Format Files (PDFs) as Artwork 272
  Specifying Colors 273
  Creating PDF Files..274
    Export to PDF: QuarkXPress 5.0...276
    Export to PDF: QuarkXPress 6.0 Through 6.5.............................277
    Print to Distiller/PDF Printer (QuarkXPress 5.0 and Above)......278
    Print to PostScript, Distill Manually...279
    Save as PDF 279
  Collect for Output 280
QuarkXPress 7.0..281
  New Features..281
  Improved Support for Photoshop Native Images..............................283
  Exporting PDF Files from QuarkXPress 7.0.....................................284
Troubleshooting 285
  What a Drag..285
  Divide and Conquer 286

Chapter Fourteen: Acrobat Production Tips 287

Acrobat Product Line 288

Where Do PDFs Come From? 289

Creating PDF Files 289

  Determining Which Type of PDF You Should Create 289

  PDF Settings and Some Important Standards 290

  Acrobat Distiller 293

  Handling Image Content 296

    Resolution Settings 297

    Compression Settings 298

  Font Embedding 299

Editing PDF Files 299

  Editing Text 300

  Editing Graphics 301

Print Production Toolbar 304

  Forensic Tools: What's Wrong with this PDF? 305

    Output Preview 305

    Preflight 308

    PDF Optimizer 311

  Repair Tools 311

    Convert Colors 311

    Ink Manager 312

    Add Printer Marks 312

    Crop Pages 313

    Fix Hairlines 314

    Transparency Flattening 315

    PDF Optimizer 315

    Trap Presets 316

    JDF 316

Using External PDF Editors 316

Appendix: Print Production Resources **319**

    Organizations 319

        User Groups 320

        Online Communities and Forums..320

        Printing Industry Organizations..322

        Packaging Organizations..322

        Technical Education Organizations..323

    Conferences and Trade Shows 324

        Printing Industry Events...324

        Design Conferences 325

        Acrobat/PDF Conferences...326

    Design and Printing Books...326

        Desktop Publishing...326

        General Design..327

        General Printing..327

        Typography...329

    Software-Specific Books 329

        Acrobat...329

        Adobe Creative Suite 330

        Freehand 330

        Illustrator..330

        InDesign...330

        Photoshop 330

        Photoshop Specialty Topics 331

        QuarkXPress...331

    Publications 332

        Desktop Publishing...332

        Design 332

        Printing Technology..333

        Tutorials...333

    Destinations 333

Index..**335**

Preface

True confession: I'm not a designer.

Oh, I can place type and graphics in a respectable arrangement on a page, but that's about it. I can't conjure up compelling concepts and award-winning designs. But that's OK. I'm not *supposed* to be a designer.

I'm a printing person. I spent the first ▬▬y years of my working life in prepress. (Oops, there seems to be a little printing problem there. But, hey—are numbers really that important?) I'm at an awkward stage in my career. I'd like to lie about my age, but I'm reluctant to abbreviate my résumé. Instead, I'll attempt to convince you that I started in printing at a *very* young age ("Is that a *baby* with an X-Acto™ knife?"). You know you've been in printing a long time if:

- Your grocery list has hanging indents.

- Your driver's license lists your eye color as PMS 5757.

- Your shoe size is 6½ plus ⅛-inch bleed.

- You refer to painting your house as a two-color job.

- You decide to write a book called *Real World Print Production*.

WHO SHOULD READ THIS BOOK

If you are a designer or a production artist who would like a better understanding of the pitfalls you encounter in using popular software, you'll find lots of pointers in this book to help you avoid problems. Almost all software provides options that are tempting to choose, but are dangerous under some circumstances. It's good to know which buttons *not* to push. And it's valuable to know *why* those buttons shouldn't be pushed.

In addition, the more designers know about the physical requirements of the printing process, the more easily they can avoid problems and missed deadlines. This book can explain why your printer sometimes asks you to modify your designs for print. Better yet, you can beat them to it, and they will compliment you on how well-prepared your jobs always are. Besides, working within limitations can sometimes lead to imaginative solutions and more interesting designs.

If you are a prepress production operator, you'll find many reminders of subtle problems that can lurk in images, page layouts, and illustration files. If you're new to printing, you'll find beneficial insights into what's happening on the other side of the pressroom door. And if you're looking for a gentle way to educate clients, well, a book always makes a nice gift, doesn't it?

As the lines between *designer* and *printer* become more blurred, some professionals don't fall clearly into a single category. Many organizations are responsible for both design and output, and it's especially important to know the whole story if you're going to shoulder such a wide responsibility.

WHAT THIS BOOK IS *NOT*

If you're in the market for a hot tips-and-tricks book, this isn't it. It's not a guide for wow-your-friends special effects, unless you consider it a special effect to get your job to print as expected. And, although this book demonstrates how to do some useful things in the most popular desktop publishing programs, it isn't strictly a how-to book either. In fact, there's so much "how *not* to" information in this book that I considered calling it *You Must Always Never Do This*.

Are there any prerequisites for using this book? Only two, really. First, you should have basic proficiency in the software you use on a regular basis. The other requirement is arguably more important: You should have a healthy curiosity about the printing process and a desire to build problem-free files.

ABOUT THE AUTHOR

You never know where you'll end up. I was a chemistry major. Really. But I had a knack for illustration, and I took some college art classes for extra credit. One of my instructors (Michael Parkes, who has since become a well-known fine artist in Europe), suggested that I change my career path from chemistry to commercial art. I thought, "Well, I'll try it for a while," and took a job at a printing plant that summer. I fell in love with printing, and never went back to the lab. Thanks, Michael.

As a prepress production person, I always enjoyed discovering new techniques and sharing those discoveries with coworkers and customers. I started in conventional paste-up, and then moved into film stripping. (It's not what you think. See the glossary in Chapter One, "Lifecycle of a Print Job.") And I was extremely fortunate to be one of the first operators of color electronic prepress systems in the U.S., so I've been pushing pixels around for a *long* time. Then, because it could do the same magic as a Scitex or Crosfield system (minus the million-dollar price tag), Adobe® Photoshop® lured me to desktop computers.

I always believed in educating customers so they wouldn't be intimidated by the mysteries of printing. Not surprisingly, that led to my second career as a trainer, consultant, and presenter at industry conferences. It's truly invigorating to answer questions, illuminate software mysteries, and solve problems for my clients and conference attendees.

ACKNOWLEDGEMENTS

I'm passing on to you some of the Basic Printing Truths imparted to me by a number of fine old printing curmudgeons. Count yourself truly lucky if you're befriended by a craftsman like Rick Duncan, who came up through the ranks, learned how to do everything the old-fashioned way, and who was always patient with a kid asking too many questions.

I'm quite fortunate to be part of an informal fraternity of graphic arts ~~geeks~~ aficionados. While we each have our specialties, our common bond is the love of learning and sharing new tricks. David Blatner, Scott Citron, Sandee "Vector Babe" Cohen, and Anne-Marie Concepción are my InDesign brethren (and sistren), going back to the days when we were considered page-layout rebels. Mordy Golding's passion for Illustrator is contagious, and he shares my devotion to enlightening designers in the mysteries of print. His URL says it all: www.designresponsibly.com. Dan Margulis is my long-time Photoshop color-correction hero (and a fine cook to boot), and I'm grateful to Chris Murphy for putting color management into mere-mortal language. Mark Atchley has been a wonderful cheerleader when I'm exhausted, and Steve Werner's insights into prepress and software arcana have given me many "Aha!" moments. Chuck Weger is in a class by himself, providing all of us the opportunity to publicly humiliate ourselves in his delightful printing-trivia game shows. (Even Chuck's jacket is in a class by itself. Well, actually it's in *quarantine*.) And I owe special thanks to Olav Martin Kvern for lending me a cup of PostScript code for the FreeHand chapter. These are some of the brightest and funniest people I know.

My appreciation to Carrie Cooper, Colin Fleming, and Maria Yap of Adobe Systems, Inc., for kind encouragement when I struck out as a freelance consultant and trainer. Adobe is also home to a number of other exceptional colleagues, including Will Eisley, Dov Isaacs, Lonn Lorenz, and Whitney McCleary. They all show a true passion for Adobe products, a realistic view of how things actually work out here in the wild, and, most importantly, an affection for users and a strong dedication to creating better software. I must also single out two of Adobe's most energetic women: My heartfelt thanks to Noha Edell for her continuing, inspirational support and encouragement, and my gratitude to Ashwini Jambotkar for her unique insights into the challenges faced by designers.

Many thanks to Cyndie Shafstall and Shellie Hall at Quark for illuminating the new features of QuarkXPress® 7.0. It's probably the best-ever version of the program.

I must express appreciation to my fellow PDF devotees Carl Young, whose conferences prove that Acrobat geeks are great rollicking fun; interactive Acrobat magician Bob Connolly for bringing PDFs to life; and to PDF Sage Leonard Rosenthol, who always knows where the best restaurant is (as well as the longest, most interesting route to get there). And Ted Padova doubles the value of his prodigious knowledge of all things PDF by always being so generous in sharing it.

You sometimes hear scare stories about the process of writing books, but you won't hear them from me. I am fortunate to be under the wing of Peachpit Press. I'm especially grateful to the incomparable Pam Pfiffner for making authorship sound like such a good idea. Thanks to Lisa Brazieal for guiding me through the foreign territory of the book-writing process, and very special thanks to Nancy Raiken for her delicate editorial touch. This is a better book for all their gentle nudges.

And for applying the last coat of varnish and polishing this book to a sheen, I must thank Owen Wolfson for his design and composition work, and Carol DeMatteis of Colleen Dunham Indexing for crafting the index so you can actually *find* information.

When I was asked to suggest technical editors, I went for the gold. Jim Birkenseer and Peter Truskier of Premedia Systems, Inc., in addition to knowing the most arcane inner workings of publishing technology, are responsible for the automation that made the stellar series of *America 24/7* books possible. I can't thank Jim and Peter enough for taking time from their brutal schedules to poke through my words and ensure that I wasn't spreading any myths. They refined, corrected, and taught me a few things in the process. They're also accomplished masters of the nose flute.

CHAPTER ONE

Life Cycle of a Print Job

People who aren't involved in the graphic arts industry probably have no idea where all that stuff in their mailbox comes from. They're blissfully unaware of the design process and give not a whit about those poor guys on third shift in the printing plant trying to troubleshoot a problem file. They don't think about the electronic design environment or the mechanical process of printing. All they think is, "Wow! That really looks good! I should buy this!" But as a designer or production artist, you need to know a bit about what happens when you're finished with your part of the job. The more you know, the more you can do to prevent problems—and missed deadlines—later in the life cycle of your job.

> **NOTE:** See the glossary at the end of this chapter for more detailed explanations of some common printing terms, both modern and historical, used in this chapter and throughout the book. Terms that are italicized in this chapter's text are expanded in the glossary, which also includes additional terms you may find helpful.

First, a little history.

THE OLDEN DAYS

Twenty-five years ago, the responsibilities in the graphic arts professions were rather clearly defined, and there wasn't much overlap of skills or responsibility. Designers knew a bit about prepress and printing endeavors, but they usually weren't required to perform any work typical of those operations. Design was a more hands-on process involving more hand drawing and pen-and-ink work. Production artists created page layouts by gluing down photo prints with wax or rubber cement to a piece of thick illustration board, creating a *mechanical* (short for mechanical artwork). We did type corrections with X-Acto® knives and rubber cement, sometimes going home at the end of a long day with words glued to our elbows and the occasional consonant stuck in our hair. Who knows—maybe that was the inspiration for refrigerator magnet poetry.

The design and print process moved at a slower pace than it does today, largely out of necessity. It's certainly not that we were more patient in those days—it's just that all that handwork took time. There was more specialization. Dedicated *typesetters* generated text using phototypesetting equipment (after the demise of lead-based *hot type*), *trade shops* employed *cameramen* to create color separations and shoot line shots of mechanicals, and *dot etchers* performed color corrections by etching film with acid solutions to change the size of the dots.

Film strippers combined line shots and color separation films from the camera to create final page film. *Page proofs* were created by exposing the final composed page films onto photosensitive materials. *Color Key* proofs consisted of individual color overlays, one for each printing ink. *Matchprint* proofs consisted of color layers laminated to printing stock. And *Cromalin* proofs were made by dusting pigment onto a sticky image. Sounds primitive now, perhaps, but we were high-tech in our day!

Proofs and film were given to the printer, where *imposition* took place (although some trade shops also did imposition and shipped plate-ready films). *Bluelines* (single-color proofs that actually weren't always blue) were exposed from the imposed *flats*, and then folded up to check the mechanics of the page contents and imposition. Plates were burned from the imposed flats, then mounted on the press. Using the page proofs from the trade shop, pressmen adjusted ink coverage on the press during the process of getting the press up to speed and the ink behavior optimal—referred to as *makeready*. Then, when everything was up to speed, the customer might be asked to attend a *press check* to assure that everything looked good. Some of these processes, such as Cromalin proofing, no longer take place. Some have morphed into digital versions. Imposed bluelines, for example, have largely been replaced by output from large-format, inkjet printers. Press makeready has been streamlined by technological advances. But you'll be happy to know that press checks are much the same as they have always been.

In those (relatively) ancient times, the workflow looked something like **Figure 1.1**. There were variations, of course. Some design houses had in-house typesetting and photography, and some trade shops supplied finished plates to printers. Some printers had in-house designers as well as prepress departments to perform trade shop functions. And then, as now, some printers used outside firms to perform specialty finishing such as *embossing, foil stamping,* and *die cutting*.

The introduction of electronic *scanners* and *color electronic prepress systems* (CEPS) revolutionized the art of color separation. What had been a nuanced and specialized undertaking involving masking, tricky exposures, and chemical baths became accessible to a wider range of graphic arts professionals. Old instincts for camera work and dot etching were channeled into scanning and onscreen color correction. It was a wonderful new world. And our hands healed up as a result.

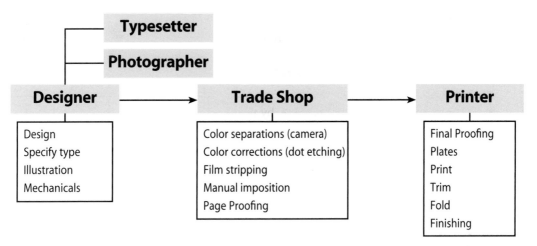

Figure 1.1 Historically, functions were divided between trades and professions that specialized in an individual aspect of graphic arts and printing. Designers designed, trade shops assembled all the pieces, and printers printed and performed finishing. Typesetters were often independent providers, although many design firms had in-house typesetting. Photography studios, while usually separate companies, were occasionally part of a design firm or a department within a trade shop providing photography services. The advent of desktop publishing changed this ecosystem radically.

BRAVE NEW WORLD: DESKTOP PUBLISHING

With the appearance of the first Apple® desktop units, computers were no longer quite so foreign and mysterious to The Rest of Us. In 1985, the advent of page–layout programs such as Ready, Set, Go!® and Aldus PageMaker® made the computer a replacement for X-Acto knives and hot wax applicators.

Adobe's PostScript® page-description language brought laser printers to life and turned them into viable output devices for *camera-ready art*. Soon, what had been the sole province of specialized craftsmen became a public playing field. The good news? Anyone with a computer, a page-layout program, and an Apple LaserWriter® could now do much of the work involved in publishing. Tasks that had traditionally been performed in trade shops were accomplished by desktop computer users. Page-layout applications began to replace the separate jobs of setting type, creating mechanicals, and stripping film. Adobe Photoshop became the most widespread tool for retouching and color correction, seriously eroding the market for the million-dollar, high-end CEPS. New desktop publishers leapfrogged the former apprentice-to-journeyman training of printing craftsmen, and hit the ground running. And while the speed of electronic systems accelerated the pace in the industry and redistributed the tasks, it also redistributed the responsibilities. The distribution of labor began to look more like **Table 1.1**.

For example, in the Old Way, designers might indicate *color break*—what color is used in each element of the page—but it was usually up to the prep workers in the color trade shop to cut masks to accomplish this, in a process called *mechanical color*. But now color break is part of a page layout or illustration. Designers have a finished product ready to print when it leaves their hands, rather than a guide for someone else's work.

JOB SUBMISSION

Your method of submitting files will depend on your print service provider's requirements. Chapter 8, "Job Submission," is devoted to these issues, including some helpful checklists to aid you, if your print service provider doesn't provide a similar guide.

SCENIC TOUR OF A TYPICAL PRINTING PLANT

Depending on the size and structure of your print service provider, some of the functions described in this section might be combined. For example, in some companies, job planning might be done by a dedicated planner, by customer service representatives, or by an estimator. And some prepress departments make no distinction between *preflight* (looking for job errors) and *production*—they just watch for problems as they prepare a job for later prepress functions. The departments are described in the approximate order in which they handle your job. **Figure 1.2** provides an aerial view of a fictional printing company to give you a general idea of job flow.

The flow of a job in a given printing company is governed by the company's capabilities and the type of work they usually perform. For example, a small printing company that specializes in business collateral such as letterheads, business cards, and envelopes is not likely to have binding equipment such as saddle stitchers or custom inline inkjet heads for on-press *personalization*.

	Designer	Photographer	Printer	Other
Design	●			
Illustration	○			○
Page layout	●			
Photography	○	●		
Scanning	○	○	○	
Color correction	○	○	○	
Retouching	○	○	○	
Imposition			●	
Page proofing			●	
Final proofing			●	
Burn plates			●	
Print			●	
Trim			●	
Fold			●	
Finishing			○	○

● = Primary vendor

○ = Possible vendors

Table 1.1 Desktop publishing's redistribution of graphic arts tasks. Traditional tradeshop tasks like retouching, for example, might be done by a designer, a photographer, or the printer.

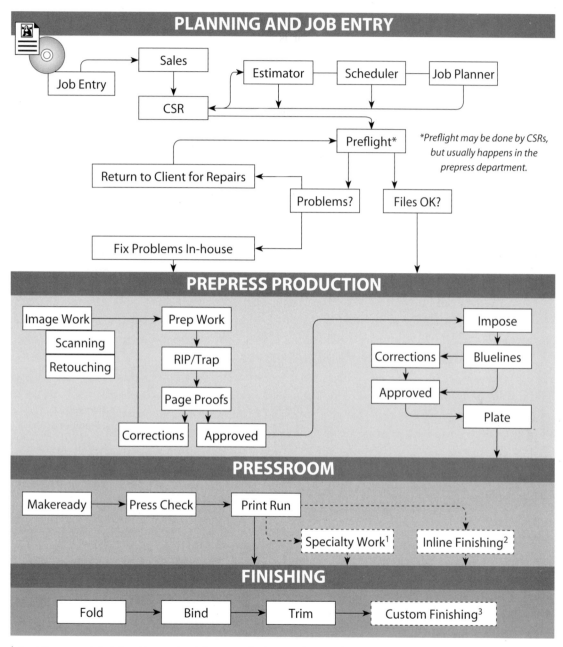

Figure 1.2 Job flow in a typical printing company. Your mileage may vary. Some printers divide departments differently, and some use external suppliers for operations such as custom finishing. *(Dashed lines indicate functions that may not be performed by all print service providers.)*

Sales

Typically, the print salesperson will be your first contact and will set things in motion for you by initiating your job's entry into the printing plant's workflow. At this early point in the life of the job, it's important to discuss any concerns you may have about the job. Learn as much as you can about the processes that will be used in manufacturing your job. If your job will require any special stock such as vellum or heavy cover stock, discuss this with the salesperson. Also discuss any special finishing treatments that will be used, such as embossing or die cutting. The salesperson will probably be the person who provides you with an estimate of job costs and gives you an idea of the timeline of the job's trip through the printing plant. Initially, the salesperson may be your primary contact, but your job will probably be assigned to a customer service representative (CSR) early in the job.

Customer Service

After you submit your job files, the CSR is likely to be your prime contact point throughout the remainder of the job. If the production staff has any questions about how job issues should be handled, they'll ask the CSR to call or e-mail you for the answer. If you need to send corrected or updated files, you may be asked to contact the CSR rather than the salesperson, since the CSR is closer to the action and more likely to know the current status of your job in the workflow. A skilled, proactive CSR is your best friend and often has the foresight to help you anticipate and prevent problems. Ideally, the CSR is fluent in both design-speak and printing concepts and can act as a translator to keep the lines of communication open between you and production staff for the duration of the job.

Planning, Estimating, and Scheduling

Once your job is accepted by the print service provider, it will be assigned a job number and some sort of identifying name. This information will become part of a printed *job ticket,* which will travel with the job materials. The job ticket will be affixed to a physical *job jacket* containing job materials such as your disks, your printed hard copy of the job, and other pertinent pieces that are accumulated during the life of the job. Eventually, the job jacket may contain intermediate proofs, printed instructions for correction cycles, and approved final proofs to be used as a reference during the press run. The attached job ticket serves as a job identifier and job information reference as the materials travel through the printing plant. Some printing plants use bar codes on their job tickets to aid in job tracking, but many rely on plant employees to note a job's process by making entries in computer-based tracking systems.

Job ticketing conventions vary between printing companies, but the job ticket will contain vital information about the job's requirements, including such information as:

- Job number (a unique identifier assigned at the print service provider)

- Client contact information

- Internal contacts (salesperson, CSR)

- Intended press

- Inks, including specially mixed inks

- Due dates (final print, as well as intermediate events, such as page proofs)

- Line screen

- Custom handling required, such as special folding or other finishing operations

Planners establish the basic flow of your job, including its timeline. The timeline identifies when each segment of the job will take place and how the print service provider can wedge your job into the ocean of other jobs occurring at the same time. They may also plan how jobs will run on press to take advantage of available time—your job may be combined with another, similar job to run simultaneously and save on the time and materials devoted to makeready.

Like air traffic controllers, *schedulers* track all the jobs running through a printing plant at any given time. They have to ensure that all the plant's equipment is kept humming and that deadlines are met. As they juggle all the live jobs in the plant, they have to take into consideration any jobs whose progress hits a snag. They're constantly rearranging indicators on large scheduling boards, which resemble huge bulletin boards or whiteboards with all jobs represented by identifying tickets or labels.

Estimators determine job costs, including labor, paper, ink, proofing materials, as well as press time and bindery time. In some plants, estimating and planning tasks are combined. Once the estimating and planning groundwork is laid, the job is often subjected to a preflight process. In some printing plants, preflight is performed by CSRs. In most plants, however, preflight is done by prepress operators when the job enters the prepress department.

Preflight

On its way to prepress production, your job will usually be run through a preflight process to check for problems with setup and content. Don't take it personally. It's better to find problems early in the job rather than later when deadlines loom. For application files such as QuarkXPress or Adobe InDesign® files, many prepress departments use dedicated preflight software such as FlightCheck® Professional from Markzware. Some departments rely on dedicated preflight operators to manually check files for problems, while some combine FlightCheck with manual checks geared toward the printer's particular workflow. To preflight submitted PDF files, many print service providers use PDF-specific software such as Enfocus PitStop, PDF/X Checkup from Apago, or the print production tools in Adobe Acrobat® Professional. However preflight is performed, when problems are found, you may be asked whether you'd like to fix the problems yourself or incur a charge for letting the printer fix them. Common problems include issues such as lack of sufficient bleed, misspelled words, overset text, incorrect or extraneous spot colors, or wrong document size.

Preflight personnel are also often responsible for organizing job files into a standard folder hierarchy used by the printing plant, which may require that they rename some files and reestablish image links in page layouts as a result.

Prepress

These days, many prepress departments refer to themselves as electronic prepress departments, a holdover from earlier days when the computer-based activities were a parallel process, and manual prepress activities such as film stripping still encompassed much of the work. But now you'd be hard-pressed to find extensive stripping capabilities in all but the smallest shops. As long as plates were still being exposed manually from large film flats, strippers would be called upon to make last-minute corrections by taping out or grafting in replacement film pieces. But with the overwhelming move to *computer-to-plate* (CTP), dedicated film strippers and their light tables are increasingly rare.

Production

Many of today's affordable desktop scanners can produce high-quality results, but some designers prefer to do quick-and-dirty FPO (For Position Only) scans to use in their page layouts while color professionals at the print service provider do the final, high-resolution scans. Once the job enters prepress production at the printer, the FPO images will be replaced with the final scans. Any silhouetting (eliminating backgrounds) will have to be performed at this point, which will add to job cost and time. If your printer does the scans and provides you with low-resolution, placeholder images to use in your layouts, replacing those placeholders with the high-resolution images will already be part of the standard job costs. Even if there are no true errors in the way the file is built, it's likely that prepress production operators will still need to tweak your job to get it ready for other parts of the workflow, such as raster image processing (RIPping), trapping, and imposition.

For example, if your job contains large solid areas of black, the prepress production operator may replace the single black ink with a rich-black mix such as C60-M40-Y40-K100 to facilitate a good outcome on the press. Another example: Gradients created in QuarkXPress are routinely replaced with Photoshop gradients to prevent a banded appearance in output. Such alterations are for the printer's convenience and are not usually charged to the customer.

Scanning

If you've supplied reflective artwork such as drawings, paintings, or photographic prints as artwork to be placed in the layout, the print service provider or an outside vendor will have to scan the artwork. Whether scanning is performed by you, the print service provider, or someone else, you should expect to see random proofs—raw, individual proofs of the artwork before the images are placed into the layout—so that you can determine at an early stage whether color correction or retouching will be necessary. Even the best scan may not be able to initially capture your intent for the image because of the limitations inherent in the scanning process and the inherent difficulty of reproducing some colors in the standard CMYK printing inks. Color correction can compensate for some of these issues, but be prepared for the limitations of CMYK (see Chapter Two, "Ink on Paper," for more on these issues). Early random proofs will prepare you for the appearance of images in the final printed piece.

Image Work

If you're not comfortable with creating clipping paths or performing other image manipulations such as retouching, color correction, or compositing, specialists in the prepress department will do those things. Often, the scanner operator is an accomplished Photoshop user with a good eye for color.

Raster Image Processor (RIP)

Believe it or not, "We RIPped your file" is *good* news. At its most basic, a RIP interprets the incoming page-description (PostScript or PDF) information and converts that data to a literal bitmap image that instructs the marking engine of the output device how to image the film, plates, or, in the case of toner-based printers, the electrostatic drum (**Figure 1.3**). Many RIPs also perform other operations, such as in-RIP trapping or the low-resolution to high-resolution image swap functions of an *OPI* workflow.

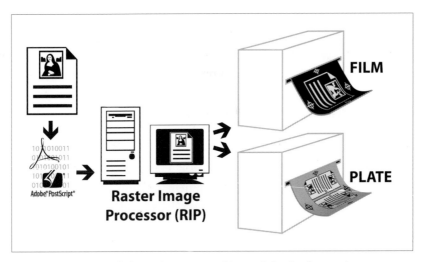

Figure 1.3 A RIP is a dedicated computer with specialized software that converts PostScript or PDF information into bitmapped information. This process drives an imagesetter to image film or a platesetter to image plates. Since each manufacturer's RIP consists of a proprietary combination of hardware and software, capabilities differ among brands.

In some workflows, individual pages are processed by the RIP, and then combined in imposition software. In other workflows, PostScript files for individual pages are imposed, and the imposed file is processed by the RIP.

Whereas RIPs usually feed on PostScript, some manufacturers' RIPs such as those from Artwork Systems Group and Global Graphics® can handle native PDF files. PostScript is actually a programming language that is used to describe and define pages so that output devices know how to image those pages. PDF files contain information that's much like PostScript (and in fact shares many of the concepts of PostScript). But PDFs can also contain information, such as transparency, which goes beyond the capabilities of PostScript. Some RIPs take in PDFs, but internally convert them to PostScript for further processing. This is the source of some imaging errors when you submit PDF files containing native transparency from applications such as InDesign or Adobe Illustrator.® RIPs that maintain PDFs as PDFs throughout the raster imaging processing, rather than converting PDFs to PostScript, sometimes do a better job of imaging PDF content. The announcement of the Adobe PDF Print Engine opens the way for true PDF-based RIPs from even more vendors.

Trapping

It's necessary to compensate for slight errors in the alignment of the printing inks as they're laid down sequentially on an offset press. Trapping provides a combination of colors at the edges of abutting color areas to camouflage any slippage. See Chapter Two, "Ink on Paper," for an in-depth description of trapping, and why it's necessary. Since trapping itself can be a complex undertaking, and because requirements vary according to printing conditions, this is an arcane art best left to prepress professionals. Aren't you glad? Whereas in the past, trapping was accomplished within originating applications such as Illustrator or QuarkXPress, or with dedicated trapping software, the majority of trapping now takes place at the RIP.

Imposition

Using the job information provided by planners, imposition operators combine individual pages in the proper pagination for plating. In some companies, separate groups handle prepress operations (such as preflight) and plating functions (such as imposition). This allows specialized operators to perform plate-related tasks while general prepress operators continue to do preflight and production. For a more detailed description of imposition, see Chapter 3, "Binding and Finishing."

Proofing

Several different rounds—and several different kinds—of proofing may occur in the life of a job:

- Random proofs of images early in the job help determine whether color correction or retouching is needed.

- Desktop printer output may be used for internal checks of the content of pages after preflight and before proceeding to prepress production.

- Color or single-color proofs (often called *bluelines*) after prepress production are used for customer markup or approval before proceeding to imposition and output to film or plates.

- Color proofs of finished pages are used for color match on press. The proofs may be single page proofs, proofs of reader spreads, or proofs of multiple pages in their final imposed position. These proofs are viewed under controlled conditions in a viewing booth, which is painted a neutral gray and uses special lights for a standardized environment. The color temperature (5000–6500° K) is intended to mimic daylight. You may be asked to sign these proofs to indicate that you approve of the color and the content of the pages. This is often referred to as a *contract proof*, since it constitutes a contract between you and the printer. Your approval of the proof implies that you're satisfied with the appearance of the proof. The printer is then expected to match the appearance of the contract proof on the press.

- Blueline folded comps, created after imposition, are used on press and in the bindery to check page position and content.

Corrections

Printer alterations are sometimes the result of mistakes that are made during production, but they can also be voluntary changes to a job to ensure satisfactory printing under the press or bindery conditions. For example, if there are large, solid color areas in a single ink, the printer may elect to print that area with two separate applications of the same ink to achieve a uniform appearance on press. Since this is elective, such an alteration is not chargeable to the customer.

Artist alterations (AAs), also called *customer alterations*, are alterations requested by the designer or the designer's client. AAs include such changes as type changes, replacing images, or moving content. Charges vary depending on the complexity of the change and the stage in the job at which the change is requested. For example, adding a comma at the preflight stage might be a freebie, whereas adding it after the job is on the press might require stopping the press, correcting the affected page, and resending it through the RIP, retrapping, re-imposing, and burning a new plate (or more if the comma affects multiple colors). The new plate (or plates) must be mounted on press, and the makeready process repeated. The expense of labor, materials, and lost press time could be considerable. Once the job is pulled off press, you've lost your slot in the production cycle and, depending on how busy the presses are, you may wait a day or more for another opportunity to run your job.

Creating Plates

In the earlier days of electronic desktop publishing, film was often output for individual pages, and then taped down in flats on large, clear carrier sheets in the proper printing position. (A flat is just that: a flat carrier sheet with one or more pieces of film in final position.) These imposed flats were used to expose printing plates with powerful light sources. Because intermediate films were stripped and combined to create the page films, and then the page films used to expose the plates (or to create huge, composite single films for each plate), some tiny details could be eroded by the multiple generations of exposures. Any errors in aligning the individual pieces would affect the quality on press.

The introduction of computer-to-plate (CTP) revolutionized this process. In a CTP workflow, the imposition is digitally created, and then the printing plate is directly exposed in a large imaging device, using no intermediate film. The photosensitive coating on the imaged plate is chemically developed much like photographic film and baked, if necessary, to harden the image for printing. This usually takes place in an inline unit attached to the exposure unit, so a finished plate emerges ready for mounting on the press. Think of the photosensitive plate coating as being a bit tender while it's still fresh. The plate is heated to stabilize the imaged coating so it will be able to stand up to the rigors of being mounted and used on the printing press.

The elimination of intermediate films reduces opportunities for error and considerably improves the process. There's less chance for loss of detail and, understandably, some cost and time savings.

A variation of this concept is on-press imaging, which is most commonly used on smaller-format presses. Unexposed plates are mounted on the press, and imaging units on the press expose the plates in position. This approach can reduce makeready time because plates are already in position on the press when they're exposed, eliminating handling and possible registration issues.

Pressroom

The printing process that will be used on your job will have some bearing on how your job must be prepared, so the choice of printing process is one more important topic in your initial conversations with a print service provider. *Offset printing* is probably the process that you envision when someone says "printing press," and it's the printing method you will probably encounter most frequently. But there are other printing methods. The choice of printing process is dictated by the end product. *Gravure* is often used for long print runs typical of catalogs and magazines. *Flexography* is used for flexible packaging such as wrappers, foil bags, and labels. *Letterpress printing* is most often used for artistic applications these days, such as invitations or special publications. You may think of *screen printing* as only for clothing, such as t-shirts, but it's also capable of producing fine-art pieces, and often used to print on irregular surfaces such as cans, bottles, and other containers.

Increasingly, *digital printing* is used for short-run printing jobs such as brochures, product literature, mailings, and small-circulation magazines. The ability to utilize *variable data* with digital printing opens up some interesting possibilities for marketing with printed pieces containing content customized for individual recipients.

Preparation in the pressroom includes adjusting the ink coverage, varying the pressure of the ink-bearing plates and the transfer blankets, and adjusting the paper-feeding mechanisms. Much of this process is facilitated by on-press technology, but the pressmen's instincts are indispensable for fine-tuning the mechanics. The term *makeready* refers to the process of getting the press up to speed and the ink behavior optimal. The press crew will be using approved *contract proofs* to guide them in setup. The color and content of the printed piece should match what the client has approved. Once everything is behaving as it should, you may be asked to attend a *press check* to approve the results, especially if there are special treatments that are difficult to simulate with a contract proof, such as custom-mixed inks or specialty stock.

Other specialty work that may take place in the pressroom includes personalization such as addressing, as well as on-press finishing that might include perforation and scoring. In addition, coatings, such as varnishes, may be applied during the press run. Even fragrances and adhesives may be applied with inline units attached to the press.

Finishing

There's some overlap between the pressroom and a dedicated bindery, since some finishing functions, such as scoring or perforation, may take place on press or may be accomplished in the bindery. But traditionally, operations such as trimming, folding, stitching, and diecutting are done in the finishing department or bindery.

Trimming

Large, heavy-duty trimming equipment is used to cut printed sheets to final size or to cut apart ganged content such as business cards. In some cases, trimming may take place before binding, although some pieces are bound first. For example, a business-reply card would be trimmed to the correct size before being bound into a publication. But the signatures of a book would be trimmed after being bound together in the final book configuration, ensuring that exterior page edges are cleanly aligned.

Folding

Simple folding may be performed inline as the printed sheet comes off the press, or it may be done in the bindery. More complex folding, such as that required for pocket folders or packaging, uses dedicated folding equipment. Some folding operations require handwork to finish the job, which adds to the cost of the job.

Stitching

When a piece requires stitching, thread may be used to anchor the pages of a *signature* for subsequent binding into a larger, finished book. But wire is often used for stitching, during which it is fed into stitching heads that feed, bend, and cut the wire simultaneously, resulting in a stapled piece. You'll often hear the term *saddle stitching*, which refers to the way a group of pages is held—as if draped over a saddle—while it is stitched.

Die Cutting

A *die* is a shaped metal cutter that is used to trim the edge of a printed piece in a special shape or to punch a shaped hole through the piece. The tabs on the edges of dividers are a simple example of die cutting. Many companies have standing dies for tab creation and can supply you with a template for creating your artwork so that it fits their existing dies. This avoids the cost of creating a custom die.

In a more complex example, a packaging piece may require that the printed sheet be scored and die cut to the final configuration for folding, creating all the interlocking panels that fold up to create the final box. If you're creating artwork for packaging, it's important to work closely with the print service provider and the die creator to ensure that your artwork is correct. Special handling is required at the intersections of panels to avoid artwork falling onto the wrong panel. Many printing companies do not create custom dies in-house, so be prepared for the cost and time involved in creating them. While the design of a custom die can be computerized, the assembly of the die itself still requires the knowledge of skilled craftspeople.

Binding

Many forms of assembly fall under the heading of binding, from stitching to bookbinding. The most common forms of binding are *saddle stitching* (see the previous section on stitching) and *perfect binding*, in which multiple signatures are combined into a bundle, anchored with an adhesive, and then bound with tape or paper binding to hold them together.

Additional binding methods include *coil binding*, *comb binding*, and *wire binding*. The binding method may require that you avoid placing artwork in a specified margin so that it clears the punching or binding area. Consult with the print service provider early in the job to determine what the practical page area will be when binding is taken into consideration.

Gluing

Binding methods such as perfect binding require gluing to keep all the pages together. But gluing is also an integral part of the manufacturing process for pocket folders and packaging that require folding. Because glue should be applied to a clean, ink-free substrate, artwork for the job needs to provide areas for glue application. Consult with the print service provider as you create your files so you'll know where glue needs to be applied. You may also request that they modify your artwork to accommodate gluing.

Fulfillment and Shipping

Some printing companies provide services beyond the production of printed pieces. Many offer mailing and fulfillment services, or they partner with other companies to provide such services. Fulfillment is especially useful for product literature and other pieces with a long life span, such as pocket folders and presentation binders. Rather than requiring the customer to store boxes or materials, the printer keeps the inventory and ships it as needed.

Printers who specialize in mailers such as catalogs often offer mailing as part of the job cost and process. This may include variable data addressing (whether on-press or offline) as well as the actual mailing.

Glossary of Printing Terms

This glossary is by no means a comprehensive record of printing terms. But it may come in handy before and during your conversations with a print service provider.

Aqueous Coating: A water-based coating applied over the entire printed area, usually by the last printing unit on a press. Aqueous coatings protect the printed ink and may enhance the appearance of the piece. For example, a pocket folder may benefit from the ability of aqueous coating to prevent scuffing as the pocket folder is repeatedly handled.

Baseline: An imaginary line at the base of a row of text. All text sits on the baseline, with descenders such as the lower case *y* and *g* extending below the baseline.

Bindery: Sometimes also called a finishing department, the bindery performs trimming, folding, gluing, and stitching for finished pieces.

Blanket: An intermediate, rubber blanket used in offset printing to transfer the printing ink to the paper surface. The inked printing plate transfers ink to the blanket, which then applies the ink to the paper. The use of the intermediate blanket is the reason the printing process is called offset printing.

Blueline: A single-color proof made by exposing photosensitive paper to a strong light source through film (usually a multipage, imposed layout for plate). Bluelines are used for proofreading, checking for scratches in film, and correct pagination of the flat. In a computer-to-plate (CTP) environment where no plate film is necessary, bluelines are often digitally output on large-format inkjet printers.

Cameraman: In the days before scanners, cameramen used masking and exposure techniques to create film color separations on large cameras. Transparencies, color prints, or original artwork were mounted on a large platen and then photographed through color filters to generate the films for the printing inks.

Camera-ready art: Ink drawings for illustrations, logos, or finished mechanicals ready to be photographed by the cameraman. The line shots of the clean, camera-ready artwork were used as the starting point for film stripping.

CEPS (color electronic prepress system): A specialized computer system for retouching and assembly of images. Marketed by Scitex, Crosfield, Linotype-Hell, and Dainippon Screen, they often cost in excess of a million dollars. Largely rendered obsolete by the advent of Photoshop and the affordability of the Macintosh.

Chase: A wooden frame that contains the metal printing components used in a letterpress printing press.

Coil binding: (Also called *spiral binding*.) Pages are punched (usually at the left or top edge), and then a single coil (spiral) of plastic or wire is threaded through the punched holes to anchor the pages together. Coil binding is useful for presentations and workbooks because pages lie flat when the finished piece is opened. One disadvantage is that there is no printable spine.

Color break: How color should be used in various areas of a page. In the days of physical *mechanicals*, colored markers were used to mark a tissue paper overlay so that *film strippers* would know how to apply color to type, rules, and boxes. Since the underlying mechanical artwork consisted of only black-and-white contents (to facilitate the shooting of *line shots*), an indication of color break was necessary. For example, headlines might be circled and marked to print as M100–Y100, and quick sweeps of a blue marker, accompanied by a written instruction, might be used to indicate that all boxes on the page should print with a mix of C50–Y15. It was sort of like coloring books for adults. The term color break is still used in discussions of page-layout contents.

Color Key™: A product of 3M, the Color Key proofing system used individual photosensitive color overlays to create proofs. Each sheet was exposed to a high-powered light source through the appropriate color separation film (for cyan, magenta, yellow, black, or a spot color). After development in a alcohol-based bath, the unexposed areas of the sheet would wash off, leaving the exposed areas to represent the printing ink. The overlays were aligned, and then taped to a white paper base. (No longer used.)

Color separations: Individual sheets of film for each printing ink to be used in reproducing artwork. In four-color designs, four pieces of film are used: one each for cyan, magenta, yellow, and black. For a duotone image, two films would be generated, one for the black ink and one for the spot color to be used. For tritones, three pieces of film would be generated, and so on. Formerly created by cameramen until the introduction of scanners.

Color temperature: A standardized measure of the value of a light source to control viewing conditions. Think of a piece of iron being heated in a furnace. As its temperature increases, the color given off by the piece of iron goes from dull red to bright red, followed by orange, and so on. The Kelvin temperature scale is used, under which water freezes at 273 degrees K (the abbreviation for *Kelvin*), and all molecular motion stops at 0 degrees K. This is, no doubt, more than you care to know. But, for reference, it may be helpful to know that a household tungsten bulb measures about 2700–2800K, and average sunlight is approximately 5000K. The sun at high noon measures between 6000–6500 degrees K. For many years, the graphic arts industry was standardized on 5000K viewing conditions, often referred to as *D50* lighting. But in recent years there has been a move toward the brighter, 6500K (*D65*) standard.

Comb binding: A binding method in which pages are punched, and then a comb-like piece of curved plastic is inserted (usually at the left or top edge). The teeth of the curved comb (hence the name) curl into the punched holes, and the curvature of the insert draws it closed. Comb binding allows the finished piece to open flat, which makes it suitable for textbooks and workbooks. Since the exterior of the bound piece is solid, the spine can be imprinted, although this isn't frequently done.

Comp: Short for *comprehensive*. A representation of the final printed piece, usually printed on a desktop printer and manually assembled to show a client (or the print service provider) how the finished piece should look. Comps are helpful for checking pagination and for planning complicated pieces such as those involving inserts, tabs, or custom trimming. Also sometimes called *mockup*.

Computer-to-plate (CTP): Direct imaging of a printing plate from digital information. CTP replaces previous methods of generating intermediate film and exposing plates. The imposition is digitally created, and then the printing plate is directly exposed in a large imaging device using no intermediate film.

Continuous tone: A smooth transition from one color to another, such as the variations of color in a color photograph. While the emulsion of a photographic print can replicate continuous tones, printing presses cannot. Instead, the printing process approximates a variety of color by using *halftone* dots (see Chapter Two, "Ink on Paper," for more information on halftones).

Contract proof: A proof intended to represent the appearance of the final printed piece. Contract proofs are used for color and content matching on press. Traditionally, they are made by exposing proofing materials through final film, but now they are usually generated digitally from the same information used to generate plates. Signing a contract proof constitutes an agreement between printer and client. The client's signature indicates that the proof shows correct color and final content. The printer is obliged to match the proof on press.

Cromalin®: A product of DuPont™, the Cromalin proofing offerings include both analog (film-based) and digital proofing options. The film-based Cromalin proofing systems use photosensitive coatings adhered to a heavy carrier sheet. A layer of photosensitive coating is exposed to a high intensity light source through film for one of the printing inks. In the positive-acting version of Cromalin, the exposure hardens areas of the photosensitive coating, leaving the remainder slightly sticky. Very fine, pigmented toning powder is applied to the proof, adhering to the sticky imaged areas. Another layer of the photosensitive material is laid down on the carrier, and exposed through the film for the next color, and so on. When the process is finished, you have a one-piece proof with all colors in place. As the printing industry moves more toward an all-digital workflow, less film is generated, so DuPont now also markets digital proofing solutions under the Cromalin name.

Cure: To dry or harden an ink or other applied material. Heat, pressure, air, or ultraviolet light may be used, depending on the material and the substrate to which it is applied. The purpose of curing is to minimize smearing or scuffing of the printed piece.

Custom-mixed inks: While the variety of ink recipes available from Pantone®, Toyo Ink, and other firms provide a huge rainbow of colors from which to choose, it is sometimes necessary to mix a custom color to get exactly the right shade. There's more involved than "a cup of this and a cup of that," since what's important is the appearance and behavior of the ink on the final printing surface under press conditions. To ensure realistic expectations, the printer should provide an ink draw-down, which is a thin film of the custom ink applied to paper (ideally, the actual printing stock) to simulate the appearance of the ink when printed.

Die cutting: Using pressure and shaped metal dies to cut a printed piece in an interesting shape. Sometimes done by the printer, and sometimes done by outside specialty companies that subcontract with the printer.

Digital press: While this term usually refers to plateless, toner-based printing devices, it may also refer to presses that enable on-press imaging of conventional plates. The output of high-end, toner-based presses rivals the appearance of offset printing, while enabling functions such as the customization of each piece.

Dot etcher: A skilled craftsperson who performed color corrections by delicately etching color-separation films in mild acid baths. The acid eroded the edges of halftone dots, which would alter the diameter and thus the amount of ink that the resulting printing plate would hold. Etching a positive film would lighten color, and etching a negative film would increase color. To prevent etching in some areas of the film, the dot etcher would paint on a varnish-like protective mask. After etching, the mask would be removed with a solvent. While this may seem primitive compared to the ease with which we now make color corrections in Photoshop, the concepts are the same. In fact, many dot etchers were quick to adopt Photoshop and excel at using the program to perform color corrections. Imagine how relieved they were to go home without acid burns in their clothes! Dot etching, alas, is completely extinct.

Dot gain: The tendency of ink to spread when applied to a substrate, resulting in a perceived darkening of the printed image. Touch a fine-point pen to a paper towel, and you'll get the idea. Dot gain is an unavoidable physical occurrence, but plate imaging and press controls can mitigate it. Contract proofs should approximate the results of dot gain so that the printed piece isn't a surprise.

Embossing/debossing: Using pressure and shaped dies to press paper into a three-dimensional relief. Embossing raises the surface on the finished side; debossing indents the surface on the finished side. When used in an unprinted area, this is referred to as *blind embossing*.

Estimator: A knowledgeable and important part of the printing plant's front line, an estimator is responsible for estimating the time, labor, paper, ink, and other materials that will be required to complete a printing job.

Film stripper: A nearly extinct breed of trained crafts-people who use tape, photographic masks, and dark-room techniques to combine type and images for final film. In some ways, the film stripper was the equivalent of a production artist of today, although the job title made for some very awkward moments during intro-ductions. "You're a *stripper*?!" This would be followed by a brief explanation to your date's parents, during which you attempted to condense the printing process into a few convincing sentences.

Finishing: The manufacturing processes that take place after the job leaves the printing press. Finishing can include such processes as folding, binding, trim-ming, diecutting, embossing, and foil stamping.

Flat: Pieces of film taped to large clear plastic car-rier sheets for subsequent exposure. Film strippers taped the component parts of a page to flats, and then exposed them in a certain order through masks to create a finished film for the individual printing inks. Platemakers taped down films for pages in the correct position as part of very large imposed flats. With the increasing use of computer-to-plate technology, these processes are rarely used. Instead, pages are created in page-layout programs, and imposition software posi-tions the pages in the correct orientation for directly exposing plates.

Flexography: A printing process that uses fast-dry-ing inks and plastic, rubber, or photopolymer plates with raised image areas carrying the ink. Flexographic printing transfers the ink directly to the printing sur-face, rather than using an intermediate blanket as in offset printing. Flexo printing, as it is usually called, is often used for printing flexible substrates such as plas-tic sheeting or thin packaging foils. While flexography may have previously been regarded as inappropriate for higher quality work, that's no longer the case. Improvements in inks and plate materials have greatly expanded the capabilities of flexography.

Foil stamping: Using pressure and heat to transfer a special, film-backed sheet of color (often metallic or iridescent) to paper. Foil stamping often uses a die to transfer a shaped design or to accentuate printed type and can be combined with embossing for elegant effects.

Folding dummy: A blank sheet of paper folded in the configuration that will be used in finishing the job. Pages are numbered to indicate the correct imposed page position. A folding dummy may be made by the planning department or by imposition operators and is used to check for correct folding and imposition.

FPO (for position only): Placeholder content (usually an image) used in the early stages of design. FPO images are later replaced by final, high-resolution images.

Ganged: The process of combining images on one mounting to be scanned simultaneously. Business cards or other similar pieces may be ganged together for simultaneous printing, and then separated when the printed sheet is trimmed apart. Ganging saves time and labor.

Gravure printing: A specialized printing method using engraved metal cylinders. Chrome-plated gravure cylinders are capable of extended printing runs, mak-ing gravure appropriate for publication and packaging applications. After printing, the chrome plating can be stripped off and replaced, so the cylinder can be reused.

Halftone: Since it's not possible to print millions of colors in a continuous-tone fashion, the predominant printing processes approximate a wide range of colors by using cyan, magenta, yellow, and black inks (usu-ally) printed with halftone dots of varying diameters. (See Chapter Two, "Ink on Paper," for a more detailed description.)

Hot type: A method of creating type with a raised printing surface by injecting molten metal into a shaped form called a matrix. Usually a combination of lead, tin, and other metals, the molten metal filled the mold and cooled to form the printing surface, called a slug. A slug might be just a single word, portions of a page, or an entire page. This process is also the source of the term *leading* (pronounced *ledding*). Thin strips of lead were placed between lines of text as shims to pro-vide space between the lines. The concepts and terms remain, although we no longer have to pour hot lead.

Imagesetter: A digitally driven device for imaging film. A RIP converts incoming PostScript information to very high-resolution bitmaps that guide the imagesetter's marking engine to expose the film with a laser or light-emitting diodes.

Imposition: Placing individual pages of a multipage document in the correct position for final printing.

Job jacket: A large plastic or cardboard carrier containing materials for a job. Usually open on one side like a big, flapless envelope, the job jacket allows the job materials to travel together throughout a printing plant. A job jacket might contain your original disks and hard copy, as well as any proofs and necessary paperwork pertaining to the job. Usually an identifying *job ticket* is affixed to the job jacket to identify it and serve as a job information reference.

Job ticket: Usually attached to the *job jacket*, a job ticket contains important information about a printing job, such as the job number, the customer name, contact information for key personnel, the number of inks used, the press to be used, and important dates in the job's timeline.

Knock out: In printing, an area where no ink prints. For example, white text *knocks out* of an area of black ink, leaving unprinted paper. The term is also used to refer to creating a silhouette of a portion of an image, as in *knocking out* an object so that its background disappears.

Laminate: To coat a printed piece with a clear film by using heat, pressure and adhesive. Laminates are used to protect printed pieces from abrasion and other wear and tear.

Leading: Pronounced *ledding*. The amount of space between the baseline of one line of text and the *baseline* of the following line of text, expressed in *points*.

Letterpress printing: Printing from a raised plate or collection of printing components that are held together in a *chase*. The pressure of letterpress printing creates a slight indentation, especially in heavy stock. It is a slow, mechanical, hand-intensive process, but creates unique pieces. Used by Gutenberg to print his famous Bibles, letterpress was once the standard printing process before offset printing began to replace it in the 1950s. Now it is used mainly for invitations, announcements, and fine-art printing.

Linen tester: A small, rectangular, folding magnifier used to check artwork, proofs, or printed pieces. It's called a linen tester because of its origins in the fabric industry.

Line shots: In the old manual days, a camera shot of black-and-white, hard-edged artwork such as type or line drawings. High-contrast film eliminated shades of gray, thereby producing a sharp image with no soft edges. The digital equivalent would be line-art scans.

Lithography: A printing process based on the mutual repulsion of water and oil. Oil-based ink adheres to areas of a lithographic printing plate that are not moistened by water.

Loupe: A small, folding magnifying glass that is used to examine small details in artwork, on a proof, or on a printed piece. A loupe folds into itself horizontally, whereas a linen tester pops up vertically.

Lower case: Uncapitalized text such as a, b, c, d, and so on. As compared to upper case (capitalized) text such as A, B, C, D. Originally, the term referred to the physical location of the wooden case containing the uncapitalized letters that were made of molded lead.

Makeready: The process of getting a printing press up to operating conditions. Makeready includes adjusting ink feed, paper tension, and blanket pressure. Also used to refer to the waste material produced during this process.

Matchprint: Originally a film-based proofing system marketed by 3M, the Matchprint proofing system became a product marketed by 3M's spin-off company, Imation. Ultimately, Kodak Polychrome Graphics purchased Imation, and now Matchprint is a digital system using high-quality inkjet proofing.

Mechanical: In the days of manual artwork creation, a mechanical consisted of hand-inked artwork and black-and-white photo prints that were affixed to heavy artboard with adhesive wax or rubber cement. Line shots of the mechanical were used by film strippers as the starting point for creating film for printing. Now, the term is sometimes used to describe a finished page-layout file.

Mechanical color: The process of cutting complicated, stencil-like masks for *color break*. Since each distinct color mix in a page required a separate mask, the process was exacting and time consuming. Fine knives were used to cut shapes in a red (Rubylith® brand from the Ulano® Corporation) or amber (Amberlith® brand also from Ulano) varnish-like coating on a thick, clear plastic backing. Once the masking shape was cut, sections of the coating were lifted and peeled off to reveal the clear plastic. Since the amber or red mask was opaque to the light used to expose the film, film strippers used these masks in the darkroom to create the final page films.

Offset printing: Offset printing is based on *lithographic* principles, which take advantage of the repellent properties of oil and water. The imaged area attracts oil-based inks, while the nonimaged area attracts water. On each revolution of the press, a thin film of water is applied to the plate, followed by a film of ink, which only adheres to areas not coated with water. The ink image is transferred to a *blanket*, which then transfers the ink to the paper. The use of an intermediate blanket is the reason the process is called *offset* printing.

OPI (Open Prepress Interface): A method developed originally by the Aldus Corporation (but also implemented by other vendors) that allows the use of low-resolution (and thus smaller) images in creating a page layout. These low-resolution images represent the original high-resolution images but take up less space on disk and print more quickly. They contain PostScript comments that identify their high-resolution replacements. During final imaging, a server- or RIP-based process replaces the low-resolution image with the high-resolution image. OPI is used less often with today's faster networks and larger storage devices, but it is still implemented in workflows that deal with high volumes of images, such as catalog production. Pronounced "oh-pea-eye," not "opey."

Page proof: A proof of an individual page, which is usually created to obtain customer approval of color and content at a fairly early stage in the job.

Perfect binding: Combines multiple signatures into a bundle, anchors them with an adhesive, and then applies a tape or paper binding to hold them together for a flat spine. The paper binding may also be a printed cover that allows a title and other information to be printed on the spine.

Personalization: A data-driven method of inserting a recipient's name or other personal information during printing. In offset print environments, this is usually done via press-mounted inkjet units, although processes such as addressing may be performed during later stages in the bindery. As data-driven processes become more sophisticated, and the inkjet units faster and more refined, it is becoming possible to personalize with more than just a few lines of type — even custom images can be applied.

Pica: A unit of measurement. There are six picas in an inch. A pica is equal to 12 points.

Planner: A printing company specialist who establishes which press will be used to print a job, how the job will be imposed for the press, and what finishing processes should be scheduled to complete the job. Planners may also be involved in job scheduling. In many printing plants, the jobs of estimating and planning may overlap or may even be performed by the same person.

Platesetter: An output device that uses a laser or light-emitting diodes (LEDs) to expose the photosensitive surface of a printing plate by using digital information.

Point: A unit of measurement. There are 72 points in an inch. Text size, leading, baseline grids, and the thickness of rules and strokes are almost always specified in points. Some designers specify everything in points and picas, but many are accustomed to specifying page sizes and the dimensions of objects in inches, and they only use points when referring to text size and rule thickness.

PostScript: A programming language used to describe the contents of a page so that an imaging device such as a laser printer, an imagesetter, or a platesetter can produce output. Developed by Adobe Systems, Inc., PostScript was the major driving force in the birth of desktop publishing. Since its advent in 1985, PostScript has gone through several revisions. The current version of PostScript is Level 3.

Preflight: Inspecting job files at an early stage of the job to find content errors that might prevent the file from printing as the customer intends. While there are dedicated software programs such as FlightCheck from Markzware, some print service providers rely on skilled preflight operators to examine files. Designers can also preflight their outgoing jobs as a check before submitting the job for print. This allows problems to be fixed before incurring repair charges from the print service provider.

Prepress: All the preparatory work that takes place before actual printing. Prepress includes preflight, production work to correct or modify files for printing, proofing, trapping, imposition, and plating. It may also include scanning, retouching, and color correction.

Press check: Once makeready is complete and the printing press is in an optimal running state, the client is asked to approve the printed output for content and color. This is often necessary when custom inks or tricky substrates are involved—components that may be difficult to represent faithfully with proofing. Since printing companies often operate 24 hours a day, you may find yourself invited to a press check in the middle of the night.

Press proof: While current proofing methods are adequate for simulating actual printed pieces under most circumstances, special add-ons such as custom inks or applied varnishes may present challenges. For exacting jobs such as complex promotional pieces or annual reports, it may be necessary to perform a small press run to determine if everything looks as expected. While this adds considerably to job cost, it may be worthwhile on a high-profile job to ensure that the finished piece meets expectations.

Printer's spreads: The printing position of pages on the press, determined by the imposition requirements of the job. While pages two and three face each other in a printed eight-page brochure, they don't print together. Instead, page two prints next to page seven, and page three prints next to page six. When the pages are bound together, they are read in the correct order. See Chapter Three, "Binding and Finishing," for more information about imposition.

Proof: A simulation of the final printed piece, used to check the content of the job. Necessary corrections should be marked on the proof, and the marked-up proof should be compared to the next round of proofs to ensure that the requested changes have been made. Signing a proof indicates that you consider everything to be correct in the proof.

Registration: The alignment of all inks printed on a press. Since each color is applied by an individual unit on press, there is some possibility of the successive colors not aligning. While modern presses have sophisticated controls for maintaining proper registration, mechanical or environmental problems may cause slight misregistration, as can stretching or deformation of the paper itself during the printing process. A multicolor fringe at the edge of color areas is a symptom of misregistration.

Raster Image Processor (RIP): A specialized computer that uses a combination of proprietary software and hardware to translate PostScript or PDF input to a very high-resolution bitmap image that drives the marking engine of an output device, such as an imagesetter, platesetter, or desktop printer.

ROOM (RIP Once, Output Many): The practice of processing a page in a RIP, and then using that same information from the RIP to generate proofs, film (if necessary), and plates, rather than reprocessing the original digital information through different RIPs for different output. Using the same data for multiple outputs ensures that no processing errors creep in. Using one vendor's RIP for proofing output and a different vendor's RIP for platesetting can result in a proof that does not represent what will be on the plate. This can lead to surprises on press. *Surprise* is not necessarily a positive thing in printing.

Saddle stitch: Binding multiple pages together with staple-like metal stitches. Often used for magazines and catalogs. See Chapter Three, "Binding and Finishing," for more information about saddle stitching.

Scanner: A device for converting reflective artwork, photographic prints, transparencies, or film negatives to digital information. Early scanners were large, expensive devices with daunting controls that required careful mounting of artwork on large, heavy clear drums. But with advances in optics and software, they have been largely replaced by flatbed scanners, and prices have plummeted accordingly.

Screen printing: A printing method in which a finely woven stretched screen carries a hand-cut or photographically exposed mask. The mask acts as a stencil, and ink is squeezed through the mesh of the screen in open areas of the mask onto the intended substrate. While you may associate screen printing only with apparel printing (such as t-shirts), it's also used for spot application of scratch-off coverings for game pieces, scratch-and-sniff areas, and printing on irregular surfaces such as molded pieces.

Scheduler: A printing-company specialist who determines when each portion of a job occurs (barring errors or other problems). The scheduler must consider how long each process takes and must factor in the effects of other existing jobs, staffing resources, and the required final deadline for the job. In some printing plants, scheduling and planning may overlap, or they may be done by the same persons.

Score: To press a groove into paper or board for easier folding. This ensures a smooth, predictable bend while lessening the chance that the paper or board will tear when folded.

Sheetfed press: An offset press that takes in single sheets of paper from a stack rather than a roll. Typical sheetfed press paper sizes are around 20 by 28 inches or 30 by 40 inches, although there are larger-format (and smaller-format) presses as well.

Signature: A printed sheet folded one or more times to create a single section of a multisection piece. Pages are imposed in the correct position so that when the sheet is folded, trimmed, and bound, the pages will be in the proper reading order. (For more on imposition and signatures, see Chapter 3, "Binding and Finishing.")

Silhouette: To eliminate the background surrounding the important element in an image. This may be done by erasing the background or (more commonly) by creating a mask or path that allows the element to display without the background. Also called *knockout, dropout, blockout, silo,* or *KO,* depending on your locale and your local printer's particular slang.

Spiral binding: see *Coil Binding.*

Trade shop: A print service provider that works for other printing providers and performs services such as scanning, retouching, and other prepress services. Some trade shops also provide printing and finishing services.

Transparency: A transparent, positive color image such as a 35 mm slide. Larger formats include 4 by 5 inches and 8 by 10 inches, but the advent of digital photography has made the use of transparencies (and the need to scan them) less common.

Trap: To create overlapping areas of common color in order to minimize gaps during slight misregistration on press. Trapping is usually performed at the RIP stage, although it's also possible to create traps manually in many applications. (See Chapter Two, "Ink On Paper," for a more detailed explanation of trapping issues.)

Typesetter: The definition and responsibilities of a typesetter changed with technological advances. Typesetters no longer handle tiny molded lead characters locked in a chase (container). Currently, *typesetter* usually refers to a specialist who uses page-layout tools to set type with an emphasis on readability and style in long documents.

UPC (universal product code): A machine-readable identifier that consists of two components — a bar code and human-readable numbers. The first six digits identify the product's manufacturer, and the remaining digits identify the product itself and provide a check digit used by the code reader to determine if the code has been read correctly. It's not difficult to generate UPC artwork with special barcode fonts or dedicated software, but you must be mindful of requirements such as minimum size, location, and color of the code itself. It's important that busy backgrounds or dark colors don't interfere with the legibility of the UPC, which is why it's often placed in a white rectangle. You'll have to plan for this when you're creating artwork for publication covers or books, as well as packaging.

Uppercase: Capitalized letters such as A, B, C and so on. As compared to lowercase text such as a, b, c, d. Originally, the term referred to the physical location of the wooden case containing the uncapitalized letters, which were made of molded lead. Capitals were kept in an upper case, hence the name.

Variable data printing (VDP): At its most basic, VDP can be the personalization of a printed piece by inserting the recipient's name and address: "Dear [your name here]." While this can be accomplished by using press-mounted inkjet heads with acceptable results, the increased use of fully digital presses opens the way for more extensive customization. Since each impression on a toner-based digital press is unique anyway, a database-driven process can insert custom text — even images — to narrowly target the printed piece to the recipient's demographic or buying history. While variable data printing is more expensive because of the programming and planning involved (as well as the cost of demographic information and mailing lists), the response rate from such targeted mailings is substantially higher than for generic mass mailings.

Viewing booth: A cubicle-like area that provides a controlled viewing environment for judging color. Although a printed piece will be viewed by recipients under a variety of lighting conditions from fluorescent or tungsten to daylight, it's important during production to have standardized lighting and surrounding surfaces so that everyone from designer to retoucher to pressman is viewing proofs and printed materials in a common environment. To prevent any influence from the surroundings, the surfaces of a viewing booth are painted a neutral, medium gray, using matte paint to avoid reflections. To ensure consistent lighting, fluorescent bulbs of a specified color temperature are used. Originally, D50 (5000 K) bulbs were used, but there has been a move in recent years to D65 (6500 K).

Web press: A roll-fed printing press. Trimming to individual sheets may take place at the end of the press on an inline unit called a sheeter, or the printed web may be rolled up onto a takeup reel for offline trimming. The size of the web press dictates the width of the paper roll it accepts.

Wire binding: Similar to comb binding, but wire binding uses wire that is bent into tooth-like prongs.

CHAPTER TWO
Ink On Paper

The craft of printing is a combination of art and science that has been developed and refined over hundreds of years. Because printing is a complicated mechanical undertaking, numerous variables affect the printing process. Such factors include the type of press, the direction of the grain in the paper as it goes through the press, the kind of ink being used, and the prevailing temperature and humidity during the press run. Stand by a thundering press that is running at full speed, watch the paper race through the printing units, and consider the tons of machinery churning out your job. You'll wonder how it ever works at all—it's an impressive feat. A skilled pressman is an artisan who can work miracles, but there are still some physical limitations to what can be achieved with ink on paper. It's a long trip from what you see on your monitor to the printed paper that flies out of the press.

FUNDAMENTALS OF BLACK-AND-WHITE PRINTING

The *black* in black-and-white printing is black ink. The *white* is the paper. When you hear a print job referred to as a *two-color job*, that means that two colors of ink will be required to print it. That may seem obvious, but here's a true story: There once was a poor, befuddled, novice print salesman who priced a black-and-white job as a *two*-color job: *black* and *white*. Understandably, he didn't last long in the trade and is probably selling used cars now. You may have heard the limerick:

> There was a print salesman named Bob
> Who quoted a "two-color job."
> But what was he thinkin'?
> There's only black ink, and
> The paper. Is that not macabre?

Printing a single ink on paper is somewhat simpler than printing a four-color job, but the same rules apply. While a black-and-white photographic print or an image displayed on your monitor is made of a continuous range of thousands of shades of gray, a printing press doesn't print thousands of shades of ink. Instead, a single color of ink is printed in tiny dots called *halftone dots*, which simulate the shades of gray by varying the diameter of the dots (**Figure 2.1**). It's a convincing illusion because, unless your eyesight is *very* good, the individual dots are not apparent. An image printed by this method is also sometimes called a halftone.

Figure 2.1 A black-and-white image looks smooth on your monitor. But it's actually printed with thousands of tiny halftone dots (right).

Screen ruling (also called *screen frequency*) is the measure of halftone-dot frequency (**Figure 2.2**), usually expressed in *lines per inch* (lpi). Typical screen rulings range from 65–85 lpi, used in newspapers, to 133–150 lpi that is often used for magazines and books. Some high-end magazines and art books are printed at even higher line screens—up to 200 or 300 lpi. The higher the screen ruling, the more faithfully images can be rendered, because finer detail can be maintained. So why wouldn't everything be printed at 300 lpi? Because printing conditions impose certain limitations. The coarse stock used for newspapers simply won't support fine line screens. Ink sinks into the absorbent stock and spreads, which is a phenomenon called *dot gain*. Try drawing small dots on a paper towel with a fine permanent marker, and you'll get an idea of the effect. The screen ruling is determined by the print service provider, based on the type of paper being used in the job.

SCREEN RULING:
LINES PER INCH (LPI)

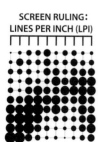

Figure 2.2 Screen ruling is measured in lines per inch (lpi).

To better camouflage the rows of dots, they are printed at time-honored angles. For example, the dots in a black and white halftone image are usually printed at a 45 degree angle (**Figure 2.3**). You don't have to create the halftone dots or figure out the appropriate angle for them. Those attributes are determined by the print service provider. The halftone dots don't come into being until the job is processed by the raster image processor (RIP).

Figure 2.3 Screen angle: 45°

If screen angles and screen frequency are the print service provider's problem, why should designers and production artists even care about such issues? Because it's helpful to have realistic expectations of the printed outcome, and both screen angle and screen ruling have an impact on printed work. Highly patterned image content, such as woven fabric, can result in an unpleasant moiré when the patterns imposed by image resolution, line screen, and screen angle combine to generate the final product.

Scanning at very high resolutions may help in some instances, but it will also produce large image files. Blurring the troublesome content may help, but is sometimes undesirable ("I thought this was a tweed jacket. It looks like *velveteen*."). Changing the screen ruling or screen angles may reduce moiré in one part of the image, but increase the effect in another area.

DPI, LPI, PPI, TLA

Because the acronyms for various forms of resolution are often used interchangeably, it's easy to get confused.

dpi (dots per inch) Used to describe the resolution of an imaging device such as a desktop printer, an imagesetter, or a platesetter. The typical desktop printer's resolution ranges from 600–1200 dpi, while the resolution of an imagesetter or platesetter is usually 2400 dpi or higher.

lpi (lines per inch) Describes the frequency of halftone dots, measured along a row of dots.

ppi (pixels per inch) Describes image resolution. For most printing applications, image resolution should be 250–300 ppi. The rule of thumb is that image resolution should be 1.5 to 2 times the printing screen ruling, but the common convention is to save images at 300 ppi.

tla (three-letter acronym)

FUNDAMENTALS OF COLOR PRINTING

While a printed color image may appear to contain thousands of individual colors, it usually consists of just four inks, referred to as *process colors*: cyan, magenta, yellow, and black (CMYK). The process inks are transparent, so when they are combined on paper, they produce other colors (**Figure 2.4**). Thus, cyan plus yellow makes green. Cyan plus magenta make violet. Yellow and magenta make red, and yellow and magenta combined with cyan makes an unattractive muddy brown. That's still a fairly small box of crayons. How can you make all the colors you need?

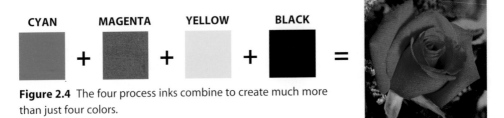

CYAN + MAGENTA + YELLOW + BLACK =

Figure 2.4 The four process inks combine to create much more than just four colors.

In traditional offset printing, the illusion of so many colors is the result of varying sizes of halftone dots, which allow different amounts of the four process colors to interact in a given area. Other printing methods use different ruses to fool the eye into seeing more than four colors, but the concept is the same: Use varying amounts of CMYK to approximate a wide range of colors (**Figure 2.5**).

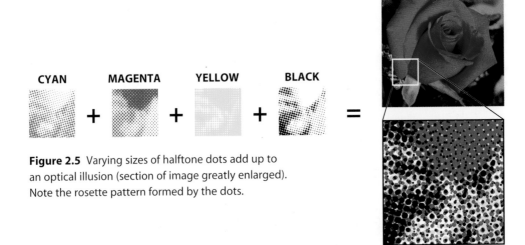

CYAN + MAGENTA + YELLOW + BLACK =

Figure 2.5 Varying sizes of halftone dots add up to an optical illusion (section of image greatly enlarged). Note the rosette pattern formed by the dots.

It's important to avoid unsightly patterns, called *moiré* (**Figure 2.6**). To see the moiré effect, put one piece of window screen on top of another, and then rotate one piece of screen. It's a challenge to eliminate an obvious pattern. That's why there are time-honored intervals of 30 degrees between the angles of the inks to create the desired rosette pattern (**Figure 2.7**). Yellow, being the lightest color, falls at a 15-degree angle away from other colors.

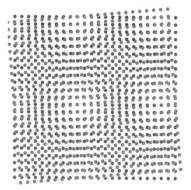

Figure 2.6 Incorrect intervals between screen angles can result in a distracting moiré. This can also be caused by a combination of screen angles and image content such as woven fabric.

Figure 2.7 Optimal screen angles add up to form a rosette pattern. Yes, it's a pattern, but it's usually not noticeable.

Screen angle preferences vary between print service providers and may sometimes be chosen to accommodate job content (**Table 2.1**).

Table 2.1 Screen angle combinations are meant to minimize patterns. Traditionally, they are 30-degrees apart (for example, 45 degrees and 75 degrees). The angle of each color is chosen to minimize interference with the other colors when all inks are combined in the printed piece.

Screen Angle Combinations

C 75°	M 15°	Y 0°	K 45°
C 15°	M 45°	Y 0°	K 75°
C 105°	M 75°	Y 90°	K 15°

Why CMYK not CMYB?

It's easy to imagine that B might be mistaken for *blue* and thus confused with cyan. But where does the K come from? One theory holds that the K is from *key*, referring to black being printed first, so other colors can be aligned to its registration marks. Another notion is that the K is lifted from the end of the word black. Whatever the true origin of the mysterious K in the acronym, it's here to stay.

Solving the Moiré Problem: Stochastic Screening

One solution for moiré is to eliminate screen angles entirely by using a printing method without the conventional grid of regularly spaced dots. *Stochastic screening*, also called *FM* (frequency modulation) screening, uses a seemingly random distribution of very small dots (**Figures 2.8 and 2.9**). If you have an inkjet printer, you have a stochastic output device right on your desk. Look at an inkjet print through a magnifying loupe, and you'll see how the scattered arrangement of tiny dots creates an image.

Figure 2.8 Stochastic screening

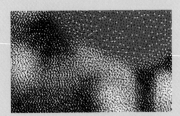

Figure 2.9 Enlarged detail of stochastic screening

After its first appearance in the 1980s, stochastic screening failed to gain much acceptance due to limitations in plating and proofing systems of the time. But it is experiencing a slight (and cautious) resurgence in the printing industry, thanks to the advent of computer-to-plate (CTP) printing, as well as increased implementation of digital (rather than film-based) proofing systems

Stochastic screening offers some interesting advantages over conventional halftones:

- Reduced chance of moiré—since there are no angles, there is almost no chance for an interference pattern to be created.
- Ability to use lower resolution images.
- Ability to print images containing more than four ink colors without screen angle issues.
- Retention of smaller details in images.
- Reduced ink usage.
- Misregistration on press is less obvious.
- Smoother rendition of skin tones.

But stochastic screening has not replaced the old-fashioned halftone dot. In fact, it's used only in a minority of printing. There are some challenges to using FM screening:

- The need for extreme cleanliness in plating: *Dust* may be bigger than a stochastic dot.
- Modifications to RIPs can be expensive ($15,000–$25,000).
- Slightly increased RIP processing time.
- On-press dot gain is higher than with conventional screening.
- The possibility of visible graininess in large highlight areas.

Consult your print service provider to determine whether stochastic screening is something they offer and whether it might be appropriate for your job. Be prepared for the possibility of increased job cost because of special handling.

Screen Values: Recipes for Color

When you need to describe a combination of cyan, magenta, yellow, and black that will print a particular color, such as the dusky blue below (**Figure 2.10**), the recipe is written in this format: C75–M50–Y25–K0. Think of halftone dots as occupying a square grid, each in its own square of the grid. The numbers signify a percentage of that square that will be filled. If the square is full, it's 100 percent. If half the area of the square is filled, it's 50 percent, and so on.

Figure 2.10 Dusty blue is 75 percent cyan, 50 percent magenta, and 25 percent yellow.

Limitations of CMYK

While an extensive range of colors can be rendered with various combinations of cyan, magenta, yellow, and black ink, there's still a limit to what CMYK can create. The human eye can see a huge range of colors—larger than even the large gamut of a computer monitor. But the total gamut of the process inks is considerably smaller than the human eye can see, or even the range that the monitor can display. Consequently, images that are quite vibrant on your monitor may print disappointingly dull. It's not because your print service provider is incompetent. It's because of the limitations of the printing-ink spectrum. In **Figure 2.11**, the large, colorful toe is an approximation of the range of colors perceived by the human eye. The solid triangular line corresponds to the range of colors that can be displayed on an RGB (red-green-blue) computer monitor. The much smaller dotted shape indicates the approximate gamut of CMYK inks. Note that the CMYK blob, while rather constricted, does not fall entirely within the RGB gamut. Some colors—bright yellows and cyan shades—fall outside the range that can be displayed faithfully on a monitor. Even a finely tuned and color-managed monitor has its limitations.

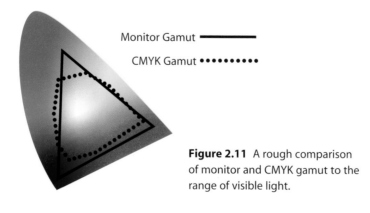

Monitor Gamut ▬▬▬▬

CMYK Gamut ●●●●●●●●

Figure 2.11 A rough comparison of monitor and CMYK gamut to the range of visible light.

This is not intended to plunge you into despondency over the limitations of the printing process. After all, disappointment is all about expectations. If your expectations are unrealistic, you're bound to be disappointed. But if your expectations are realistic, you can be prepared for the limitations of CMYK. And, equally importantly, you'll know when you need to step *outside* the world of cyan, magenta, yellow, and black to get what you want.

Spot Colors

A *spot color* is used when it is necessary to print colors that fall outside the range of CMYK inks. While it's fairly intuitive that inks such as fluorescent colors and metallics can't be faithfully imitated by process colors, there are also some rather common colors that fall outside the CMYK universe, such as bright orange and navy blue.

You're probably familiar with the Color Formula Guides from Pantone® Inc. The terms *spot color* and Pantone are often used interchangeably, although that's not strictly correct. A resource such as the Pantone Matching System swatchbook is actually a recipe book for print service providers. It provides ink-mixing formulas for creating over 1,000 standard colors, many of which cannot be accurately rendered in process colors. It's forgivable that the name Pantone has become synonymous with spot color, since the fan-like Pantone swatchbooks are probably the most common reference for specifying color. But there are other spot-color resources, such as the Toyo Color Finder from Toyo Ink, and the DIC guide from Dainippon Ink and Chemicals, Inc., (used predominantly in Japan). And there are Pantone swatchbooks that *don't* depict spot colors, such as the Pantone 4-Color Process Guide, which contains only colors created by combinations of cyan, magenta, yellow, and black.

While adding a spot color to a four-color job may slightly increase the cost of printing because of the need to create an additional plate and purchase additional ink, it ensures that important colors will print as desired. Using a spot color can also eliminate problems caused by slight misregistration on press. Consider a job containing elements in a burgundy color consisting of a process-color build of C10-M100-Y35-K50. Even the most conscientious pressman can find it challenging to keep fine elements such as small type and narrow rules in register across a large press sheet. It can also be difficult to keep the balance of four inks consistent from one part of the paper to another or from one press sheet to another in a long, multipage job. Any variation will result in color shifts, which would be especially noticeable in facing pages. Replacing the process build with a single ink, such as Pantone 209, simplifies both registration and color-consistency issues. The small increase in printing costs (as opposed to a four-color job) might be justified by the improved outcome.

CV, CVC, CVU, M, C, U: Many Acronyms, Just One Ink

It's time to dispel some urban myths about spot-color designations. The terms *Coated* and *Uncoated* refer to *paper*, not ink. Pantone 185C is Pantone 185U is Pantone 185M (apologies to Gertrude Stein). The C represents coated paper, U signifies uncoated stock, and M indicates matte paper, whose surface texture falls between that of coated and uncoated. These designations are primarily intended to keep you oriented as you view color on your computer monitor. For example, you may notice that a U version of a Pantone color looks a bit less saturated compared to the C version. It's just an attempt to mimic ink behavior on different stocks. In the olden days, CVU meant computer video uncoated, and CVC meant computer video coated. But recent DTP software has simplified this to U and C, and added the enlightened M for matte.

Process Color Guides

Since its inception, the **TRUMATCH Colorfinder** from TRUMATCH, Inc., has provided only CMYK builds.

The Pantone Corporation also provides several CMYK-based color specifiers:

PC: Solid to Process. Uses the same familiar Pantone numbers but indicates process builds.

EC: Solid to Process (Euro). Same concept as PC, but with slightly different CMYK equivalents.

DS: Process Specifier. Does not use ancestral Pantone numbers, which may help avoid confusion.

Approximating Spot Colors with Process

It's a widespread practice to pick colors from a swatchbook such as the Pantone Color Formula Guide, even for jobs that are intended to print as process. Just because everyone does it doesn't mean it's right. (Sorry. That sounds like your mother.)

The problem with this approach (as with so many things your mother warned you about), is that it can lead to disappointment. Remember that the purpose of spot colors is to render colors that fall outside the range of CMYK. Understandably, process approximations of spot colors are often unsatisfactory.

For example, a CMYK translation of a dark blue such as Pantone 286 can become a purplish blue (**Figure 2.12**). It's unfortunate, but this is as close as a combination of cyan, magenta, yellow, and black can get to the navy blue that should be used for the Brand X logo. As long as you know to expect this color approximation, you aren't shocked by the printed piece. But the president of Brand X will certainly be disappointed.

Figure 2.12 The Brand X logo is supposed to print in Pantone 286, a navy blue. But approximating that color with CMYK results in an unsightly purple. If you have a Pantone swatch book, compare the real Pantone 286 swatch with the CMYK version at left.

In the interest of realism on process jobs, consider selecting colors from a purely CMYK-based swatchbook instead, such as the TRUMATCH Colorfinder or one of the Pantone process guides. If you want a single-source swatchbook showing Pantone spot-color formulas next to their closest process equivalents, the Pantone Color Bridge™ provides helpful, side-by-side swatches.

PRESS ISSUES

Although it's a highly developed endeavor, the application of ink to paper on a printing press is still a high-speed, physical process. As such, it's subject to the vagaries of temperature, humidity, and craftsmanship. Factor in cantankerous machinery, and it's amazing anything ever gets printed. While you can't run the press, you can anticipate some common problems and build your files to facilitate printing.

Registration

Since printing inks are applied to paper in succession, not simultaneously, accurate alignment of the printed inks (referred to as *registration*) is crucial. While a small amount of misregistration can be easily camouflaged within the natural variation of colors in images, it can be a glaring problem in some special cases. This is most apparent when dissimilar color areas meet with no ink in common. In **Figure 2.13**, the reversed letters of the two-color logo fall apart if it's printed badly out of register. Is it unreasonable to expect the pressman to maintain tight register? Of course not. But keeping such art in very tight register in two dimensions over a large press sheet can be challenging. Even under the best-controlled press conditions, paper is subject to small amounts of stretching due to the physical stress of traveling through the press. Admittedly, the illustration shows a press sheet that is flagrantly out of register, which indicates two important facts: Press conditions are awful, and you need to start looking for a new printing company. However, even under ideal conditions, such art may suffer at least very small shifts, and you should be emotionally prepared. How can you compensate? If you're allowed to do so, print such artwork in shades of a single color. Then, registration isn't an issue (**Figure 2.14**).

Figure 2.13 Even slight misregister in a two-color logo can be fairly ugly. (Here, bad register is exaggerated for dramatic effect.)

Figure 2.14 One solution to registration challenges: Print the logo in a single color.

If you're designing a logo or other art element, you should keep this issue in mind. If possible, design to minimize the heartbreak of misregistration by ensuring that color areas share at least one common ink; or, better yet, print in a single ink.

The two-color, Brand X logo in Figure 2.13 is an extreme example of artwork that suffers when there is poor registration. But since printing is a high-speed mechanical process, it's unrealistic to expect utterly perfect registration, especially across a large press sheet. Even with very tight controls, slight misregistration can occur.

Trapping

One symptom of misregistration on press can be unsightly gaps between color areas that don't share a common ink (**Figure 2.15**).

The remedy for this problem is to use *trapping,* which involves creating a rim of common color between the dissimilar color areas. In **Figure 2.16**, the C100-M100 trap is greatly exaggerated for illustrative purposes. In practice, trap thickness is usually around 0.003 of an inch and fairly unobtrusive. Trap thickness may vary depending on press conditions and the conventions of the print service provider.

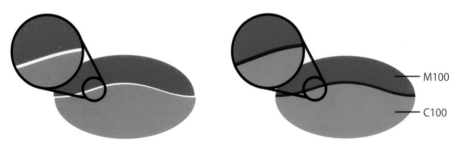

Figure 2.15 Misregistration can cause gaps between color areas that don't have an ink in common.

Figure 2.16 Trapping between two dissimilar colors (here, greatly enlarged).

Here's some great news: *It's not your problem.* Trapping is an arcane pursuit that's best left to the print service provider, who uses specialized trapping software. Many trapping circumstances can be complex to resolve, such as those involving metallic inks or neighboring gradients. And some trapping decisions depend on the order in which inks will be printed. You kids don't know how good you have it; we had to hand-carve traps, in the snow, barefoot.

In trapping, the darker color defines the edge of objects being trapped to each other, and that determines which objects *spread* (expand), which objects *choke* (contract), and which objects remain *sharp* (unchanged). In **Figure 2.17**, you can see that different approaches to trapping are required for different circumstances. The trap line consists of a combination of the adjacent colors, and it is usually not as obvious as it is in the illustration. There's some exaggeration in Figure 2.17, to call attention to the trap itself. However, sometimes it is desirable to subdue the visible trap line, especially when lighter colors combine to create heavy trap line. In version D, the color in the trap area is reduced from C100-M60 to C50-M30 to make it less noticeable. In version E, trapping is unnecessary because the objects have colors in common, so there's unlikely to be an unsightly gap in printing.

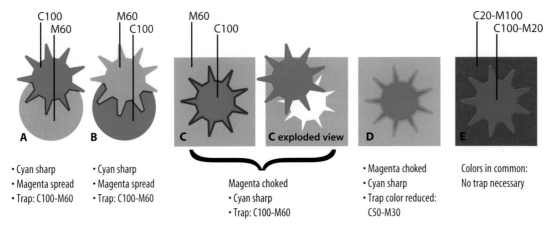

Figure 2.17 Depending on the color, a shape may be *spread* (expanded), *choked* (shrunk inward), or left *sharp* (neither spread nor choked). The darkest color defines the edge, so lighter colors are spread into darker colors.

Even though trapping is the responsibility of the print service provider, you should keep it in mind as you design. If you feel that trap lines will mar the appearance of your artwork, consider creating artwork with common colors, so that trapping is unnecessary. Also, as you examine proofs, you're usually looking for large errors such as missing elements or incorrect color. But, as you can see, it behooves you to also be mindful of the little things such as traps.

Large Ink Coverage Areas

Moving from tiny traps to the opposite end of the size spectrum, you'll discover that large color areas present some problems as well. (You're probably starting to wonder, "Is there *anything* that's easy to print?") Most ink is translucent, not opaque, and its thickness when applied to paper is measured in ten-thousandths of an inch. Consequently, covering a large area with a single spot-color ink can be challenging. Think of painting a wall. It often takes two coats to achieve smooth color coverage. Similarly, one solution is to apply two passes of the ink (called a double hit). But this can increase the cost of the job because it involves an additional unit on the press, as well as extra ink. Depending on the ink color, the first instance of the color might be a screen tint (say, 50 percent) rather than a solid, to avoid an overly heavy final appearance.

If the job already uses a four-color process, a less expensive alternative is to create a process equivalent of the screened underlay described in the previous paragraph, then run a single pass of the spot color on top of it.

Before you take the law into your own hands and start trying to solve these problems on your own, have a conversation with your print service provider about the issues involved. Don't over-engineer the job in an effort to help. Either seek guidance from the print service provider's prepress department, or leave it to the professionals to handle your job appropriately for their printing conditions. While you may incur some additional cost, these special treatments pay off in a more professional finished piece.

Rich Black

You don't have to be running spot colors to have large color areas requiring special treatment. Solid black areas bigger than, say, one square inch, usually need to be beefed up or they will appear anemic. The solution is referred to as *rich black*, but the definition of a rich black varies by print service provider. In some cases, just adding a bit of cyan (40 to 60 percent) is considered sufficient, although this can result in a cool black with a bluish tinge. To avoid a color cast to the rich black area, many print service providers add a neutral balance of the three other process colors. This author was raised to believe that C60-M40-Y40-K100 constituted rich black, but your mileage may vary. And your print service provider may fervently disagree with that recipe. As always, consult your print service provider for guidance.

If artwork or type knocks out of a rich black area (also called *reversing out*), it will require special handling to keep edges sharp to avoid an ugly appearance (**Figure 2.18**). Once again, press misregistration is the culprit.

Figure 2.18 Misregistration in a four-color rich black can be ugly. This calls for special handling.

Remember that, in trapping, the darkest color defines the edge. The case of rich blacks might be considered a sort of reverse trap. You want only *one* color to define the edge of the type or other white artwork: the black ink. To accomplish this feat, it's necessary to pull back the other colors so that if there is any misregistration, they don't peek out and create a pink, blue, or yellow halo at the edge of the reversed type.

As you can see in **Figure 2.19**, the white type is knocked out of all four plates of a rich black area. Since the black plate defines the edge of the type, its knockout is sharp (not choked or spread). But the knocked-out type is pulled back in the cyan, magenta, and yellow (hence the bloated appearance). This same approach is used for type or art reversing out of a double-hit spot color.

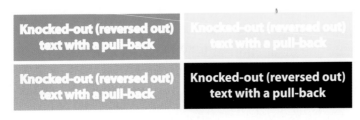

Figure 2.19 Special treatment for text reversed out (knocked out) of a four-color black.

Here comes the familiar, comforting reminder. Setting up this pull-back treatment is the print service provider's responsibility. But it's good for you to be aware of these complexities as you design. All this trapping, knocking out, spreading, and choking (sounds kind of violent, doesn't it?) may be part of the daily grind for the print service provider, but if your job requires a lot of special handling, you may incur extra charges and extended deadlines as a result. Be mindful of your print service provider's specifications for minimum type size that can be safely reversed out of a multicolor build such as a rich black.

Problem Inks

Inks are a mysterious amalgam of pigment, the vehicle carrying the pigment, solvents, waxes, and extenders. Ink problems can be caused by multiple issues, including inadequate drying time, absorbent stocks, and poor adhesion. But some problems arise from the pigments themselves. Because of its common use and stubborn personality, perhaps the best-known is Reflex Blue, which is roughly a navy blue. Reflex Blue is notorious for scuffing, smearing, and slow drying times. Navy blue seems to be a primal human favorite. Naturally, everyone wants to use *lots* of it—witness all the flags and logos that use it.

If you use Reflex Blue in your job, be prepared to tack on an extra day or so for additional post-press drying time. Additives can speed up the drying process. Depending on how heavily the color is used in your job, you can also expect slight surcharges for protective coatings (discussed later in this chapter). An aqueous coating, applied on press, is a common solution. Clear aqueous coatings usually cover the entire printed area, preventing scuffing without changing the color of the piece.

While Reflex Blue is used in formulating many of the dark blue Pantone colors, it's most troublesome by itself. It may also contribute somewhat to slower drying times and scuffing to some extent in inks mixed with it, but not as aggressively as when used alone.

Specialty Inks

Metallic and fluorescent inks can add visual interest to a printed piece. Metallic inks, while somewhat expensive, are still less costly than using *foil stamping* (a special finishing process involving heat, pressure, and thin sheets of metallic foil. See Chapter Three, "Binding and Finishing," for more information on foil stamping). The problems they pose are once again due to key pigments. Actual aluminum or bronze (zinc/copper) powder provides the basic metallic appearance, while additional pigments introduce other tinges. Metallic inks as accents are not too troublesome but such inks can mottle over large areas. Unlike most inks, metallic inks are almost opaque, which affects trapping and the order in which the ink is printed. Usually, metallic inks are printed first because of their tendency to adhere poorly to previous inks. While metallic ink will never be as shiny as foil stamping, it's most convincing on coated stock and may almost completely lose its metallic appearance on very absorbent uncoated stock. Varnishing metallic ink will not make it shinier (in fact, even gloss varnish will slightly diminish the metallic appearance), although it will subdue metallic ink's tendency to scuff and flake. If you're creating stationery, be very cautious about using metallic inks. The stress of being passed through a laser or inkjet printer can cause metallic flakes to dislodge and find new homes deep inside the printer.

Because of the metallic content, the inks are also subject to oxidation (especially the bronzes). While varnishing (discussed on the next page) may slow down the process, be emotionally prepared for some dulling over time. Also be prepared to consider somewhat extended drying times as part of your job timeline.

Fluorescent inks can add a vibrant punch, but their pigments have a limited life span, especially if exposed to sunlight for extended periods. Printing a double hit of the ink can enhance its vibrancy, since fluorescent inks tend to be transparent. They are also sensitive to heat, so such inks are not the best choice for stationery that will be run through a laser printer or copier because of the heat involved in fusing.

Custom Mixed Inks

If you just can't find a Pantone, Toyo, or DIC ink to match the color you want, your print service provider can custom-mix an ink that's just right for your job. Expect to pay more for this service since it involves extra labor and may consume extra ink (mixed as insurance for the print service provider). If you anticipate reprinting the job at a later date, tell the print service provider up front so they can retain the recipe for future use. It's not practical to "mix enough for later." Unlike wine, ink does not improve with age.

Coatings and Varnishes

Coatings are applied for two reasons: for special visual effects or to protect ink from scuffing or rubbing off. There are three general categories of coatings in print:

- **Aqueous** coatings are, as the name hints, water-based coatings. They're applied on-press, and cover the press sheet uniformly with gloss, matte, satin, or dull finishes. They behave best on coated or matte stocks, since the inherent coating on such stocks provides an even surface and consistent absorption. Aqueous coatings can be applied to uncoated stock, but there is the risk of mottling due to the nonuniform surface of uncoated stock. Perhaps surprisingly, aqueous coatings actually provide better scuffing protection than varnishes.

- **Ultraviolet** (UV) coatings are cured by UV light for quick drying. Available in matte, dull, satin, and gloss, they can be applied inline on a specially equipped press and can also be applied by silkscreen (which costs more because it's applied by separate equipment after the paper has been printed, but can achieve higher gloss).

- **Varnishes** are also applied on-press (either as the last ink or in a second pass through the press), and are also available in the standard assortment of gloss, dull, satin, and matte. Varnishes are usually applied overall, but special effects can be obtained by using spot varnishes to highlight artwork. Spot-gloss varnishes, for example, can highlight artwork to make it stand out from the page, especially on matte stock. Applying a spot-gloss varnish on a square-cut image is fairly painless, but there's a bit more work involved in spot varnishing silhouetted artwork (**Figure 2.20**). The separate plate used for a spot varnish is handled like a spot color.

Figure 2.20 Adding a spot varnish can accentuate part of an image, but creating the varnish plate requires some work (you'll have to imagine that the palm tree is *very* shiny).

Note that since varnishes and aqueous/UV coatings are sealants, it's necessary to apply the varnish or other coating as the last pass. Pieces requiring gluing (such as pocket folders or packaging) require *spot application* of such coatings, since gluing and folding take place after varnish or other coatings are applied. Spot application applies the varnish much like an ink, isolating it to certain areas (rather than applying it as an overall coat), so that glued areas are free of ink and varnish. This allows the glue to adhere correctly.

DIGITAL PRINTING

Some of the rules change when you step outside the world of old-fashioned offset print-ing. As you've seen in some of the preceding sections, the behavior of ink on paper has a lot to do with the appearance of your final job. And the limitations of the ink-and-paper relationship have an inescapable effect on what you can print successfully. Digital printing is subject to restraints too. It's just that the restraints are slightly different from those of the offset world.

In their earliest iterations, digital printing devices were not much more than glorified laser printers. The toner-based engines were beefed up to print faster and bigger, but they were still prone to have all the characteristics of laser printers. Color consistency between impressions was quite problematic, innocent environmental influences such as humidity were mortal enemies of registration, and halftone reproduction on high-speed, black-and-white machines was, to be charitable, miserable. While digital printing has always offered advantages such as relatively affordable short runs and the ability to print variable data, it was initially deemed appropriate only for basic direct mail or text-only pieces because of the superior quality of offset printing.

Digital Printing Advantages

The gap between digital and conventional offset is closing, and the premium digital print offerings from vendors such as Xeikon, Kodak, Xerox, and HP Indigo are beginning to rival the appearance of offset printing while still offering the additional appeal of custom-ization and short runs.

Short Runs

Cranking up an offset press requires a large minimum number of impressions because of all the attendant hardware. Plates have to be burned and positioned on the press, and a fair amount of time is devoted to getting the multiple inks up to optimal behavior and registration. The time and materials that are expended to reach that optimal behavior are referred to as *makeready*. Toner-based digital printing offers some advantages here. There are no plates to burn, so the minimum run for a digital job can be 200 or less, rather than 10,000. This may lower the threshold for color printing for many jobs.

Variable Data

We've all received those compelling personal letters: "Dear [Your Name Here]." Such customization is the most basic form of *variable data publishing* (VDP), but it's just a hint of what can be done with VDP. Since each impression of a document on a toner-based digital press can be different, images and other artwork can be customized for very targeted direct-mail pieces. Preparing such a piece requires quite a bit of planning, and the VDP software used by the print service provider is rather expensive. However, you may find the added expense and complexity worthwhile, since it's been shown that customized direct mail pieces elicit much higher response than generic mailings. If you have used the mail-merge features available in a word processing program, or the Data Merge features offered in PageMaker and InDesign, you have done basic variable data publishing. The complexities of setting up VDP work are outside the scope of this book.

Digital Printing Issues

Although offset printing benefits from at least 100 years of refinement, digital printing is a relatively recent undertaking. Digital printing solves some problems, such as the need for short runs. But it introduces new challenges, such as the behavior of toner on paper and paper size limitations. Large areas of uniform color are still problematic on most toner-based systems. For example, a brochure cover that is printed with a full-bleed build of C100-Y80 will look mottled compared to the same piece printed on a conventional offset press. For now, it's just one of those things that you have to anticipate. Design around the limitation by using a collage of images or smaller areas of color in which any mottling will not be glaringly apparent (**Figure 2.21**).

Figure 2.21 A screen build that covers large areas uniformly on a conventional offset press (left) may appear mottled when printed on a toner-based digital press (right).

However, you may find it surprising that rich blacks are not necessary on most toner-based presses. Not only is the dense black nature of toner sufficient for complete coverage, adding three other colors can interfere with the toner's adhesion to paper, and will actually make things worse.

Most toner-based printing lacks the inherent shine we're accustomed to seeing in printed pieces, even on coated stock. This is due to the nature of the toners themselves. The HP Indigo presses use a slurry of toner in a carrier (called HP ElectroInk), so their output often more closely resembles traditional offset printing. But all of the toner-based output can be coated, either via extra imaging units, or through coating stations attached to the press. Standalone coating equipment can also be used, but this requires that the printed pieces be moved to a separate coating machine and fed through it.

There are other differences between digital, toner-based printing and conventional offset printing. For example, most digital printing processes do not require trapping since toner is usually placed onto a carrier, and all colors are transferred to the paper in one impression, which often eliminates misregistration. Many digital presses use stochastic screening rather than conventional halftone dots and angles. These differences contribute to digital printing being a viable alternative to offset.

Registration

On most toner-based digital presses, toner for all four process colors is accumulated on a carrier that is held by the strange miracle of electrostatic force, then deposited as a single transfer to the paper. As a result, registration is somewhat easier to maintain than on offset presses, which apply each color separately from individual inking units. Sophisticated internal monitoring in these modern presses also ensures consistency. These devices demand tight environmental controls. Slight changes in humidity and temperature can play havoc with output, so toner-based digital presses are usually sequestered in specially constructed rooms that are engineered to maintain a constant environment.

Spot Colors on Toner-Based Digital Presses

Currently, spot-color offerings are limited on toner-based digital presses. Although HP Indigo and Xeikon presses do offer additional units for available spot colors (which include several metallics and fluorescents), not every Pantone color is available for these presses. However, this limitation is not as dire as it sounds. Even though the primary toner colors are called cyan, magenta, yellow, and black on these devices, the pigments are not identical to those used in offset process colors. In some ways, this is actually *good* news. The toners are often more vibrant than standard process inks, so they can simulate a wider range of

Pantone colors without resorting to actual spot colors. At this writing, Pantone provides a digital chip book certified for two Xerox digital presses, the iGen3™ and DocuColor™ 8000.

Paper Requirements and Limitations

Most digital presses are sheet-fed and have much smaller mouths than their offset brethren, which generally limits their output to approximately tabloid sizes. Roll-fed devices such as the Xeikon presses, however, cut the paper only *after* printing. And while the imaging width is about 19 inches, the total length of a piece can be banner-sized.

While there is a wide range of paper certified for toner-based digital presses, stock choice isn't unlimited. Consult your print service provider for samples of supported stock before you get your heart set on a particular paper that is subsequently not deemed appropriate. The complicated paper paths in such devices preclude the use of extremely thin (or extremely heavy) stock. And the high heat of fusing the toner to the substrate can cause curling or waving. In the interior of a digitally printed piece, this may not be so noticeable, but covers may require the extra step of lamination to keep them from curling.

Cracking and Flaking

Toner is fused to the surface of paper rather than being partially absorbed as conventional offset ink is. Consequently, it's sitting on top of the paper like a coat of inflexible paint and is prone to cracking during any folding or creasing processes. Consider this as you design for toner-based digital output, and avoid large instances of crossover art if possible. A rule here and there or the occasional line of headline text shouldn't be a problem. But the more toner encrusting the paper along the fold, the uglier the outcome can be.

Resolution and Screen Ruling

For conventional offset presses, *platesetters* are often used to digitally image plates. Data-driven lasers expose the photosensitive surface of a plate, which is then developed and mounted on a press. *Imagesetters* are used to expose film, which is then used to create an image on a printing plate (see Chapter One, "Life Cycle of a Print Job," for more information on imagesetters and platesetters). Whereas imagesetters and platesetters achieve resolution of 2400–3600 dpi, most toner-based electrostatic systems fall between 600–1200 dpi. Consequently, while these systems are capable of fairly high line screens (150–200 lpi and higher, depending on the vendor), be cautious about using infinitesimal line weights or type that has extremely fine serifs. It's a good idea to ask your print service provider to provide specifications so you know the limitations of their printing process before you go too far in your design.

YOUR MONITOR IS NOT MADE OF PAPER

Seems hardly worth mentioning: Your monitor uses transmitted light to display a semblance of your design piece, whereas the final printed job consists of ink on physical paper. When you think of things in those terms, you shouldn't be surprised that the two realities don't look the same. Yet, it's easy to forget the fundamental fact that your monitor is not displaying ink on paper, and it can be tempting to make color decisions based on what you view on screen. Wouldn't it be great if your monitor could more closely match the printed outcome of your job? Your monitor will never be identical to the printed piece, but it is possible to control your software and your monitor for a much closer match.

A Quick Overview of Color Management

It's a challenge to modify your monitor's display to simulate ink on paper. It involves *color management*, which is the science of *profiling* one device (such as a monitor) to match another device (such as a press). Profiling is the process of using specialized (and often expensive) equipment to evaluate devices such as scanners, monitors, proofing systems, and presses to determine the color characteristics of each device. Once these characteristics are known, the information can be used by software such as Adobe Photoshop to display an image on screen in a way that more realistically represents how the image will appear when it is printed. Implementing color management is not cheap, it's not easy, and it's not for the faint of heart. Using color management gets easier as more software incorporates support for it, but it's best left to dedicated color-management consultants to set up a color-managed workflow. Even then, the setup must subsequently be maintained with conscientious calibration of monitors and printers in order to have optimal results.

An in-depth exploration of color management is outside the scope of this book. For an excellent—and very readable—resource on color management, buy a copy of *Real World Color Management, 2nd Edition* by Bruce Fraser, Chris Murphy, and Fred Bunting (Peachpit Press, 2004), and take it to the beach with you.

Feeling a bit intimidated by the concepts of color management? Don't feel bad—that's normal and appropriate. But here's some good news: Even if you fall short of a fully color-managed workflow, you can still benefit by implementing some simple procedures in the interest of consistency between the color on your monitor and the appearance of ink on paper.

Control Your Environment

- **Minimize lighting interference.** Subdue the ambient light in your work space, and avoid glare on your monitor screen. Beware of incidental light reflected from brightly colored painted surfaces. Strive for consistency despite the changing light of day, and if you're like most of us, half the night. The ideal solution is to block windows, have a neutral gray room, and install lights that meet the color temperature of sunlight. (More about lighting in a bit.)

- **Subdue that psychedelic monitor background.** Vivid surrounding colors complicate color judgments when viewing images. And consider the after-effects of constantly staring at a brightly colored desktop. Your eyes' color receptors grow weary, which affects what you view afterward. For example, stare at a bright green square, then shift to a white piece of paper. You'll see a pinkish cast to the paper. So, dull as it may seem, an old-fashioned gray desktop is your best bet. If that makes you cringe, compromise by using a grayscale image, and tell your friends you're going through an Ansel Adams phase.

- **Calibrate and profile your monitor.** For best results, consider using a colorimeter such as the GretagMacbeth Eye-One Display 2, or the MonacoOPTIX XR by X-Rite. These solutions utilize specialized measuring devices and companion software to build custom color profiles for your monitor.

  However, if you're not ready to invest in such hardware, you can at least use the basics: The Adobe Gamma utility installed with Adobe Photoshop on Windows® (Start > Control Panel > Adobe Gamma) or the built-in Macintosh® color utility (System Preferences > Displays) (**Figure 2.22**). Whichever approach you choose, you should allow your monitor to warm up for at least 30 minutes, and set it to display at least "thousands of colors." It's best if your monitor is set to 24-bit color ("millions of colors"). Each utility guides you through appropriate setup, including which settings to use for the contrast and brightness of your monitor.

  Calibration is not a one-time endeavor. Monitors—whether they are flat-screen LCDs or conventional CRTs—drift over time. Consequently, CRTs should be calibrated every 80–120 hours of use, and LCDs should be calibrated approximately every 200–250 hours. Even so, monitors have a finite life and eventually must be replaced when they can no longer be kept within reasonable values.

Figure 2.22 Basic monitor-calibration utilities: Adobe Gamma on Windows (left), and Macintosh OS X Displays utility (right).

- **Treat your desktop printer kindly.** Despite the temptation of buying discount paper and inks, you'll find that you get the most predictable printing results by using recommended brand-name paper and ink cartridges. Yes, it's true that printers are cheap because the intention is to get you hooked on ink cartridges. But printer manufacturers put considerable research into creating colorants and substrates that work well together. What you save on off-brand refills and cheap paper will be offset by frustration when your output looks lousy.

- **Invoke printer profiles.** Even if you can't afford custom profiles for your devices, use the aforementioned monitor profiles and the canned printer profiles that are added when you install a printer, so that at least you'll be in the ballpark. Current versions of most graphics software offer color-management controls that make it fairly easy to plug in canned printer profiles when you print.

Realistic Expectations

If your expensive monitor is freshly calibrated, you've profiled all of your printers, painted your room a neutral gray, and you wear nothing but nonreflective black clothing…well, you're very stylish. But even the best monitor and most expensive desktop printer are, at best, an approximation of what will happen when your job goes to press. It's important to have a realistic idea of how your job will look, and everything you can do to improve its appearance on your monitor and your in-house output is beneficial. You don't want any surprises late in the game.

Consequently, your *final* judgment on job appearance should be based on *contract proofs* created by your print service provider.

Contract Proofs

Before a commercial print service provider cranks up a multimillion-dollar press for your job, *proofs* will be generated to check color and content. Internally, print service providers may use various kinds of proofs to check various aspects of a job. For example, desktop inkjet or laser output is used to check for problem fonts or mechanical issues, large-format prints are used to check imposed pages, and film-based proofs or digital proofs are used for color matching. Whereas in the olden days, print service providers generated film to create proofs, we've moved into the age of *computer-to-plate* (CTP) printing, so film output is increasingly rare. But don't feel that a digital proof is somehow less official than a film-based proof. In fact, if digital proofs are based on the same data from the *raster image processor* (RIP) that creates plates, they should be even *more* reliable for content. However, not all digital proofs show halftones, so you may be unable to check for problems such as moiré. And it may not be possible to generate a digital proof on all paper stocks.

A signed contract proof carries obligations (hence the name *contract*). The designer's signature says "this proof accurately reflects my intended design. Match this on press, and I'll be happy." And the print service provider's responsibility is to match the color and mechanical content of the contract proof on press.

In addition to portraying the mechanics of the piece, such as type flow, image crop, and page content, contract proofs also represent final color on press. If you're going to be viewing proofs in your own office or a client's office, it's important that the viewing conditions be as close as possible to those used by the print service provider. This avoids a phenomenon known as *metamerism*, wherein two colors may appear to match under one light source but don't match under different lighting conditions. For example, a sample paint chip and a piece of fabric might appear very close in color under a store's commercial lighting, but look very different in your living room. There are companies such as GretagMacbeth that specialize in color-viewing solutions, and your printer's viewing booth will give you an idea of industry standards. There are also suppliers who sell lighting (although not specific to the graphic arts industry) that falls in the desired 5000–6500 K color temperature range. For more information on viewing conditions and color temperature, see Chapter 1, "Life Cycle of a Print Job."

If the printed piece doesn't match the proof you signed, you have a legitimate gripe with the print service provider. If you miss something important on the proof, but the print service provider faithfully matches it, you're at fault. So it behooves you to very carefully inspect a contract proof before signing off on it.

CHAPTER THREE

Binding and Finishing

Getting ink on paper isn't the end of the story. The printed piece must be trimmed to its final size and subjected to any required folding and gluing. Build it the wrong size in the beginning, and you'll suffer the slings and arrows of irritated bindery operators later on. Layout repairs cost money and time. The mechanical alterations required to mend incorrect page size or configuration can be much more complex (and expensive) than just changing a font. Even if your artwork is perfect, you must keep in mind that trimming, folding, binding, and fancy finishing treatments such as embossing are all physical processes. Environmental influences such as temperature and humidity, coupled with the stresses of moving paper through printing presses, folding equipment, and trimming devices, can result in errors in the final piece. As a designer, you can't control those physical processes. But if you take those possibilities into account as you prepare artwork and create page layouts, you may be able to minimize adverse effects.

ONE SIZE DOES NOT FIT ALL

Even if you don't sew, you can nonetheless anticipate the unfortunate results of using a defective pattern. The old adage "measure twice, cut once" applies to any manufacturing process, whether it's sewing or printing (**Figure 3.1**).

Figure 3.1 Careful planning when creating a pattern can mean the difference between being stylish (left) and facing public humiliation (right).

Building your files without considering the finishing processes (like trimming and binding) can cost you money and delay your job. Consequently, the more you know about folding, trimming, binding, and imposition, the better prepared you'll be to correctly build files. Let's start with two dimensions—width and height—and work our way up to the challenge of designing in three dimensions. Think of it as one of those fun, spatial reasoning games that you loved as a child. (Or maybe you didn't. In that case, you'll hate this part of the book.) And all games have rules….

Rule Number One: Build to the Correct Trim Size

If you're creating an odd-sized piece—say, a 5-by-4 inch invitation—don't put it all alone in the middle of a letter-sized page. Create a custom page size that matches the final trim size of your piece. In a page layout program such as Adobe InDesign or QuarkXPress, specify the size as you begin the document (**Figure 3.2**).

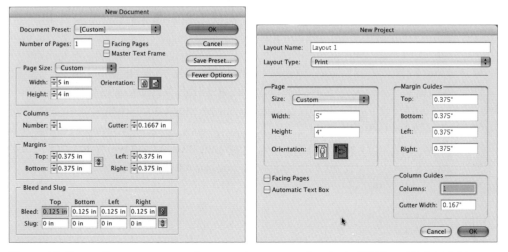

Figure 3.2 To specify a custom page size, enter the correct values in the Width and Height fields as you create a new file in InDesign (left) or QuarkXPress (right).

Slang Terms

There's a lot of colorful language in printing, and much of it has to do with the arts of trimming, folding, and binding: creep, dummy, bleed, guillotine, jogging, nipping, perfect, shingle, twist, punch, bust… (I believe some of these were also dance crazes in the 1960s).

If you're using a drawing program such as Adobe Illustrator or Adobe (formerly Macromedia) FreeHand®, the page limits that you see are just imaginary paper. Only the actual drawing's dimensions count. For more information on the way illustration programs handle page size, see Chapter Ten, "Illustrator Production Tips," and Chapter Eleven, "FreeHand Production Tips."

Why is this important? Take a simple business card as an example. The print service provider doesn't feed little individual 3.5 by 2 inch pieces of paper through a press to create cards one at a time. Your business card doesn't float alone in the middle of a press sheet as in **Figure 3.3**. Instead, multiple copies of the card are printed simultaneously—imposed— for a press sheet, which is subsequently trimmed to final size. That's why it's important to supply artwork of the correct size (**Figure 3.4**). Prepress technicians need to position your artwork accurately in the imposed layout. If they have to modify your file to do so, it costs money—and threatens your deadline.

Figure 3.3 Incorrect: A single business card on an oversized page.

Figure 3.4 Correct: A single business card built to correct size: 3.5 by 2 inches.

If you supply business card art as a lonely card on a letter-sized page, a prepress operator will have to copy the card art into a new page of the correct size (or change the dimensions of the existing file) so it's correct for everything down the line. In addition to requiring an extra, time-consuming step, this also introduces the possibility of error—not copying some little detail or moving something in the process. Figure 3.13, later in this chapter, shows one method of imposing business cards. The imposition used by your print service provider might be different, depending on their press and the size of paper used.

Rule Number Two: Provide Bleed

Trimming is the finishing process that chops the printed piece to the correct final size. Since this is a mechanical process, it helps to have some margin for error in both the printing and trimming processes. Consequently, any time there is artwork intended to extend to the edge of the page, it's necessary to provide *bleed*—extra image beyond the edge of the true page size. Commonly, bleed extends one-eighth of an inch (.125 inch or 9 points) beyond the trim line, but your print service provider may request a different bleed value. As with all issues, it behooves you to check the print service provider's specifications as you begin the job.

However, Rule Number Two does not invalidate Rule Number One, which stipulates that you should build to the correct trim size. Start with the correct trim size, and then add the extra image (or flat color) beyond the trim limits by yanking on the edges of the appropriate frames. In a page-layout program like InDesign or QuarkXPress, it's a simple matter to pull on the handles of image and tint frames to extend them beyond the page edges for sufficient bleed (**Figure 3.5**).

Figure 3.5 Extending artwork to provide bleed. The document is built to the correct final trim size, and the bleed extends beyond the trim.

In a drawing program, such as Illustrator or FreeHand, the visible page edge doesn't necessarily indicate the limits of what you can draw. Depending on how you export your artwork from Illustrator or FreeHand, objects beyond that edge may be maintained, or they may be eliminated. This behavior is particularly confusing when you're trying to make sure that you're building your artwork to the correct size, with appropriate bleed. For specific information about handling this issue, see Chapter Ten, "Illustrator Production Tips," and Chapter Eleven, "FreeHand Production Tips."

Rule Number Three: Stay Away From the Edge

You may have your heart set on that adorable doggie paw print border, but placing it too close to the edge or fold may result in disappointing results if there's any error in printing, folding, or binding. The closer your artwork is to the trim edge, the smaller the margin (literally) for error, and the more obvious any inaccuracy will be. What to do?

Don't place artwork perilously close to the edges (both internal and external). But, if you just must, make the margin as wide as possible to camouflage any problems. A small trimming error is less obvious against a larger total margin (**Figure 3.6**). Which leads us to Rule Number Four.

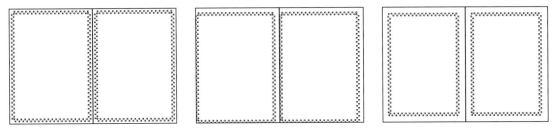

Figure 3.6 In an ideal world, your cute little paw-print border will print and trim perfectly. But a slight misregister during printing, combined with binding and trimming errors, can produce disappointing results (middle). The effect is exaggerated for dramatic effect, but you get the idea. A larger margin (right) makes it easier to camouflage a binding error.

Rule Number Four: Follow the Print Specifications

Your print service provider should provide folding and trimming specifications to guide you as you create your work, including such information as:

- Minimum distance from edges and folds for artwork
- Minimum amount of bleed (usually $1/8$ of an inch)
- Suggested sizes for panels in folded pieces

FOLDING: HIGH-SPEED ORIGAMI

Consider something as simple as a three-panel, letter-fold brochure. If all panels were the same width, the innermost panel would buckle, and the piece would never fold completely flat—the brochure would spring open or the oversized panel would crinkle when forced (**Figure 3.7**). You can demonstrate this for yourself by folding a sheet of paper into approximate thirds, as if you were going to stuff it in an envelope.

The solution? Make the fold-in panel more narrow (**Figure 3.8**). Sounds simple, but think of the effect on your design: You have to build your design to accommodate the shorter third panel. The sanest way to do this is to build such a piece as a two-page job—one page for the outside and one for the inside. Don't build such a piece as a pair of three-page spreads because this provides no way to create the narrower panel (page layout applications only allow one page size per document).

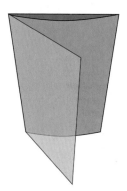

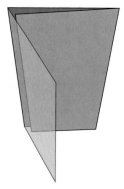

Figure 3.7 Wrong: a three-panel piece with equal-sized panels. The inner panel buckles, so the piece can't fold properly.

Figure 3.8 Right: three-panel piece folded so the innermost panel is narrower. Now the piece folds flat.

For example, if the finished, open flat width is 11 inches, build the file with two panels that are 3 11/16 inches wide and one panel 3 5/8 inches wide. Keep in mind that the inside and outside of the piece are mirrors of each other: The outside of the brochure will need the short trim panel on the left, and the inside of the brochure will need the short trim panel on the right (**Figure 3.9**).

Before starting, ask your print service provider what panel sizes they suggest, based on the paper stock to be used on the job, and the requirements of their equipment. Some folding configurations don't require short panels (**Figure 3.10**).

BINDING METHODS

There are many ways of combining multiple pages into a single, finished piece. At home, we use staples, paper clips, or binder clips to consolidate sheets of paper. The methods used in printing plants are rather more elaborate.

Saddle Stitching

Take another look at the magazine that we've been using as an example. The staples that anchor the pages at the spine of the magazine are actually created from a spool of wire. For the binding process, the loose sheets of printed pages that constitute the magazine are draped together over a saddle-like holder (hence the term *saddle stitching*). The wire is fed into position, cut to a short length, bent into shape, and then the legs of the staple are driven through the pages. Finally, the legs are bent into the final staple shape (**Figure 3.22**). Of course, this all takes place at high speed, in about the same amount of time it takes you to say the word *magazine*.

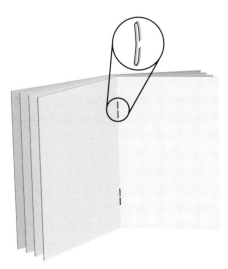

Figure 3.22 In saddle stitching, wire is fed from a roll, and then cut to form staples, which are driven through a sheaf of paper and then crimped.

Perfect Binding and Case Binding

There is another method of binding—perfect binding—that is used for larger publications such as textbooks (and some high-page-count journals). In perfect binding, creep is not as large an issue as it is with other binding methods, although it can still occur. Whereas magazines might combine over 100 pages in a saddle-stitched issue, when perfect binding is used, pages are gathered in much smaller groups—such as 16-page signatures—which are likely to result in less-pronounced creep. Then, multiple signatures are stacked together, trimmed (or ground off), and glued at the spine (**Figure 3.23**). Finally, a cover is added to enclose the pages, which is held in place by glue along the spine. For larger books such as textbooks, the spine is reinforced by adhering a cloth strip to the spine of the gathered signatures before affixing a hard cover. This is called *case binding*.

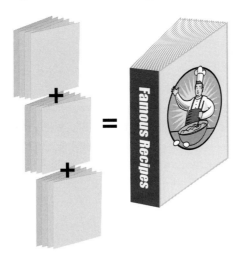

Figure 3.23 In perfect binding, individual signatures are stitched with thread to keep their pages in place. Then, multiple signatures are gathered together and anchored with adhesive on the common spine. Finally, a cover is added.

Although the smaller constituent signatures in a perfect bound book are not subject to the degree of creep that you might see in a magazine, you still have to consider some of the side effects of combining a high number of pages with the relatively stiff spine of a perfect binding. Even in a comparatively slender magazine of 192 pages, there is pronounced pinching of the pages at the center of the finished magazine, making it difficult to read some text near the interior bound edge. You can compensate for this by using wider inside margins when you build your pages (**Figure 3.24**).

Figure 3.24 Anticipate the pinch of perfect binding by setting wider inside margins (right).

Comb Binding

Often used for publications such as cookbooks, textbooks, and workbooks, *comb binding* allows a book to be opened flat. Rectangular holes are punched in the pages of the book, and then the teeth of the plastic comb are pushed through the holes. Because the combs are coil-like and curly, the teeth curve back under a spine-like collar that forms a solid spine for the bound book (**Figure 3.25**). The plastic combs themselves come in a variety of colors and diameters. Comb-bound books usually use heavier stock for the front and back covers, or they use clear plastic sheets as a protective first page.

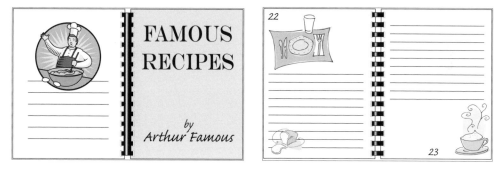

Figure 3.25 Comb binding allows books to be opened flat. It's great for cookbooks and workbooks, but makes it challenging to add a printed spine.

Comb binding has one disadvantage: It's a challenge to put a title or other copy on the spine. It's possible to apply adhesive labels or even imprint the plastic combs by using silk screening at extra cost.

In preparing artwork for a publication that will be comb bound, you have to provide sufficiently wide inside margins so the punched holes won't damage any content. Your print service provider can give you specifications for their punches.

Most print service providers and many office-supply stores can perform comb binding for you. But if you frequently produce short-run books or other small-quantity publications that require comb binding, you might consider purchasing punching and binding equipment of your own.

Coil Binding

In coil binding, a spiral of wire or plastic is threaded through round holes punched in the book (**Figure 3.26**). As with comb binding, coil binding (also called spiral binding) allows a piece to lie flat when open. However, there's no way to imprint a spine, and you must create a wide inner margin as you design the piece so that the printed area of the page will clear the punch holes.

Figure 3.26 Coil binding is suitable for notebooks, cookbooks, and textbooks. While this binding method allows a book to lie flat when open, there's no way to imprint a spine.

Other Binding Methods

If you're creating textbooks or notebook-like workbooks, you'll encounter other punch–and–bind methods that are similar in configuration to comb and coil binding. *Wire binding* uses tooth-like loops of wire similar in appearance to the teeth of comb binding, but it produces a sturdier binding than the plastic combs. By now, you're probably reciting the mantra, "Use wider inner margins to avoid the punch holes." Hold that thought. It applies to most specialty-binding methods.

For heavy-duty books with constantly changing content, such as a wallpaper sample book, *post binding* may be the most appropriate solution. In this binding method, metal posts are pushed through punched holes in the book and anchored with bolts that thread into the post centers. This method has the advantage of allowing you to add or replace pages, and it's possible to have an exterior cover with an imprinted spine.

Special presentations or other artistic publishing concepts may involve custom binding solutions such as handmade covers or cases and decorative binding devices such as screws or ribbons. Such pieces are usually used in very limited print runs and entail a considerable amount of handwork. Consequently, these undertakings require extremely careful planning.

MOVING BEYOND TWO DIMENSIONS

When you start building more complicated pieces—such as pocket folders—it's really helpful to create a dummy of some sort, so you can visualize the finished piece. It's easy to think of how the finished piece will *look*, but you need to consider how the piece will *print* and *fold* so you can create it correctly. An anatomically correct dummy will let you visualize both the *inside* and *outside* and will shed light on the difficulties of positioning tricky artwork. In fact, the challenge of lining all that stuff up in your head may force you to simplify your concept.

Consider a pocket folder (**Figure 3.27**). Folded, its configuration resembles a simple, two-page spread. But take a folder apart so you can see how the pocket and its glue flaps are positioned, and you'll see that the printed piece is rather more complex. Any art falling over the pocket has to be carefully aligned with art on the inside of the piece, and this can present a challenge in design as well as in printing and finishing.

Figure 3.27 The outside of the finished pocket folder looks like this…

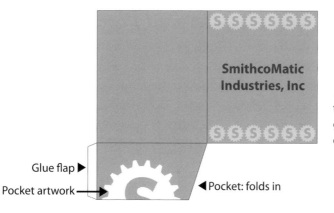

…but it should be created like this. Note that the pocket and glue flap affect the dimensions of the piece.

How do you build such a piece? Think of it as having an inside and an outside, and build it as a two-page document. As with all printed pieces, build to trim size. But you also have to think in three dimensions, to take into consideration the physical processes of folding and gluing.

The compl ex trimming for a piece like a pocket folder requires a shaped cutter called a *die*. If possible, obtain artwork for the finished *die line* to use as the basis of your file, as well as an example of the final configuration. A die line is a drawing of the open, flat piece, with all the folds and cuts indicated. This will help you visualize how the artwork must be positioned on the panels of the pocket folder. You'll also learn a lot about how your files must be created if you disassemble a printed example of a finished pocket folder. You'll see how the thickness of the heavy stock affects artwork at the folds, and you'll see how you must accommodate gluing requirements in your design.

Most print service providers who specialize in printing pocket folders can provide vector artwork for standard die lines, which you can use as a guide for building your piece. Since the glue area must be blank to allow glue to adhere to unprinted stock, follow the print service provider's guidelines for the size and position of the unprinted area to ensure that no artwork falls within it (**Figure 3.28**).

Figure 3.28 The inside of the finished pocket folder may look like this…

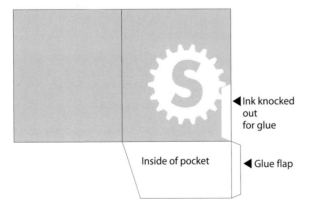

Inside of pocket   ◀ Glue flap

◀ Ink knocked out for glue

…but it prints like this. Ink must not be applied in areas that will be glued.

In addition to considering the unfolded size of the folder, you must include the glue flap in the overall size of the piece. In **Figure 3.29**, the *folded* size would be 9-by-12 inches, but the *actual* size of the artwork is 19-by-16 inches to accommodate the one-inch glue flap and the four-inch height of the pocket.

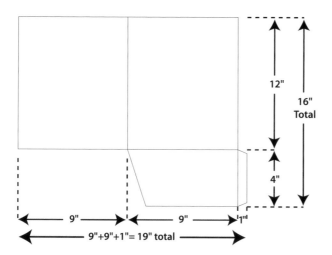

Figure 3.29 The dimensions of pocket-folder artwork must include the glue flap and the pocket area. It's helpful to take apart a printed example that is made from the cutting die that will be used on your job. This helps you visualize how the artwork should be created.

Die Cutting

When your design requires specially shaped edges or complicated folding and assembly, special *dies* must be created to *score* and cut the printed piece. Scoring is the act of pressing an indentation into the stock to facilitate folding the final piece. Die cutting is the process of cutting the printed piece into a custom shape. Packaging and pocket folders are examples of pieces that require both scoring and die cutting. Scoring ensures predictable folding, and die cutting creates the shape necessary for the printed piece to become a pocket folder or package. The die itself consists of sharp steel cutting edges anchored in a sturdy wooden base. Although much of the design of cutting dies is now assisted with computer-driven manufacturing, there is still considerable handwork and skill involved in making a successful cutting die. Provisions must be made to ensure that cuts are clean and complete, scoring is correct, and excess material is safely removed without clogging or damaging the cutting edges.

The cutting die is mounted on a specialized, die-cutting press, which uses pressure to score and cut the stock. Most die-cutting devices are platen-based, meaning that the die is a flat surface. But there are also rotary die-cutting presses, which require that the die be affixed to a cylinder. Not all printing companies perform their own die cutting. Some opt instead to contract with companies that specialize in such custom finishing.

If you intend to create a specialized piece for which the printer has no existing die, work closely with their finishing department (or the outside finisher, if that part of the job is being outsourced) to ensure that your artwork is built correctly. They can help you understand finishing issues affecting your job, and their advice can steer you away from problematic designs. It's important that you obtain a die line before you finalize your artwork (**Figure 3.30**). It may be supplied as an EPS or imaged on clear film. Carefully follow the dimensions of the die line as you plan your design, and you'll minimize problems during the finishing process.

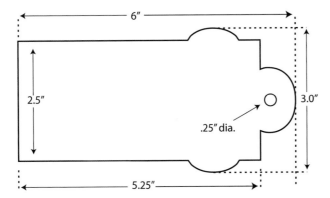

Figure 3.30 Die-line artwork shows the dimensions of the finished piece and indicates any scores, punches, or perforations.

Creating correct artwork for a die-cut piece can sometimes require that you create custom bleed areas that consider the irregular trim of the finished piece. Bleed on a diecut piece is more than just a concentric rind around the trim. A beveled approach is required where colors meet some trim points, in an effort to minimize the chances of color falling in the wrong place on the finished piece (**Figure 3.31**). Die creation is a combination of art and engineering. Don't embark on creating the art for a piece that will be elaborately die-cut without first consulting with your printer's finishing department or finishing supplier. They may have an existing die line that you can use as a basis for designing your piece, which would reduce job cost.

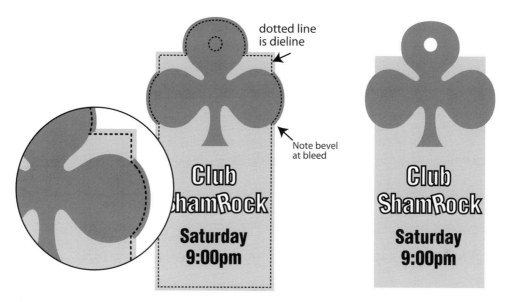

Figure 3.31 Die-cut pieces like this hang tag may require complicated bleed construction. Note beveled treatment where two colors meet (left). Finished piece (right).

Embossing

Embossing adds dimension to paper by pressing the paper stock between shaped metal pieces, resulting in a raised surface on the top (reading side) of the paper. Heat and pressure help push the paper into the shape of the embossing dies (**Figure 3.32**).

Figure 3.32 Heat and pressure combined with a pair of shaped dies (top) are necessary to produce an embossed effect on paper (bottom, shown in cross section).

Debossing is the same concept, but the shape of the dies creates a convex shape, pushing the surface of the paper *down* rather than raising it.

There are several variations on the concept of embossing:

- *Blind* embossing is an embossed effect in an unprinted area of the paper, thus creating artwork solely from the shape of the embossing.

- *Registered* embossing is aligned with a printed area already on the paper. While registered embossing heightens the dimensional effect, it requires more precision than blind embossing.

- *Glazed* embossing describes the shine that may appear as part of the embossed effect, especially on dark stock. Sometimes glazing is induced intentionally, although the higher heat often used to produce the effect can lead to scorching, and thus must be cautiously applied.

If you plan to use embossing to enhance your printed piece, consult with the print service provider and any participating outside finishing supplier to ensure that the effect you visualize is possible with the stock you intend to use. Understandably, the stock must have sufficient weight to withstand the embossing process. The pressure and heat used to shape the paper can weaken the paper, especially when attempting to force it into extreme or highly detailed embossing dies. The paper must be flexible enough to accomplish the effect, but strong enough to hold up to the deformation. Any texture inherent in the paper must also be taken into consideration, as well as any other finishing effects (such as folding or perforation) occurring close to the embossed area.

The embossing dies themselves are based on artwork such as an EPS file or raster artwork. As you prepare artwork to be used as the basis for embossing, consult with the finishing experts to ensure that you provide artwork in the appropriate format. It's likely that skilled artists will modify your artwork to create the dies and perform handwork on the metal dies themselves to ensure that the final embossed piece matches expectations. Plan for the extra time and cost involved in creating and refining embossing dies. Something this elaborate can't be hurried, but the results can be stunning.

Foil Stamping

Often used as an accent for book covers and packaging, foil stamping uses a heated, raised metal die to transfer decorative foil from a roll of carrier material onto the underlying paper. The foil may be metallic, colored, or iridescent. Some foils are holographic in nature, creating a rainbow or three-dimensional effect when applied. The best results are achieved on smooth, coated papers, since pronounced texture may prevent the foil from adhering uniformly. In addition, foil may not adhere to some coatings such as some waxy varnishes, so you should use aqueous coatings or nonwaxy varnishes before foil stamping.

As with embossing, artwork must be created to serve as the basis for the foil stamping die, and it's important to consult with knowledgeable specialists as you begin the process. Foil stamping is most effective in reasonably small areas such as type or patterns. It can be difficult to cover large areas successfully with foil stamping. But if you want a realistic metallic effect, foil stamping can accomplish what could never be equaled with metallic inks. And combined with embossing, foil stamping can create some beautiful effects.

CHAPTER FOUR
Preparing Raster Images

Whether you acquire an image from a scanner, a digital camera, a royalty-free CD with 1,000,000 images, or a stock photography vendor, it's made out of pixels. **Pixel** is shorthand for *picture element*, the smallest unit of information in a digitized image. Even though pictures on your monitor look like smooth transitions of color, zoom in sufficiently and you'll see all the little square pixels that actually make up the image (**Figure 4.1**).

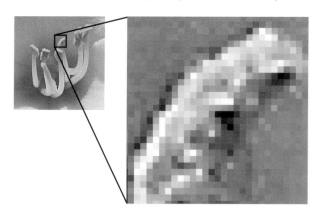

Figure 4.1 Images are made of pixels. Think of them as little-bitty mosaic tiles.

ANCIENT TIMES: B.P. (BEFORE PIXELS)

In the olden days of graphic arts, enormous cameras were used to capture artwork such as drawings, reflective photographic prints, transparencies, or painted illustrations. Highly skilled cameramen commandeered these monstrosities, some of which occupied entire rooms. The use of colored filters, masking, and exposure methods to produce color separations (a separate piece of film for each printing ink) was rather arcane and required years of apprenticeship and study to perfect. And since every step required the use of specialized film, there were a lot of trips to a darkroom to develop the results in chemical baths. It all seemed very high-tech at the time (well, compared to cave paintings), but the process was quite time-consuming.

Now: A.P. (All Pixels, All the Time)

Film has given way to pixels, and we are now beginning to keep our family photos as shoeboxes full of CDs rather than dog-eared color photographic prints. What was once the province of the darkroom became a daylight venture, and the tools of the craftsmen have become available to anyone brave enough to wade in.

Scanners

While early scanners still required highly skilled graphic arts professionals to operate them, they greatly speeded up the process of capturing artwork for color separations. Early analog models used photomultiplier tubes and a daunting array of knobs and buttons to perform the same job that had been done by the huge cameras. The first scanners were petite only by comparison to their gigantic camera ancestors: Many could easily dwarf a Volkswagen. It was necessary to mount artwork on a heavy, clear plastic drum, and then painstakingly ensure that there was no dust or a trapped air bubble to mar the scan. Scanner operators came from the ranks of color-separation cameramen, and their years of finely honed instincts for camera separations translated well to the newer photomechanical methods. The first scanners still produced film output, not pixels. But the next development was the move to digital capture and storage of image information, resulting in the introduction of the pixel and the advent of digital retouching.

In the mid-1990s, improvements in the capabilities and simplicity of flatbed scanners, coupled with the introduction of Adobe Photoshop, led to a major change in the way color separations were performed. It was no longer necessary to mount artwork on cylindrical drums, and the numerous knobs were replaced with onscreen buttons and dialog boxes. The digital imaging revolution was underway. Suddenly, people who weren't sure what *color separation* meant were *making* color separations.

As flatbed scanners have become more automated and less expensive, it's relatively easy even for novices to make a decent scan. But the more you know about what constitutes a *good* image, the better the chance you can create a *great* image from the pixels generated by your scanner.

Digital Cameras

Today's scanners capture transparencies, reflective images, or illustrations and express them as pixels. But now we're undergoing another revolution. High-end digital cameras now rival—or exceed—the ability of film-based cameras to capture photographic detail. Digital photography also cuts out the middleman. The image captured by the camera is a digital original, so there's no need to scan a print. Of course, the better the camera and the photographer, the better the image. Your mobile phone isn't up to the job.

Imaging Software

Once you have captured pixels, it's likely that you'll want (or need) to *do* something with them. The industry standard imaging application is Photoshop, and for good reason. Photoshop provides controls for color correction that enable a knowledgeable user to achieve results equal to those of a knob-twisting scanner operator. And its retouching tools surpass the capabilities of the original, million-dollar dedicated systems. If you're just beginning to learn Photoshop, you won't lack for educational resources. You could probably build an addition to your house from the books and magazines devoted to exploring Photoshop. You can add Chapter 9, "Photoshop Production Tips," to the pile.

Photoshop is arguably the most versatile and widely accepted application for image manipulation, but there are other applications that perform useful imaging functions as well.

Adobe Photoshop Album is intended for casual snapshot photographers who want to clean up family photos and create slide shows. It has no support for CMYK images.

Adobe Photoshop Elements might be regarded as Photoshop Light, but it still packs a hefty arsenal of retouching and color-correction tools. The product is geared toward enthusiasts rather than professional photographers and lacks support for CMYK images.

Adobe Lightroom™ is engineered for use by photographers working with raw digital images. It provides sophisticated tools for organizing and color correcting images. As of this writing, Lightroom is in public beta for Macintosh, but will soon be a shipping product for both Macintosh and Windows.

Apple iPhoto® offers features similar to those in Photoshop Album. Geared toward hobbyists, iPhoto has organizational tools and limited color-correction capabilities, but no support for CMYK. As you might expect, iPhoto is available only for the Macintosh operating system.

Apple Aperture is targeted to photographers working with raw digital files. It provides organizational tools as well as color correction controls. Aperture is Macintosh-only.

These are not the only solutions that exist for manipulating images. There are painting programs, such as Painter™ and Paint Shop Pro® (both from Corel®), which let you easily make images resemble watercolors or oil paintings. There are countless plug-ins that enhance the Photoshop toolset. Imaging tools for consumer and hobbyist photographers increase on a daily basis. Even Microsoft® has entered the market with the Digital Imaging Suite. However, most of these programs don't offer support for CMYK images, so they're not the best tools if you're preparing images for print.

RESOLUTION AND IMAGE FIDELITY

The resolution of an image is generally measured in pixels per inch (ppi) unless you speak metric, in which case it's expressed in pixels per millimeter. Determining the proper resolution for Web images is simple: 72 ppi at final size. But there are strongly held (and hotly debated) beliefs regarding the appropriate image resolution for printing. Some hold that 150 percent of the final screen ruling value is sufficient, and some believe twice the final ruling is preferable, largely because it's easier to calculate the resolution. For example, an image that will be printed at 150 line screen should have a resolution of 300 ppi. When typical hard drives held 80 MB, networks were glacially slow, and RIPs choked on 15 MB PostScript files, it was important to trim off every little bit of fat, so we agonized over resolution. But now, with hard drives measured in hundreds of gigabytes, and RIPs with much more robust digestive tracts, we can afford the luxury of a few extra pixels. That said, there's rarely an advantage to exceeding 300 ppi, even for higher line screens such as 175 lpi printing. So put away the calculator. For most circumstances, 300 ppi at final size is adequate and provides a bit of elbow room if you have to slightly reduce or enlarge an image.

Scaling Up

When enlarging or reducing an image, consider the pertinent word in the previous paragraph—you may *slightly* reduce or enlarge an image. When an image is scanned or captured by a digital camera, the number of pixels contained in that image is fixed. As long as the original digitizing process netted sufficient pixels for your intended use, fine. But when you enlarge an image in an image-editing application such as Photoshop, you're attempting to generate missing information, a process called *interpolation*. This interpolation process works reasonably well (considering that you're asking it to make something out of nothing), but the result is never as good as a proper-sized original scan. And the more drastic the transformation, the less satisfying the outcome (**Figure 4.2**).

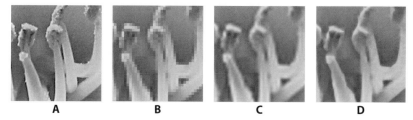

A   **B**   **C**   **D**

Figure 4.2 You can't truly make something from nothing. Notice the loss of detail in the scaled-up versions.

A: Original 300 ppi scan
B: Original 72 ppi scan
C: Results of increasing resolution of B to 300 ppi
D: Results of increasing resolution of B to 300 ppi by using a specialized fractal-based scaling plug-in to enhance the results

Because of the limitations imposed by resolution, it behooves you to anticipate how the image will be used and to set your scan percentage accordingly. For typical image content, you can probably scale up to 120–125 percent. If the image is background content without much detail, such as a soft-focus landscape or a gauzy sunset, you have more leeway and you can probably get away with scaling up to 150–200 percent. Conversely, if you need to maintain very small details, you may be limited to less than 120 percent.

Scaling Down

Remember that scaling *down* also requires interpolation. While the loss of data may not be quite so obvious when you reduce the size of an image, there *will* be some softening of detail (as shown in **Figure 4.3**), so it's still best to plan ahead, and make your initial scan as close as possible to the dimensions at which you intend to use it in a page-layout program. Generally, if you find it necessary to scale an image down below 50–75 percent in your page layout, consider rescanning. And, as with enlargements, try to use an even scaling factor, such as 120 percent rather than 119.6954 percent.

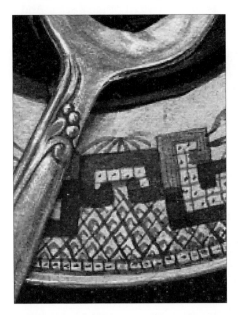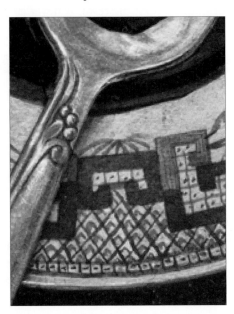

Figure 4.3 Surprise! Even scaling *down* an image can slightly soften detail. The image on the left was scanned at 25 percent. The image on the right was scanned at 100 percent, and then scaled down to 25 percent. If detail is important, it's better to scan to the correct final size.

Planning Ahead

Now that you're terrified to scale an image up *or* down, what is the safe path? If you do your own high-resolution scans, and you anticipate doing a lot of experimentation with image size as the design develops, you might consider just doing quick-and-dirty FPO (for position only) scans to start. Since such images are meant to be used only as placeholders, they can be low resolution (72–100 ppi). Build and tweak the design, scaling images as you wish. Then, when the layout is finalized, note the image scale factors, do the final scans to size, and replace the FPO images with the real scans. (Digital photographs are discussed shortly.)

Alternatively, if you want to do all your scanning at one time, but still would like some flexibility in scaling, scan one large and one small version of each image at the outset and work with those.

If you rely on the print service provider to perform scanning, the responsibility may be on their scanner operator's shoulders, not yours, depending on the workflow. Previously, when desktop scanners produced considerably lower-quality scans than those of service providers, there were two common approaches to placing scans.

In one approach, the printer was given transparencies and an indication of scan size, usually via markings on the transparency sleeve (since there still had to be some notion of final size, however sketchy). The printer then provided low-resolution FPO scans to be used in designing. When the job was submitted, the printer substituted the high-resolution images for the FPOs. This approach is still used frequently in catalog production, since it's saner for the print service provider to color-correct and manage the large repositories of images that are used in multiple publications. This low-resolution/high-resolution swap is usually referred to as *OPI* (Open Prepress Interface), Automatic Picture Replacement (APR, a Scitex solution), or just plain *image swap*. It's a bit more complicated than simply reducing the resolution of the images used as FPO scans. In these image-replacement workflows, the low-resolution images contain internal PostScript comments that identify them as low-resolution versions of particular images. Special server-based processes are required to perform the high-resolution substitution when the job is imaged. Because the high-resolution scans have already been done, it's advisable to avoid scaling images outside the standard 75-125 percent range in your page layout. If your design demands scaling beyond those limitations, let the print service provider know. They may need to rescan the image, and then supply you with a new low-resolution placeholder image for best results.

> **NOTE:** *There is a significant issue to be considered when using OPI/APR workflows for work incorporating transparency, such as that available in Adobe InDesign or QuarkXPress 7.0. The short story is that high-resolution final images need to be in place in layouts when the job is imaged or exported to PDF. If your printer is supplying OPI-based, low-resolution images to you, ask them to advise you of the best way to approach this issue. It doesn't mean you can't use transparency. It just means some special handling may be required. For an extensive discussion of transparency in InDesign, see Chapter 12, "InDesign Production Tips."*

The second approach is to do your own FPO scans, resizing to your heart's content in a page-layout application. Supply the transparencies and other art (such as reflective prints or original artwork) to the print service provider with 100-percent-sized printouts of your job, and let them do the scans and image replacement.

In both of these scenarios, it's important to note that you can't do anything useful to the low-resolution FPO images themselves. Any retouching, color-correction, compositing, or silhouetting would have to be re-created on the high-resolution scans, thus wasting any work performed on their low-resolution representations.

Digital Photographs

As digital photography displaces film-based work, the prepress workflow may change a bit, but the basic rules are still the same. Photographers who formerly supplied transparencies are increasingly providing digital images, which eliminates the scanning step. While direct digital images lack the visible grain that would be apparent in extreme enlargements of transparencies, they're still subject to showing visible pixels when enlarged beyond the recommended 125 percent mark.

Since there is no film original to rescan, and it's rarely feasible to reshoot, try to avoid any extreme enlargements with purely digital shots. Or at least be prepared to deal with the pixelated consequences. Fractal enlargement plug-ins such as Genuine Fractals from onOne Software may give you slightly better results with extreme enlargements, but they can't miraculously transform a tiny, low-resolution scan to something appropriate for a magazine cover. Nothing beats a healthy original image, chock full of detail.

Cropping and Transforming Images

It would be great if you could anticipate the exact size, crop, and angle at which you'll want to use an image in your page layout. But it's difficult to see that far down the line at the moment you're slipping a transparency under the lid of your flatbed scanner. Oh, and watch out for that little gust of wind that comes along just as you're putting the lid down…

Cropping

Should you crop your images during scanning? Maybe. You probably should crop if you're fairly certain about future image use. Leave a reasonable rind around the image area you intend to use, to provide some elbow room when you place the image in the final page. However, if you think you'll want to crop the image more generously in the near future—maybe you're not sure if you might want to show a row of four buildings instead of just the one in the middle—then it's worth scanning the whole shebang. But don't feel compelled to scan an entire image just to get the two-inch golf ball that you're going to silhouette anyway.

Rotating Images

Almost any transformation, whether resizing or rotating, will require interpolation of pixel information. The only safe rotations are 90-degree increments—anything else will result in softening of detail (see **Figure 4.4**). Think of those rows and columns of pixels, much like the grid of a needlepoint pattern. Imagine what a challenge it would be to redraw that pattern at a 42-degree angle. It should give you a little sympathy for the math Photoshop has to do.

 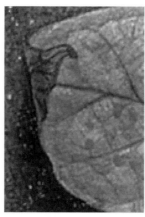

Figure 4.4 Rotation at anything other than 90-degree increments degrades detail. An image scanned at the correct angle (left) is sharper than an image rotated 42 degrees after scanning (right).

All these cautions about transforms such as scaling and rotating are not intended to strike terror in your heart. Don't be afraid to enlarge, reduce, or rotate if you need to. Just be prepared for the unavoidable loss of detail and the degradation of the image's appearance. Try to resize in even increments, and beware of oblique rotations such as 1.25 degrees in the interest of maintaining as much information as possible.

Successive transformations—scaling and then rotating, for example—are particularly destructive. Let your conscience be your guide. How important is the detail in the image? If it's a key product shot, it's worth rescanning (if possible). If it's a less important image, such as a ghosted background or a decorative bit, you needn't feel quite so guilty about the transformation.

Where to Transform: Image Editor versus Page Layout Application

If you *are* going to transform digital images, does it matter where the transformation takes place? If you use Photoshop to scale an image, is the result superior to the outcome of scaling within your page-layout application?

The answer is an unqualified, "It depends."

If you perform your scaling and rotation in Photoshop or another image-editing application, and then place the resulting image in a page layout at 100 percent with no rotation, you do have a pretty good idea of how the finished piece will look.

If, however, you induce the scaling or rotation in a page layout, you've only *requested* those transformations. They don't really take place until the job is processed by the RIP. This adds a bit to the processing time and job complexity at the RIP, and it also puts you at the mercy of that RIP's implementation of scaling and rotation algorithms. Even if you generate and submit PDFs, the transformations within that PDF are still pending, and they are implemented only when the PDF is processed by a RIP.

Be comforted by the fact that late-model RIPs can chew a lot more information in a shorter time than they used to. Rotating a few images here and there won't prevent the processing of your job. However, despite the improvements in RIP technology, it is still possible to build a job that can't be processed by a RIP. (Please don't take that remark as a personal challenge.)

Keep in mind, too, that if you've rotated an image in Photoshop, and then subsequently applied additional scaling or rotation in a page layout, you've transformed it twice. It's not the end of the world, but you may see some slight softening of detail in the finished piece.

APPROPRIATE IMAGE FORMATS FOR PRINT

How you should save your raster images is governed largely by how you intend to use them. Often, you will be placing images in a page-layout or illustration program, so you're limited to the formats supported by those applications. The application may be willing to let you place a wide variety of file formats, but the most commonly used image formats have traditionally been TIFF and EPS. However, native Photoshop files (PSD) and Photoshop PDF files are also frequently used. (We'll discuss vector artwork formats in the next chapter.)

TIFF

TIFF (tagged image file format) is perhaps the most widely supported image file format. It's happy being imported into QuarkXPress, InDesign, Adobe PageMaker, Microsoft Word, some text editors—almost any application that accepts images. The TIFF image format supports multiple layers as well as RGB and CMYK color spaces, and even allows an image to contain spot-color channels.

Photoshop EPS

While many people equate *EPS* with vector artwork, the *encapsulated* part of the format's name gives a hint about the flexibility of the format. It's a *container* for artwork. An EPS can contain vectors, rasters, or a combination of raster and vector content. EPS (encapsulated PostScript) is, as the name implies, PostScript in a bag (see sidebar, "EPS: Raster or Vector?"). The historic reason for saving an image as a Photoshop EPS was to preserve the special function of a PostScript-based vector clipping path used to silhouette an image.

As applications and RIPs have progressed, it's no longer strictly required to save such images as Photoshop EPS. Pixel for pixel, a TIFF is a smaller file than an equivalent EPS, so if disk size is important, stick with TIFF, with one exception. If you are creating a duotone image—usually an image consisting of black and a spot color—it should be saved as a Photoshop EPS. The TIFF format does not support duotone images, even though it allows spot-color channels. This may seem contradictory, but duotones (and tritones, quadtones, and so on) are special creatures. Under the hood, they are still grayscale images, but they contain special information saying, in effect, "When you output me, use my special recipe for generating spot plates." The TIFF file format doesn't know how to contain that special recipe, but the EPS format does.

EPS: Raster or Vector?

It may be a bit confusing that there are raster-based EPSs (saved from an image-editing program such as Photoshop) and vector-based EPSs (saved from a vector drawing program such as Adobe Illustrator or Adobe [formerly Macromedia] FreeHand. The uninitiated sometimes think that saving an image as an EPS magically vectorizes it. Not so. Think of the EPS format as a type of container. The pixels within an EPS are no different from those in their TIFF brethren. They're just contained and presented in a different way.

Photoshop Native (PSD)

Historically, the native PSD (Photoshop document) format has been used solely for working files in Photoshop. Copies of those working files were flattened and saved in TIFF or EPS formats for placement in a page-layout program. While PageMaker allowed placement of native Photoshop files (although it did not honor transparency), QuarkXPress required TIFF or EPS instead. And since QuarkXPress has been a prominent page-layout application for nearly 15 years, TIFF and EPS have been the standard of the industry.

However, InDesign can take advantage of the layers and transparency in Photoshop native files, eliminating the need to go back through two generations of an image to make corrections to an original file. The working image and the finished file are the same file. QuarkXPress 6.5 allows the placement of native PSDs but does not recognize transparency. QuarkXPress 7.0, however, honors transparency in layered, native Photoshop files.

> **TRANSPARENCY TIP:** Although InDesign accepts and correctly handles opacity settings in a placed Photoshop native file, it does not correctly handle blending modes in a Photoshop file. The most common example is a drop shadow created in Photoshop. While the shadow will correctly darken image content beneath it in Photoshop, it will knock out of content beneath it in InDesign. The result is an anemic and unrealistic gray shadow —not what you want. There are some workarounds detailed in Chapter 12, "InDesign Production Tips," but a simple solution is to omit the shadow in Photoshop, and generate it instead in InDesign. InDesign's own shadows behave correctly, darkening content beneath the shadow as you intended.

Photoshop PDF

A Photoshop PDF (Portable Document Format) contains the same pixels as a garden-variety PSD, but those pixels are encased in a PDF wrapper. There's usually no reason to use a Photoshop PDF when a TIFF, EPS, or PSD will suffice, but a Photoshop PDF has special features. It can contain vector and type elements without converting the vector content to pixels, a process called *rasterizing*. And a Photoshop PDF allows round-trip editing in Photoshop. While a Photoshop EPS can contain vectors and text, the vector content will be converted to pixels if the file is reopened in Photoshop, thus losing the crisp vector edge. As a result, you lose the ability to edit text or vector content, since it's been converted to pixels. A native Photoshop PSD can contain vector components, but page-layout programs rasterize the content. However, Photoshop PDFs maintain vector content when placed in other applications. For vector content, Photoshop PDF is the solution, because it is able to hold both transparency and vector components (see **Table 4.1** for a feature comparison of common image formats).

Table 4.1 Image format features

Supported Feature	TIFF	EPS	PSD	PDF
RGB color space	X	X	X	X
CMYK color space	X	X	X	X
Grayscale	X	X	X	X
ICC profiles	X	X	X	X
Clipping paths	X	X	X	X
Layers	X	—	X	X
Alpha channels	X	—	X	X
Spot color channels	X	1	X	X
Duotones	—	X	X	X
Bitmap (bi-level content)	X	X	X	X
Vector data	2	3	2	X
Transparency	X	—	X	X

1 Must save as DCS2 (a variant of the EPS format)
2 Page-layout applications rasterize vector content in TIFFs and PSDs
3 EPSs cannot be re-opened in Photoshop with vector content intact

Moving to Native PSD and PDF

As the major page-layout applications increasingly support native PSDs and PDFs, is there any compelling reason to continue using old-fashioned TIFFs and EPSs? It may seem adventurous to use such new-fangled files, but workflow is changing. The demarcation between photo-compositing and page layout is blurring, and designers demand more power and flexibility from software. RIPs are more robust than ever, networks are faster, and hard drives are huge. It's still important to know the imaging challenges posed by using native files (such as transparency), and wise to communicate with your print service provider before you embark on the all-native path. You're still at the mercy of their equipment and processes, and if they're lagging a bit behind the latest software developments, you'll have to be governed by their capabilities.

Special Case: Screen Captures

If you're creating software documentation for print, or you want to show an image of a Web page in your project, you may need to include screen captures in your page layouts. Screen captures are easy to make using a system utility or special screen-capture software, but they require some special handling to print clearly. Especially when they're part of software documentation or instructional materials, it's important that the details are as sharply rendered as possible.

Funny thing about screen captures: Whether you take them by using your system's built-in screen-capture functionality or a third-party screen-capture application, you are merely intercepting information that eventually becomes pixels on your monitor. Whatever your current monitor resolution, there is a one-to-one relationship between the fixed *number* of pixels that the system generates and the number of pixels you see on your screen. The *size* of the image you see is just a function of your current monitor resolution (**Figure 4.5**).

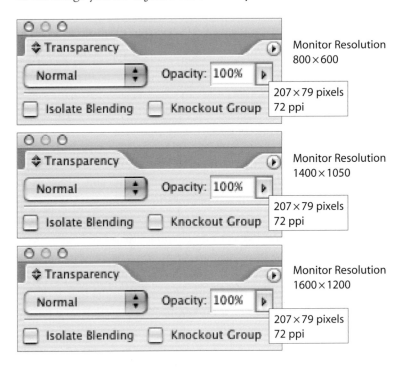

Figure 4.5 The resolution setting of your monitor has no effect on the number of pixels captured in a screen capture. Although this palette was captured at three different monitor resolutions, the three captures are identical, each consisting of exactly the same number of pixels.

An application palette that measures 208 pixels by 80 pixels may appear larger when your screen resolution is set to 800 by 600, and it appears almost unreadably small when your monitor is set to 1600 by 1200. However, the palette itself is made of exactly the same *number* of pixels in both instances. So it doesn't matter at what resolution your monitor is set, or how large the palettes may appear on screen. You'll capture the same image regardless of monitor setting, and the resulting image will be 72 ppi.

Since it's been drilled into you that 300 ppi is the Holy Grail of image resolution, it's tempting to try to improve screen captures by increasing the resolution. Unfortunately, this usually makes them look *worse* by softening small details during interpolation.

If you plan to use a screen capture at 100-percent enlargement, just leave it at 72 ppi. Yes, the print service provider's prepress department will raise a flag, but the examples below show why screen captures are not improved by increasing their resolution.

As you can see in **Figure 4.6A**, the original 72-ppi screen capture seems a bit coarse, but it's readable. Increasing the resolution to 300 ppi in Photoshop may sound like a good idea, but as shown in **Figure 4.6B**, the interpolation will soften detail in the image.

If you do feel compelled to increase the resolution of a screen capture, there is an approach that may yield better results than resampling up to 300 ppi. In Photoshop, choose Image > Image Size, and then set the resolution to an even multiple of 72, such as 288 ppi. In that same dialog, set the Resample Image option to Nearest Neighbor (**Figure 4.6C**). This avoids interpolation by simply *repeating* pixels rather than attempting to *create* pixels. It's not an appropriate approach when scaling images of a photographic nature, but it's a helpful solution for screen captures, because of their special nature.

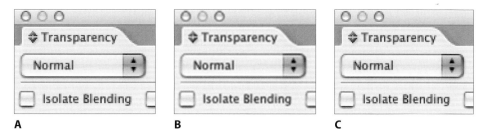

A   **B**   **C**

Figure 4.6 Increasing the resolution of a 72-ppi screen shot (A) to 300 ppi in the traditional way does not improve its appearance (B). However, using 288 ppi (72 ppi multiplied by 4) and the Nearest Neighbor resampling method increases resolution while avoiding the softening effects of interpolation (C). The resampling controls are in the Photoshop image resizing dialog box (Image > Image Size).

Converting Screen Captures to CMYK

Since screen captures are generated as RGB images, they must be converted to CMYK for print. When performing that conversion, a special approach is recommended to maintain the best rendering of black type. The default conversion of RGB to CMYK in Photoshop will render black as a four-color mix (**Figure 4.7**), with the possibility that slight misregistration on press will turn tiny details to mush.

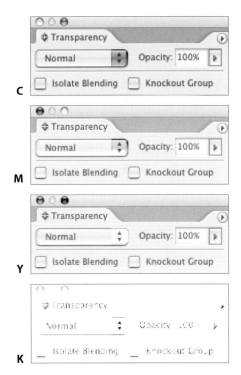

Figure 4.7 A conventional conversion from RGB to CMYK produces four-color equivalents of the gray and black parts of a screen capture. Press misregistration will turn text and other black or gray elements to an out-of-focus rainbow. Festive, but hard to read.

To simplify printing of screen captures, use a color-separation recipe that ensures that all neutral black or gray areas of the image will print only in black ink during the RGB-to-CMYK conversion. Neutral areas in an RGB image are those areas in which the RGB values are equal; for example, R128–G128–B128 would constitute a midtone gray.

To create this custom, screen-capture conversion recipe in Photoshop, choose Edit > Color Settings to access the color-separation controls. Under Working Spaces, choose Custom for the CMYK setting. In the Custom CMYK dialog box, select Maximum Black Generation (**Figure 4.8**). The curve you see may seem odd, but it merely indicates that all equivalent RGB values are being replaced with black. The appearance of color elements won't be compromised.

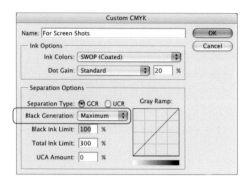

Figure 4.8 Use the Custom CMYK option in Photoshop to access the Maximum Black Generation option.

Color elements will be composed of four colors in the final CMYK image. But black and gray elements will be rendered only in black (**Figure 4.9**). While this may look odd, it results in cleaner printing of the screen capture, since there aren't four colors gumming up the works in most of the image.

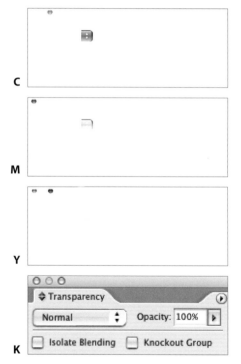

Figure 4.9 By setting the Black Generation option (on the Custom CMYK dialog) to Maximum, all gray and black content images only on the black plate.

RGB versus CMYK

Since the dawn of desktop scanning, it's been unquestioned that Thou Shalt Convert to CMYK. Those who submitted RGB files were considered uninformed, even uncivilized. But here's a secret: Scanners and digital cameras see in RGB. High-end production scanners such as those from Fujifilm/Enovation and Kodak produce CMYK files only because they utilize software to perform the conversion from RGB to CMYK on the fly.

As shown in Chapter 2, "Ink on Paper," the RGB gamut is larger than that of CMYK. Consequently, it's often preferable to perform color corrections and compositing with RGB files, converting to CMYK as late in the process as possible. If you are participating in a fully color-managed workflow, you will likely keep your images as RGB with ICC profiles. The International Color Consortium (ICC) was formed by a group of graphic arts industry vendors, with the goal of promoting the use and standardization of color management tools. ICC profiles are methods of describing the characteristics of devices such as scanners, presses, and printers for optimal results. Conversion will not take place until the job is imaged. Much of today's software offers sophisticated support of color management. For example, when exporting a PDF or printing, InDesign will perform the same conversion of RGB to CMYK that Photoshop would (assuming consistent and correct profiles).

Some print service providers and their customers have fully adopted color-managed workflows as part of their regular operation. But many print service providers (especially in North America) expect CMYK when you submit your job, believing that it's what Nature intended. Consult with your printer to see what they prefer. If you're using digital photography or scanning your own artwork, they should be able to provide you with their preferred settings, so you can make appropriate conversions to CMYK.

INAPPROPRIATE IMAGE FORMATS FOR PRINT

Some image formats are intended primarily for onscreen and Web use. **Portable Network Graphics** (PNG) images can contain RGB and indexed color, as well as transparency. While PNG can be high resolution, it has no support for CMYK color space.

The Windows format **BMP** (an abbreviation for bitmap) supports color depths from one-bit (black and white, with no shades of gray) to 32-bit (millions of colors), but lacks support for CMYK. BMP is not appropriate for print.

Graphics Interchange Format (GIF) is appropriate only for Web use because of its inherently low resolution and an indexed color palette limited to a maximum of 256 colors. Don't use GIF for print.

JPEG (Joint Photographic Experts Group), named after the committee that created it, has an unsavory reputation in graphic arts. Just whisper "jay-peg," and watch prepress operators cringe. It is a *lossy* compression scheme, meaning that it discards information to make a smaller digital file.

Assuming an image has adequate resolution, a very slight amount of initial JPEG compression doesn't noticeably impair image quality, but aggressive compression introduces ugly rectangular artifacts, especially in detailed areas (**Figure 4.10**).

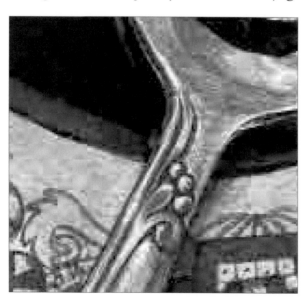

Figure 4.10 Overly aggressive JPEG compression produces unattractive rectangular artifacts. A slight amount of JPEG compression, however, is not noticeable. So don't fear JPEG compression. Just don't overdo it.

Each time you re*save* an image as a JPEG, you re*compress* it. Prepress paranoids will shriek that you're ruining your image, and there's some truth to that. While it's true that repeatedly resaving an image with low-quality compression settings would eventually erode detail, the mere fact that an image has been saved as a JPEG does not render it unusable. Despite the reputation, JPEGs aren't inherently evil. They *can* be decent graphic citizens, even capable of containing high-resolution CMYK image data. That said, when you acquire a JPEG image from your digital camera or a stock photo service, it's still advisable to immediately resave the image as a TIFF or PSD file to prevent further compression. However, JPEGs intended for Web use are low-resolution RGB files, inappropriate for print.

CHAPTER FIVE
Vector Graphics

While raster images are made up of pixels, vector graphics are refreshingly pixel free. As such, vector graphics are not subject to the scaling restrictions that plague raster images (**Figure 5.1**). The smooth shapes of a purely vector drawing have no inherent resolution, so it can be enlarged and reduced with no penalty.

Figure 5.1 Vector drawings (top left) are mathematically generated smooth lines, whereas raster images (top right) are composed of pixels.

Vector art can be scaled up with no limit (bottom left). Raster images, however, don't fare well at extreme enlargements (bottom right).

VECTOR FILE FORMATS

Since the File > Save and File > Export dialogs of popular drawing programs offer a dizzying list of prospective file types, it's important to know what's acceptable for print and what's not.

Encapsulated PostScript (EPS)

The most common file format for containing vector artwork is EPS. In fact, the acronym EPS is so deeply associated with vector graphics that new entrants to the mysteries of graphic arts sometimes believe that merely saving an image in the EPS format magically converts it to vectors. They're subsequently disappointed when they discover that they must instead use the dreaded Pen tool to create vector art. See Chapter Four, "Preparing Raster Images," for an explanation of raster EPS versus vector EPS files.

Encapsulated PostScript is, as the name implies, a container for PostScript information that allows it to be understood by other applications. An EPS file contains drawing information, of course, but it may also contain font information as well as embedded raster images. A preview image is also usually included to provide an appearance for the file when it's placed in a page-layout program. However, if you travel off the beaten path and attempt to use EPS artwork in word-processing or presentation programs, you may find that the artwork does not appear correctly because the program can't correctly read the preview image that represents the contents of the EPS. And some programs can't correctly send out the PostScript information itself, resulting in poor output. It isn't the fault of the EPS—it's the application's inability to utilize the PostScript contents. The preview is akin to a label on an opaque package: It represents what's inside.

EPS files can be placed in a wide range of applications such as the dedicated page-layout applications QuarkXPress and Adobe InDesign, which understand how to display and print EPS content. However, page-layout programs can't directly interact with the contents of an EPS, so any editing must be performed in the originating application, such as Adobe Illustrator or Adobe (formerly Macromedia) FreeHand.

EPS files are usually used for placed artwork, but are also used as files for output. (Some print workflows are based on EPS files rather than application files.) Since PostScript is a published specification and thus available to any software developer, *any* application can potentially generate EPS files. However, not all applications create EPS files that are intended to be opened by drawing applications. It is generally *not* advisable to open an EPS generated from QuarkXPress or InDesign in Illustrator or FreeHand. Yes, it's an EPS, but it is intended only for *placement*, not for *editing*. You *may* successfully edit such an EPS, but don't count on it. You may damage font embedding or inadvertently make changes that won't be apparent until the job images. As they always say in B-rated science fiction films, "We were never meant to go in there."

There are cautions, even when opening up EPS files generated by the most popular drawing programs. FreeHand can safely open up EPS files created by FreeHand. Illustrator can successfully open its own Illustrator EPS files. This may not seem surprising, but it only works because each application adds extra information to create an editable EPS, which allows it to be reopened in the originating application.

If you attempt to use Illustrator and FreeHand to open up each others' EPS files, the translations are not always successful. Text may become point text (little isolated clumps of editable text), and some special features such as shadows may not translate correctly. Some elements may completely disappear or become rasterized. It's best to keep such files in their own species to avoid problems.

Why is this? PostScript is a programming language that provides instructions for imaging. Thus, an EPS is more than a drawing in some sort of container. In essence, it's a tiny computer program. So, just as one programmer might not understand another's style of coding, one application may not correctly interpret an EPS produced by another program. Man was never meant to reopen EPS files, but you know what always happens in sci-fi movies. They just *have* to pry open that EPS. They just *have* to go into that darkened room. With a flashlight. In a nightgown. Thus, some real-world advice: Make edits in the originating application. Don't try to pry open an Illustrator EPS in FreeHand, or vice versa.

> **TIP:** When saving an EPS from Illustrator, choose TIFF 8-bit for the preview option. In addition to providing better cross-platform support, it also prevents a known problem in InDesign versions through Creative Suite 1 (CS). If you place an EPS with a Macintosh preview in InDesign and then add a drop shadow, the shadow will follow the edge of the graphic frame, rather than the edge of the graphic. If, however, you save the EPS with a TIFF 8-bit preview, the shadow will correctly follow the shape of the vector graphic itself. It's just one of life's little mysteries. If you use native Illustrator files, or you're placing EPS files in InDesign CS2, this isn't an issue.

Native File Formats

In the olden days, it was necessary to save a vector drawing twice—once as an EPS for placement in a page, and once in the application's proprietary, native format for rework. Since FreeHand and Illustrator are able to reopen their own EPS files, this is no longer strictly necessary (see the above section on reopening EPS files). Then why would you ever save a vector drawing as a native application file rather than an EPS, since EPS seems to offer the best of both worlds?

If you're planning to place the artwork into an InDesign page, there is some motivation to go native. InDesign honors transparency and blending modes in a native Illustrator (AI) file. This means that a placed Illustrator file can interact with other artwork in InDesign, allowing you to create some interesting opacity and blending effects that would not be possible with an EPS, whose internal contents are opaque to other applications.

While InDesign offers this special functionality, you'll still need to save in the EPS format for placement in QuarkXPress layouts or for use in other applications. And neither QuarkXPress nor InDesign allows the placement of native FreeHand files, so FreeHand artwork must be saved as EPS for placement in page layouts.

Adobe PDF

If you are creating vector artwork for placement in another application such as a page lay-out file, there's usually not much reason to save your file as a PDF. However, if you are creating vector art in Illustrator CS or CS2, you can selectively reveal or hide layers of the drawing in an InDesign CS2 page, if you save the file as an Illustrator PDF (more about this in Chapter 10, "Illustrator Production Tips").

If the vector art is not destined for placement in a page layout, but will be submitted as finished art, saving it as PDF allows you to protect your artwork from unwanted editing. And under most circumstances, saving as PDF eliminates the need to supply fonts with your job (assuming you're using fonts that don't forbid embedding).

In all cases, before you send your job as PDF, ask the print service provider to provide detailed specifications for PDF creation.

Vector Formats Not Appropriate for Print

Not all vector formats are created equal. While page-layout programs may allow you to import them, some vector file formats do not print satisfactorily.

Microsoft Windows Metafile Format (WMF)

WMF is intended for placement in applications such as Microsoft Word or PowerPoint.® While WMF can contain both vector and raster content, it offers no support for CMYK content. Curved shapes are rendered as choppy, chiseled sections (**Figure 5.2**). WMF is a very limited format and simply isn't appropriate for print.

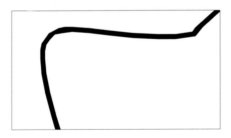

Figure 5.2 WMF renders curved shapes as choppy approximations. While it may be acceptable in a Microsoft Word or PowerPoint file, WMF should not be used for print.

Enhanced Metafile Format (EMF)

EMF, like WMF, is intended for use in applications such as Word and PowerPoint. While curves are smoother than those in a WMF, strokes become concentric shapes. EMF offers no support for CMYK, and some vector artwork may be rasterized. And, like WMF, EMF is not appropriate for print production.

Raster Formats

FreeHand and Illustrator both offer options for exporting to raster formats such as TIFF, JPEG, PNG, and BMP. Of course, a vector format provides more flexibility and sharper output. But if you do need to rasterize the content of a vector artwork file (say, for Web use), you may find that a drawing program's direct export is superior to the results of using Photoshop to rasterize an EPS.

HANDLING TEXT

When you include text in your vector artwork, you have to take steps to ensure that it will print as expected. Of course, you can use the same approach that's recommended for page-layout applications: Gather up the fonts and include them when you submit your vector artwork to the print service provider. FreeHand provides a "Collect for output" option (File > Collect for Output), which harvests fonts and linked images, and then places them in a designated folder. While Illustrator doesn't naturally do this, the Art Files plug-in from Code Line Communications adds the functionality for Illustrator 8.0 through CS2. (As of this writing, the Art Files plug-in is available for Macintosh only.)

The more common methods for dealing with needed fonts in vector graphics, however, are *embedding* and *outlining*.

Embedding Fonts

Provided that the font creator has not forbidden embedding, Illustrator and FreeHand can embed fonts in an EPS *for placement in other programs*. This means that font information should be available for display and printing, but it does *not* make the font available for editing text in the EPS. To edit text in an EPS, you'll need the appropriate fonts active on your system, and you should open the file in the originating drawing program. (Recall the earlier cautions about the dangers of attempting to cross-pollinate between FreeHand and Illustrator.)

Not all applications can embed fonts in the EPSs they generate. QuarkXPress, for example, does not embed fonts in an exported EPS. However, a number of XTensions provide this functionality, including XPert Print from ALAP (a lowly apprentice production, inc.), the assets and products of which have been acquired by Quark. (By the way, marketing materials from ALAP consistently displayed the company name in all lowercase letters. We were torn: Should we capitalize, as we were itching to do, or should we follow their example?)

It may come as a surprise to you that not all fonts *can* be embedded. Some font vendors prevent embedding by placing a nonembed flag in their fonts. This won't prevent you from using these fonts to create artwork, nor will it prevent printing. But you will be unable to embed the font in any EPS or PDF that you export. This means you have to ensure that the print service provider also has the necessary fonts to print your job (more about this thorny issue in Chapter Six, "Fonts").

Even if you *can* embed fonts, there is no guarantee that the embedding will survive what the print service provider might do to your poor, innocent EPS. If there is a problem that requires editing the EPS, they'll need to open the file. Opening the EPS without the necessary fonts loaded will result in the font embedding being munged.

You also have to consider the various processes that affect your job as it passes through the print service provider's workflow, even if nobody attempts to perform surgery on your EPS. Some smaller printers do informal imposition by positioning EPS or PDF files in a page-layout application. Trapping, imposition, and RIP software all must correctly interpret font information. Each step has the potential to drop font information. Don't freak out, these are worst-case scenarios. But the prospects are worth considering.

Now that you fear for the safety of your fonts, what can you do to ensure successful imaging? Well, you might consider converting your text to outlines.

Outlining Text

Fonts contain information, called *hinting*, which refines the display and printing of text. Consequently, some purists hold that those who outline text should be tarred and feathered. These are people who apparently don't have to actually get their jobs printed. Converting text to outlines eliminates hinting, so text may display onscreen as if slightly bloated and will print slightly heavier on desktop printers. However, the fattening is *not* usually apparent when outlined text is imaged on high-resolution devices such as imagesetters and platesetters. It's worth mentioning that very small text or type with delicate serifs may lose definition when outlined.

> **NOTE:** Please read the section on font licensing in Chapter 6, "Fonts." Not all font vendors allow you to outline text. This is probably a surprise to you, but it's an issue that you must consider.

Realists (by which we mean "people who convert their text to outlines") believe that ensuring the safety and portability of artwork is worth enduring the condescending snorts of purists. Converting text to outlines eliminates the worry that font embedding might be undone by incautious editing or a process that fails to honor the embedded fonts.

Realists also have the foresight to save a second version of the file without outlined text to use as a working file, in anticipation of possible corrections or the sobering discovery of a misspelled word.

INCORPORATING IMAGES INTO VECTOR FILES

It's possible to place images in vector drawings in much the same way they're placed in page layouts. It's accepted practice in page layout to *link* the images rather than *embed* them, and this same approach is an option when incorporating images in vector artwork. However, linking images rather than embedding them can cause some problems when the finished artwork is placed into another document, such as a page-layout file. If, in the heat of battle, you neglect to send the linked images along with the parent vector file, things will understandably fall apart.

The alternative is to embed the image in your vector drawing as you create the EPS, so that it can't fall by the wayside. Embedding, as you might expect, increases the size of the resulting EPS file. It's pretty easy math. If you've embedded a 2 MB image, you'll be adding 2 MB to your final size. But you have to remember to choose the option to embed images, rather than link them.

Fortunately for us, we live in civilized times. Whereas earlier versions of FreeHand and Illustrator didn't do so, current versions present users with the option to embed images as they export an EPS. You can then fearlessly send your EPS out into the world, fully outfitted with its outlined text and embedded images. By the way, it's also possible to embed images in native Illustrator and FreeHand files, if you just feel compelled to put all your eggs in one digital basket.

What if it's subsequently necessary to color correct an image embedded in an EPS or drawing file? If you created the file, and still have the image, just do the corrections and replace the image in the drawing. But if there's no access to the original image, what do you do?

FreeHand allows the extraction of embedded images via the Links option in the Object panel (Window > Object). While Illustrator doesn't offer such a straightforward method for image extraction, you can cheat. Select the embedded image in the Illustrator file, and then copy it the clipboard. Launch Photoshop and choose File > New. A new, blank document is created that's the same size as the clipboard contents. Select Edit > Paste, and voilà (which is French for *"add extracted image"*), there's the image.

Imported images aren't the only pixel-based content that is possible in drawings. As vector-drawing programs have evolved, they have increasingly offered painterly effects that don't look at all like vector artwork. That's because they *aren't* vector artwork—they're made of pixels. Effects such as feathered edges, blurs, and soft shadows are generated as pixels, and, as such, are subject to the same restrictions that apply to scanned images. Artwork containing such elements should not be scaled up in page layouts or other applications beyond a reasonable level.

> **NOTE:** For more details on issues pertaining to creating and imaging these special effects, see Chapter Ten, "Illustrator Production Tips," and Chapter Eleven, "FreeHand Production Tips."

AVOIDING UNNECESSARY COMPLEXITY

RIPs are more robust than ever, but there are still reasons to simplify vector artwork. Simpler drawings usually result in a smoother appearance, and they're easier to edit later. If you've used the drawing tools in Illustrator or FreeHand, you know that vector art is made of straight and curved lines called Bézier shapes. The anchor points and direction handles that allow you to modify such shapes are fairly confusing when you first use them. So, in our timid early experiments in drawing programs, we tend to tiptoe around shapes, using a bazillion clicks to create a drawing. Eventually, we become more comfortable with the tools, and learn to do more with less.

Simplify Your Paths

Stop clicking. Really. Right now. More points do not equal a better drawing. In fact, *fewer* points—if they're the *right* points—result in a smoother drawing, as you can see in **Figure 5.3**. Of course, in the early stages of learning vector drawing tools, it's difficult to draw so elegantly. But even if your drawing is a bit lumpy, there are tools in both Illustrator and FreeHand to smooth and simplify paths.

In the early days of desktop drawing, it was crucial to minimize the number of points in a drawing to ensure successful imaging. The overly busy shamrock on the top row of Figure 5.3 might have been called a RIP-buster in those ancient days, resulting in glacially slow print times and the possibility that it would produce the dreaded limitcheck error and fail to be processed by the RIP. Modern RIPs are much more robust and computers are exponentially faster, but smoothness is still a strong motivation to master the Zen of fewer clicks while drawing. And your mouse will last longer.

OpenType Fonts

OpenType fonts are single-file fonts and do not have separate screen and printer fonts to keep track of. But here's where the real font fun begins. OpenType fonts are cross platform. This doesn't mean that Adobe Garamond Pro comes in a Macintosh version and an identical Windows version. Instead, the *same* font file can be used on a Mac or on a PC with no special handling.

But, as the late night TV ads say: Wait, there's more. Whereas PostScript fonts are limited to a paltry 256 characters (isn't that *enough?*), OpenType fonts can contain more than 65,000 *glyphs*. A glyph is any distinct letterform, such as a number, a lowercase *p*, or an ampersand. This allows a font designer to include swashes, contextual ligatures, titling alternates—even fractions—all in one font. The entirety of a font family that previously required separate expert and titling sets can now be contained in one font. See **Figure 6.1** for a glimpse of just a few of OpenType's possibilities.

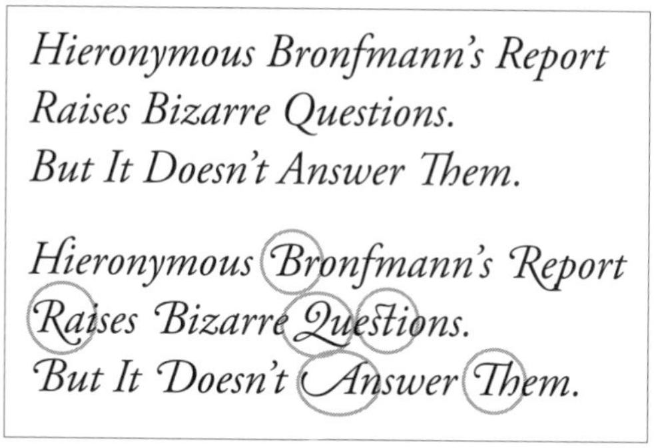

*Hieronymous Bronfmann's Report
Raises Bizarre Questions.
But It Doesn't Answer Them.*

*Hieronymous Bronfmann's Report
Raises Bizarre Questions.
But It Doesn't Answer Them.*

Figure 6.1 Adobe Garamond Pro is a lovely font even without invoking its special OpenType features (top). But look what happens when Swashes and Discretionary Ligatures are turned on (bottom).

Not all OpenType fonts contain glyphs in every one of those 65,000 available character positions. For example, one font may have swashes, but another may not. However, the adherence to Unicode mapping ensures that a character exists in the same position from font to font. *Unicode* is a standard that provides a unique universal identifier for every character, regardless of language, application, or platform. For more information, visit the Unicode Web site (www.unicode.org). If you set text using some of the special diacritical characters in Caslon Pro, for example, and then change the font used to Garamond Pro, the diacriticals are intact because they exist in both fonts.

You can use OpenType fonts without fear of imaging problems. They are compatible with all recent RIPs, and all current font-management software supports OpenType. Not using font-management software? OpenType fonts can be activated by the built-in Font Book application on the Macintosh and by the Windows Fonts control panel. Or you can drop them in the Macintosh system fonts folders to make them available to all applications (although it's preferable to use font management software). And having OpenType fonts doesn't mean you have to stop using the PostScript and TrueType fonts you already have.

The benefits of OpenType extend far beyond typographic beauty. One of the motivations for the OpenType format was to provide multilingual support. In **Figure 6.2**, you can see the extensive character set in just one font, Myriad Pro from Adobe Systems.

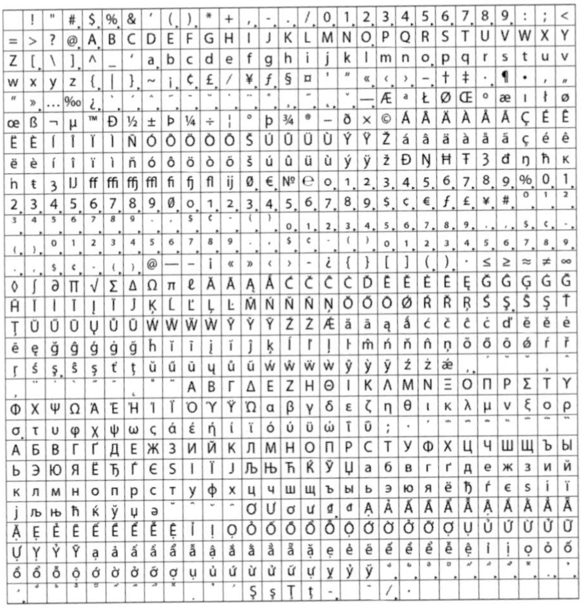

Figure 6.2 Multilingual support available within the OpenType font Myriad Pro, viewed in the InDesign Glyphs palette.

You won't be able to use all 65,000 glyphs unless you're using software that recognizes the additional features. Adobe InDesign, Illustrator, and Photoshop can see and use the entire contents of an OpenType font, whereas QuarkXPress through version 6.5 has blinders on, and it can only utilize the same old 256 characters. QuarkXPress 7.0 offers support for the complete range of OpenType features.

Adobe has converted its entire font library to OpenType and will no longer be offering PostScript Type 1 fonts. It's easy to spot OpenType fonts from Adobe: They have *Std* or *Pro* as part of their names. Adobe is not the only font vendor marketing OpenType fonts. Most major font vendors now offer OpenType. Given the linguistic support and the enhanced typographic features offered by OpenType fonts, it's easy to see that it's the font format of the future. And it's here today, unlike those flying automobiles we've been waiting for.

NOTE: *The* Std *is short for Standard, indicating an Adobe OpenType version of a previously available PostScript Type 1 font. Adobe OpenType fonts with the* Pro *indicator have more expanded glyph sets and are often the result of combining what once were expert font sets and their base companions.*

Glyphs and Characters

It's easy to confuse the terms *character* and *glyph*, but they describe different concepts. A *character* corresponds to a single position in the Unicode standard, which is a uniform, agreed-upon mapping system for the contents of a font. A *glyph*, however, is a distinct letterform. Multiple glyphs may exist for a single character position in an OpenType font, such as *Q* and *Q* for the uppercase Q in Adobe Garamond Pro Italic.

Macintosh OS X System Fonts

Macintosh system fonts such as Geneva, Monaco, Chicago, and Charcoal had traditionally been easy to spot because of their distinctive names. But with the introduction of OS X, Apple threw a monkey wrench into the font wars by including system fonts named Helvetica, Helvetica Neue, and Times Roman, just like their PostScript cousins. Under the hood, these are TrueType fonts, but you'll see them described as *dfonts*, a moniker derived from the fact that the fonts are data-only, and not a two-headed file consisting of a data fork and a resource fork. (If this doesn't mean much to you, don't worry.)

Macintosh dfonts aren't inherently evil, but they are problematic because their names are indistinguishable from their PostScript counterparts. If the job is created by multiple people who are using different versions of a font, this may result in font substitution and consequent reflow. Since they're system fonts, they're active by default. To use the PostScript fonts of the same names, you have to sneak up on the dfonts to control their activation or deactivation by using dedicated font-management software as described in the earlier section, "PostScript (Type 1) Fonts."

Additionally, dfonts don't work under OS 9 because they're not recognized as fonts by the OS 9 operating system or its font-management schemes. If you're still jumping back to OS 9 to use earlier versions of software such as QuarkXPress 4.x or 5.x, this can complicate your font usage. Imagine that you have used a dfont in a QuarkXPress 6.0 file created in Macintosh OS X, and then saved the page-layout file down for QuarkXPress version 5.0. A user of QuarkXPress 5.0 will open the file under OS 9, and the dfont will not be available. They'll be forced to substitute a similar font, possibly leading to text reflow. One solution is to use the dfontifier utility from Mark Douma (http://homepage.mac.com/mdouma46/dfont/dfont.html) to convert dfonts to a font format that is recognized under OS 9.

OpenType fonts are innocent bystanders in this battle. Their names distinguish them from TrueType, PostScript, and dfont files. As you can see in **Figure 6.3,** the OpenType version of Times is named TimesLTStd, making it much easier to pick it out of the pack.

Figure 6.3 Sign of the Times. On the left, Macintosh OS X icons for PostScript screen font (left) and printer font (second from left). The OpenType icon is in the center, and Macintosh dfont is on the right. The icons aren't exactly obvious, are they?

Windows System Fonts

PC users may now revel in the fact that, starting with Windows 2000, their system fonts are OpenType fonts. In fact, the birth of OpenType is the result of a collaboration between Adobe Systems and Microsoft. The Arial system font has the ability to display an extensive character set, including Greek, Hebrew, and Arabic characters.

Multiple Master Fonts

The term Multiple Master probably elicits as much fear in a prepress department as yelling "TrueType," and for much the same reason—fear of the unknown. Adobe's Multiple Master fonts were a great idea: Start with a PostScript font, and then give users the ability to create multiple weights, angles, and widths (such as condensed or extended) of a single font. It was an enlightened idea. The problems arose from a lack of education. It wasn't obvious how to make all the cool variants, how to collect the variants necessary for your job, or how to ensure that the print service provider knew how to use them. So the Multiple Master concept sort of died on the vine. Its creative promise was never fully realized, and it's been phased out as an available font product. However, Multiple Master technology is still used for display and printing when fonts are missing in a PDF and for displaying text when fonts are unavailable for an InDesign or Illustrator file.

Substituting One Font Species For Another

A variation on the old joke:

PATIENT: I didn't have the necessary PostScript font, so I used my TrueType version. The type reflowed and the line breaks are all wrong now.

DOCTOR: Don't do that.

When you collaborate on designs, try to avoid substituting a TrueType version of a font for a PostScript version, or vice versa. Don't use an OpenType font instead of the file creator's original font choice, despite your conviction that it's somehow better. You may get lucky, but you're risking type reflow.

This is particularly treacherous if you move a job between platforms. A Windows font and its Macintosh namesake may both be PostScript, but that's still no guarantee that they were created by the same foundry with the same nuances.

ACTIVATING FONTS IN THE OPERATING SYSTEM

Just having a font somewhere on your hard drive isn't enough. You must activate it to make it available to all the applications on your computer. Both Windows and the Macintosh provide built-in font activation. If you tend to use the same fonts, and don't need to frequently add fonts, the built-in font activation schemes may be sufficient for your needs.

Apple Font Book

Apple's free Font Book utility ships as part of OS X. If you're using a limited selection of fonts for the majority of your work and don't need the control afforded by creating font sets, Font Book is probably adequate. It may appear to be a font manager, but earlier versions of Font Book did some ugly things. Fonts were moved into the system library, and then deleted from their original location. (There goes your job folder!) And it never deactivated a font that was removed from Font Book's collections. Fonts remained in the system, eternally activated.

Mercifully, this uncivilized behavior is somewhat improved under OS 10.4 (Tiger). Font Book now copies rather than moves font files. And it actually deactivates fonts when Font Book's collections are disabled or removed. However, it still leaves a duplicate of the font files in the your Library/Fonts folder.

Windows Control Panel

PC users can activate fonts by placing them in the Fonts folder of the Control Panel. Much like Apple's Font Book, the Fonts control panel provides a common system location so that fonts are available to applications. Deleting a font from Windows' Fonts control panel puts it in the Recycle Bin. There is no provision for creating sets of fonts. Activated fonts are stored together in a single folder, and they're all awake, all the time.

FONT MANAGEMENT PROGRAMS

It's important to note that the font activation methods provided by your operating system are just that—font *activation*, not font *management*. As an application launches, it takes note of all the activated fonts. Do you really need to have 500 fonts awake all the time? If you have hundreds of fonts active, you're adding to system overhead and slowing down all your applications. If you're tired of taking ten minutes to get from the *A*s to the *H*s in font listings, it's a sign that it's time to adopt some sort of font management.

Font management programs allow you to selectively activate and deactivate fonts as necessary to reduce system overhead. These programs also allow you to create custom sets of fonts, so you can easily activate all the fonts needed for a job or a particular customer with just one click.

Some of the commonly used font-management applications include Extensis Suitcase (Mac/PC), Extensis Suitcase Fusion (Mac-only as of this writing), FontReserve (Mac/PC; also owned by Extensis), FontAgent Pro from Insider Software (Mac only), and Alsoft's MasterJuggler® (Mac only). Which solution should you choose? There's no easy answer: It depends on your own tastes. These products provide approximately the same functionality, so your choice will likely depend on your fondness for a particular interface. Download a trial version of the software, give it a spin, and see if it fits with your workflow and requirements.

> **NOTE:** As expected after their purchase of FontReserve, Extensis seems to be merging it with their venerable Suitcase product. As of this writing, the Macintosh-only Suitcase Fusion is the first product of that cross-breeding. Suitcase and FontReserve for Windows may have been merged into a Windows version of Suitcase Fusion by the time you read this.

Automatic Font Activation

In addition to allowing you to create and activate font sets, some font-management solutions provide the ability to automatically activate fonts as needed when document files are launched. Occasionally, autoactivation conflicts with other plug-ins in some applications. Symptoms may include minor effects such as display glitches or pauses while fonts are activated. Such glitches are rarely dangerous, but be prepared for them.

Font Conflicts

Imagine you're asked to pick up a can of BeanCo black beans at the grocery store. Sounds easy. But while the shelf tags read "Green Beans," "Lima Beans," and "Black Beans," all the BeanCo cans are labeled simply "Beans." You dare not go home empty-handed, but there's no assurance that you will find the correct can of beans.

That's how your font-management software feels when it encounters PostScript, TrueType, and Macintosh system fonts—all named Helvetica. If one flavor is active, and you attempt to activate another, things get exciting, as shown in **Figure 6.4**.

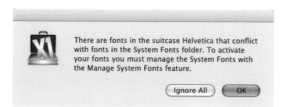

Figure 6.4 Attempting to activate a PostScript version of Helvetica prompts an alert because the OS already has its own version of Helvetica. Fortunately, font management software (Extensis Suitcase shown here) allows you to sneak around and fix this.

To rectify this conflict, you need a third-party font management solution such as Extensis Suitcase, Suitcase Fusion, or FontAgent Pro. (These are the most frequently used programs, but there are other solutions as well.) They allow you to perform an end run around the operating system so you can manage the system fonts as you do all other fonts. It also pays to perform some font house-cleaning. Use a utility such as Morrison SoftDesign's FontDoctor™ to check for damaged and duplicate fonts. FontDoctor also organizes fonts into a sensible library to make your font life easier. You can discard TrueType versions of fonts in favor of the PostScript duplicates.

As you contemplate purchasing fonts, it's strongly recommended that you consider OpenType. While its typographic and linguistic features alone are compelling, OpenType is also a handy solution to the font-conflict dilemma. Since OpenType fonts have distinctive names, you won't have to worry about any naming conflicts.

FONT LICENSING ISSUES

You probably don't think of fonts as software, but that's how fonts are distributed and licensed. They're not just little drawings of letters. Fonts also contain instructions for font appearance and imaging. Consider the prodigious amount of work that goes into creating a font, and perhaps you'll understand why you shouldn't just freely distribute fonts. Each character must be painstakingly drawn. The designer must take into consideration how characters fit together, how they will look at various sizes, create hinting information, and much more. Professional font-creation software is expensive and complex because designing fonts is not a simple undertaking. Consider that a copy of the FontLab font editing application costs $650—that should give you an idea of the nontrivial nature of font creation and font editing!

End User License Agreements (EULAs)

Yes, you'll find EULAs with fonts that you purchase (you *did* purchase them, didn't you?), although there's a good chance you've never read them. Most font foundries allow use of a purchased font on several workstations and one or two printing devices, so if you've bought a font for a three-person workgroup that shares one networked printer, you're probably abiding by the EULA (commonly pronounced *yoo-la*).

But the licensing situation is more complex than you may have realized. When you send your job to a print service provider, you gather up all the necessary files, including fonts. Surprise—you're probably in violation of the EULA for doing so. Here's an excerpt from a major font foundry's EULA:

> You may send a copy of any font along with your documents to a commercial printer or other service bureau to enable the editing or printing of your document, *provided that such party has informed you that it owns a valid license to use that particular font software.* [Italics added]

In other words, to be in compliance with the EULA, both you and the print service provider must have purchased licenses for the font. You may have never read the fine print, but this is indeed the letter of the law when it comes to font licensing.

Embedding Fonts in PDFs

You may think that no font vendor would object to an end user embedding a licensed font in a PDF. Well, some do. (The surprises just keep coming, don't they?) While we're not aware of any method for extracting a font from a PDF, apparently some font vendors fear that it is (or may become) possible. To forestall such thievery, some have included clauses in their EULAs that prescribe that fonts must be *subset*, which is a good idea, font licensing issues aside. Subsetting embeds only the characters needed to image the PDF file, rather than the entire font. They further stipulate that only one copy of the PDF must be supplied to the recipient. But beyond these two fairly harmless requirements, they insist that the PDF must contain security settings to allow only viewing and printing.

These strictures don't sound unreasonable until you consider an important aspect of securing PDFs. To make security settings stick in a PDF, you must use at least a permissions password to protect the security settings themselves. Otherwise, the recipient could just remove the security limitations. However, to place a secured PDF into a page, or to use it in an imposition process, the recipient will have to know the password to allow the file to be used. This defeats the purpose of imposing security, and seems to put both the creator of the PDF and the print service provider in the position of violating the EULA. So, once again, the legally acceptable solution is for the print service provider to purchase a license for the font. Note that some font vendors sell what is called a *service bureau license* at a reduced price, which is considered an extension of your license and may be exercised by the print service provider only for output of your jobs. Yes, it's a complex subject. But the proprieties of font licensing are widely overlooked.

Several EULAs suggest submitting PostScript files to the print service provider. While this would certainly force a designer to painstakingly check files before setting them in digital concrete, it's a fairly draconian approach, and offers no provision for corrections.

The sanest legal approach is to truly read the EULAs for fonts you own, and take the measures necessary to be in compliance with their stipulations, even if it means purchasing additional licenses for your print service provider. It's a small addition to job cost in the interest of unquestionable legality.

Converting Text To Outlines

By now you're probably thinking, "Surely I can just convert my text to outlines and completely avoid the Font Police." Surprisingly (or perhaps not, at this point), converting text to outlines does not sidestep the provisions of the font vendor's EULA. In fact, while some font vendors' licensing allows conversion of text to outlines, many expressly forbid it.

Additionally, you must consider that, even if a font vendor's EULA permits outlining fonts, you may see some slight loss of quality when converting to outlines, especially with small, serif text.

What's a concerned citizen to do? First and foremost, read the license before you purchase fonts. If you're purchasing fonts online, the vendor should make the EULA available to you before you commit to purchasing a font. You'll find that some font foundries are less restrictive than others on issues such as font embedding and outlining. Either patronize those with less stringent EULAs, purchase fonts for your print service provider…or learn how to create your own fonts. *That* will give you some sympathy for font designers!

And don't name your firstborn child Eula, or she won't be able to go *anywhere* or do *anything*.

Sending Fonts to the Print Service Provider

If you have studied the fine print in the licensing agreements for all the fonts you're using in a project, and you've determined that you and your print service provider are in full compliance with any applicable licenses, remember to gather up all the necessary fonts when you submit your files for printing. See Chapter Twelve, "InDesign Production Tips," and Chapter Thirteen, "QuarkXPress Production Tips," for specific information on preparing page-layout files (including fonts) for the print service provider.

If you submit PDF files, make sure you've correctly embedded the fonts. See Chapter Fourteen, "Acrobat Production Tips," for general information about font handling in PDF files. For detailed information about creating PDF files from an individual application, see the appropriate chapter:

- Chapter Ten, "Illustrator Production Tips"

- Chapter Eleven, "FreeHand Production Tips"

- Chapter Twelve, "InDesign Production Tips"

- Chapter Thirteen, "QuarkXPress Production Tips"

CHAPTER SEVEN

Cross-Platform Issues

Allegiance to an operating system can be a tribal issue, rivaling politics as a trigger for heated discussions, innuendo, condescension, and insults regarding parentage and one's fitness for procreation. It's part of the fun of using computers.

In the early 1990s, this chapter would not have been necessary. In fact, it would have been fairly pointless. (Depending on your platform preference, you may feel that it's pointless *now*.) In those days, if you were involved in graphic arts, you were using a Macintosh. Period. End of story. Windows users were treated like second-class citizens when they dared take their jobs to a print service provider. If you wanted to clear out a prepress department in 1992, all you had to do was yell "PC job!" It was much like yelling "Fire!" in a crowded theater.

Fast-forward to the present day: It's not a Macintosh-only world. The major graphics applications such as Adobe InDesign, Illustrator, Photoshop, Acrobat, FreeHand and QuarkXPress are almost indistinguishable across platforms. But while the applications themselves are generally compatible, operating system issues still must be addressed if we're all to get along peacefully. Now, put down that wooden stake.

CROSSING THE GREAT DIVIDE

Gone are the days when we needed special translation software to even read files from The Other Side. Whereas network connections once required arcane geek incantations and burnt offerings, mere mortals can now point, click, and magically access a networked PC from their Mac. We live in wonderful times.

But that doesn't mean things are perfect or painless. Windows users have to accept that many Macintosh users consider file extensions equivalent to obscenities. Macintosh users must learn to avoid florid naming conventions. And everybody *still* needs to gather up the fonts before they send a job out the door.

While setting up a network is outside the scope of this book, the assumption is that you've figured out some way to get your stuff to wherever it needs to be. We've come a long way from floppies (Grandma, what are floppies?) and SyQuest drives. It was very chic to have huge whopping 44 MB SyQuest cartridges ten years ago, and blank CDs cost nearly 20 dollars apiece. Now, we have large-capacity CDs, DVDs, and memory sticks, and none of the current methods is platform-specific. Pardon the flashback. The author suddenly feels very, ah, mature.

FILE NAMING

It's great to be creative while you're designing an annual report or sales brochure. But when it's time to name and save files, control your imagination. Both Windows and Macintosh computers, as well as popular server platforms, are more forgiving than in the days of old eight-dot-three naming conventions (eight-character file name, followed by a three-letter file extension). In those days, a Macintosh user wanting to share with a PC user had to be fairly creative to come up with file names. AnRepCov.eps, AnRepCv2.eps. You get the idea.

Let's Have a Lot of Brevity

The ancient eight-dot-three limitation has long been lifted. Given expanded file-naming freedom, some of us get a little carried away. Here's a file from one of the author's clients, slightly altered to protect the innocent: **SSGC holiday wreath photos and logos -- Publisher (10-19-05).pub**. Because spaces, periods, and parentheses also count, that's a 64-character file name. Windows and Macintosh OS X platforms both currently allow a total of 255 characters, which is perhaps overly generous. That's an entire paragraph.

While Windows allows file names of 255 *characters*, it limits a total *path designation* to 260 characters. Path designation is the literal pathway to the file's location. For example, a file named Test.doc stored at the root level of a PC's C drive would have a path designation of C:\Test.doc, a total of 11 characters. File extensions like .doc or .pdf are included in the total character count for a file name.

If you're a Macintosh OS X user, you may not think of OS 9 as another platform, but in many ways it is. Users of OS 9 are limited to 31 character filenames, so if you're sharing files with colleagues who are still languishing under OS 9, you'll have to take that into consideration, and keep your file names appropriately brief.

Filenames Don't Need Punctuation. Period.

Length is not the only issue affecting proper file naming. There are certain characters—even certain *names*—that should be avoided. A good rule of thumb is this: Don't include any characters traditionally used in comic strips to indicate profanity, such as !@#$★% (pardon my language). Stick to solely alphanumeric contents—uppercase and lowercase letters, coupled with numerals, spaces, underscores, and hyphens. There's an urban myth that spaces are forbidden in file names, but this doesn't usually matter in a graphics/print environment. If you embark on Web work, however, omit spaces from file names.

Avoid colons and slashes, since those characters are reserved to mark directory breaks. Although the Macintosh won't prevent you from naming a file with forward or backward slashes, you won't be able to copy it to a Windows drive. PCs prevent the problem by stopping you in your tracks when you press either slash key, displaying an alert listing forbidden characters. And even Macintosh CD-burning applications will convert slashes to underscores during the creation of a data CD.

If you're creating your job on the Mac and sending it to a print service provider who will be handling it on a Mac, why should you care about slashes? Because they'll probably copy your job to a server for storage. If it's a Windows server, they'll have to rename your files to even allow copying, which will then munge all your image links, forcing them to update your images. Ouch. Since you have no control over where your files may land, forestall such problems by getting in the habit of using safe file names.

Both Windows and Macintosh OS X prevent you from typing colons in filenames, and neither operating system allows you to begin a file or folder name with a period. An initial period renders a file invisible under Unix.

Although current operating systems prevent much of this file-naming misbehavior, beware of legacy files created before the Macintosh adopted Unix under the hood. While files whose naming began with a period were not problematic under OS 9, they'll cause problems when you attempt to use them under OS X. They'll disappear.

While some file-naming purists object to using multiple periods as visual separators in file names, such as *Smith.Brochure.new.pdf*, newer Windows and Macintosh operating systems don't care, although this practice may cause problems with some persnickety applications. Some older server processes may modify the name by substituting underscores for extra periods, or by truncating the file name. Rather than risk this reaction, consider using underscores (*Smith_Brochure_new.pdf*) or capitalization (*SmithBrochureNew.pdf*).

Watch Your Language

Although the Macintosh has no objection to using them in file names, some combinations of letters and numbers are reserved by the Windows operating system. Names such as com1, com2, all the way through com9 are reserved for communication ports on the PC. If you were to create a Word file named com1.doc on the Mac, you might successfully copy it to a Windows drive, but you'd be unable to open it under Windows. Other forbidden names include lpt1 through lpt9 (reserved for printer ports), as well as prn, con, and nul.

Include File Extensions

Like two-button mice, file extensions (for example, .txt and .doc) have long been considered by some Macintosh users as symptoms of consorting with the Dark Side. Under previous Macintosh operating systems, file extensions were not required. In those days, files consisted of two forks, a data fork and a resource fork. The data fork held the true guts of the file, while the resource fork told the system which icon to use and how to open the file. Under Unix-based OS X, the Macintosh does not yet require file extensions to determine which application should be used to open a file, and which icon should represent the file — that can be accomplished with the Get Info palette. But file extensions are still helpful for human identification of files, and crucial for cross-platform compatibility. On both Macs and PCs, you can choose to hide those extensions, but they are there nonetheless.

Most file extensions consist of three letters (for example, .rtf, .pdf, .tif), but some applications create four-letter extensions such as .html (Web page), .fh11 (FreeHand MX) and .indd (InDesign). A period always separates the file name from its extension, as in Image.tif or Brochure.indd.

Failure to append the correct file extension on the Macintosh can prevent a Windows user from opening the file by double-clicking it. In addition, lack of a file extension may prevent accessing such a file in other ways, such as attempting to import or place the file in another document. Of course, it's easy to add the extension if you encounter this problem, but it's better to just develop the habit of adding the extensions when you save the file. All Windows applications and most Macintosh OS X applications are smart enough to do this for you. Some applications, such as Photoshop, provide an option in the dialog box you encounter as you save a file.

Whereas even the most ancient Windows file will be sporting a file extension, Macintosh files saved under OS 9 (or earlier) may be extension-free. So as you dig up old files for new jobs you're creating under OS X, either manually add the appropriate extension or open the file in the appropriate application by choosing File > Open from within the program. Then resave the file with a shiny new extension.

FONTS

Macintosh-specific fonts don't function on PCs, and Windows PostScript or TrueType fonts don't work on a Mac (usually, see the "Font Trick" note below). That's why there are a number of utilities to convert PC fonts to Macintosh fonts, and vice versa.

The most common motivation for such gyrations is to submit a Windows-based job to a Mac-based print service provider. There is only one correct way for the print service provider to treat the job, but unfortunately it's not what usually happens. The solutions range from bad to bearable to acceptable.

- **Bad Idea:** Copy the job to a Mac and use the closest available fonts. "Hmmm… Helvetica is pretty much the same as Arial, isn't it?"

- **Bearable Compromise:** If the font vendor's licensing agreement allows it, convert the PC fonts to Macintosh versions with a high-end font-editing program such as FontLab or Fontographer (both now owned by FontLab). Check the converted file carefully against hard copy; or, better yet, a PDF supplied by the creator of the file.

- **Best Approach:** Keep the files in their native habitat. Bite the bullet and learn the basics of Windows, and avoid any conversion. PCs are really not as scary or neurotic as they used to be. If you're designing on Windows computers, have a heart-to-heart conversation with the print service provider before submitting your job. Elicit some assurance that they will not use either of the first two approaches above. If that assurance is not forthcoming, consider submitting print-ready PDFs to avoid font issues.

FONT TRICK: Windows TrueType fonts can be used under OS X if placed in Macintosh HD/Library/Fonts. To use both Windows TrueType and PostScript fonts in Adobe applications on the Mac, place them in Macintosh HD/Library/Application Support/Adobe/Fonts. You can place the font in an individual Adobe applications Fonts folder, but it will then be available only to that single application. You have to be pretty bored or fontless to do this, and you must check the font vendor's licensing agreement to see if this is legal.

Of course, the niftiest solution to the old font wars is to switch to OpenType fonts. As you've seen in Chapter 6, "Fonts," they're completely cross-platform and full of tempting typographic features.

GRAPHICS FORMATS

All current graphics formats—including TIFF, PSD, EPS, AI, JPEG, FH11, and PDF are perfectly happy jumping platforms. Just don't forget the file extensions. That was easy, wasn't it?

CHAPTER EIGHT

Job Submission

The planning that goes into your job should begin long before you hand your job files to the print service provider. As you've seen in the preceding chapters, it behooves you to anticipate the challenges presented by the physical processes of printing. It's less traumatic to prevent problems early in the game than to frantically fix something as the deadline looms. And it's not just the big stuff that bites you. It's no fun to be leaning blearily over a printed sheet on a 3:00 a.m. press check and have a pressman remark, "Hey, didja notice that this guy's name is spelled three different ways in this brochure—is that right?"

In the heat of battle, it's easy to overlook the basics while you're focused on the tricky parts of the job. And tunnel vision can cause you to lose sight of the big picture. But if you break the process into several smaller chunks, it's easier to catch problems at each stage.

This chapter serves as a reminder of some of the issues you've read about in earlier chapters and provides a number of checklists to review while you're preparing to send your job to the print service provider.

PREPARATIONS DURING THE DESIGN PROCESS

It's exciting to get started on a new project, and there's no such thing as too much time to do a job. However, before you wade right into the project, take a breath. Take two.

Lean back and consider the end product. Try to isolate the most challenging aspects of manufacturing the printed piece. Does it involve spot colors or varnishes? Does it require special finishing treatments such as die cutting or embossing? Is it an odd size? Does it involve multiple, collateral pieces that have to fit together, such as a pocket folder with inserted literature and a business reply card?

As you sketch out the prospects in your mind, start having conversations with the printer. In the very earliest stage of the job, you may not always have the luxury of knowing who the print service provider will be. But as soon as you do, start paving the way for a successful print project by opening up the lines of communication. Their staff can help you build your project successfully, and you will have prepared them for the incoming job. In printing, as in any kind of manufacturing, *surprise* is rarely a good word.

TALKING WITH THE PRINTER

Your first contact at the printing company will probably be with a salesperson. The ideal salesperson asks questions about your expectations for the job, advises you of any potential problems if your job contains some challenging aspects such as special stock or fancy finishing requirements, and gives you a realistic idea of the outcome. The salesperson will gather your initial information and will provide you with an estimate of job costs and a proposed timeline for the steps along the way. Those steps will include such events as when your files must be submitted, when you can expect the first proofs, when the press run will take place, and when the final job will be delivered. Finally, the salesperson will hand you and your job off to a customer service representative (CSR).

If you're fortunate, your CSR will be an experienced print professional who can give you some insight into your job's special needs. If you find yourself dealing with someone who seems to know less about the print process than you do, you might try diplomatically to expand your list of contacts at the printing company. A few print service providers frown on allowing customers to talk to production personnel, but it really does make life easier for everyone if you can deal with knowledgeable operators. Your salesman may be able to smooth the way if necessary. But speaking as a production person, I'll volunteer that most production personnel welcome a customer who's interested in providing a job that's not a nightmare. But there's a fine line between being a conscientious client and being a pest. You, of course, would never cross that line. You shouldn't call the prepress department unnecessarily (they'll start hiding from you), and it's important that you keep the CSR in the loop if you are allowed to contact production staff directly. The CSR is the common contact point for jobs, and is expected to know everything about a job, so don't forget to inform the CSR if anything about the job needs to be changed.

In your initial conversations with the CSR, make sure they're aware of any special issues with your job. Here are a few topics you may need to discuss:

- **Unusual stock.** Substrates such as metallic stock or paper with pronounced texture or of unusually thick (or thin) weight may require additional time to order, and may also dictate which press will be used for the job.

- **Special mixed inks.** If you need something beyond what's available in the Pantone, Toyo, or other swatch libraries, you may want to see ink draw-down samples on the final stock. A draw-down sample is created by spreading a thin coating of the desired ink on the intended stock to present a realistic preview of how the ink will look on press.

- **Varnishes or other coatings.** Special add-ons such as spot varnishes, aqueous coatings, or scratch-off spots require planning.

- **Custom finishing.** Operations such as perforation, die cutting, embossing, foil stamping, or unusual folds require advance planning and equipment setup. Since custom finishing can take extra time, adequate time must be included in the schedule for the job. Complicated folding may also require modifications to the standard configurations of the folding equipment to ensure that the folds occur in the proper manner. See Chapter 3, "Binding and Finishing," for more information on finishing processes.

- **Unusual content.** If you require special print add-ons such as customized content for variable data printing (VDP) or custom addressing, it may be necessary to add time for programming and acquisition of data such as mailing list files.

For your sanity—and theirs—make sure you obtain the following crucial information:

- A detailed schedule that includes dates for intermediate events such as random proofs, page proofs, bluelines, and any press checks. Yes, the final delivery date is important, but unless you're aware of all the intermediate dates, you'll jeopardize the final goal.

- Contact information for all the people who are (or should be) familiar with your job, including the salesman, the CSR, and any prepress staff you've been told you can call with questions. Make sure that they know how to contact *you* if questions arise. And keep in mind that printing plants often operate 24 hours a day. You may not be accustomed to phone calls after midnight, but if your job is on a tight schedule and there's a problem during night shift, your phone may ring. This prospect alone may be a strong incentive to check your job thoroughly before you submit it.

PLANNING FOR PRINT

As your files take shape, it's important to build from the ground up. It's not much fun to deconstruct a complex file and then reassemble it because it was built one-half inch too big or all the artwork uses the wrong six spot colors. Before you choose File > New, make sure you've established the following important specifications:

- **External document size.** If you're printing letterheads, that's easy. But if you're creating a piece that folds, such as a trifold brochure or a pocket folder, whip out the ruler and make sure you know the correct external dimensions before you go too far.

- **Adequate bleed.** While one-eighth of an inch is standard bleed, some print service providers may request a larger value, especially on packaging or large-format output.

- **Internal panel sizes.** In folding pieces such as trifold brochures, remember that you have to allow for shorter panels that fold in (see Chapter 3, "Binding and Finishing"). In your page-layout program, set up guidelines to help you position content. Your print service provider may be able to provide a template to use if you're building to a common size.

- **Artwork interactions with folds, perforations, or die cut trims.** If artwork stops at a fold, special handling may be required to ensure that it doesn't dribble over onto the next panel, especially on packaging. Your print service provider can provide some guidance for preparing artwork, especially if you're printing on heavy stock whose thickness has a bearing on how wide the folded edge will be.

- **Correct number of pages.** In a common-format, multipage document (facing pages), the number of pages should usually be divisible by four. If you were inspired to pull the staples out of a magazine while you were reading Chapter 3, look at the loose pages and note that each loose sheet consists of four pages — two front, two back. In a longer document, such as a textbook, you (or the printer) can take up the slack by providing blank pages for notes.

- **Correct inks.** If it's not a 27-color job, there shouldn't be 27 colors in your application's color palette. Delete unnecessary colors, or convert them to CMYK if they're not intended to print as spot colors.

Checking Raster Images

As you've seen in Chapter 4, "Preparing Raster Images," it's important that your images are of sufficient resolution at final size, and that you've saved the images in an appropriate format and in the correct color space—CMYK for many print service providers, or RGB images containing the correct, embedded color profile if you're working in a color-managed workflow.

If the images you're creating are your final art (that is, they're not being placed into an illustration or page-layout application), check them in Photoshop or the application in which you created them. Consult your print service provider to make sure you know their requirements, but here are some general guidelines:

- **Resolution.** Raster images should usually be at least 300 ppi (pixels per inch) at their final imaging size. However, there are exceptions. For example, large-format output such as posters, store signage, and billboards. Since readers will probably be at least several feet away from the finished poster or large sign, the net effect is the same as viewing a smaller image at a shorter distance. In other words, a 150 ppi image viewed from a distance of several feet is the equivalent of a smaller, 300 ppi image viewed up close.

  It may be necessary to create images of higher resolution for high line-screen work (200 lpi or higher). If you are creating images for special printed pieces such as art prints or art books, you may be asked to supply images at higher than 300 ppi. Keep in mind that it's best if the original scan or digital photograph is of adequate size and resolution. Scaling up or increasing resolution through interpolation never produces results equivalent to healthy original images.

- **Color space.** Images usually come in one of five major flavors for printing purposes: CMYK, RGB, grayscale, monochrome (bitmap black and white, with no shades of gray), and duotone. Unless you're working in a color-managed environment, you'll be asked to provide CMYK images for color images. If your print service provider utilizes color management, ensure that you've tagged your RGB images with the appropriate color profile. Make sure that grayscale images are truly black-only files, not gray-appearing RGB or CMYK images.

- **Retouching.** If you're not comfortable performing retouching work beyond simple blemish removal, let the print service provider know that you'd like them to perform the work instead. It's helpful if you print the image(s) in question, and then indicate the problems you'd like them to fix. It's likely that you'll incur additional job charges for this service.

- **Rotations and scaling.** You'll achieve the best results if your scans or digital photographs are created at the proper size and rotation for final use. But let's be realistic. You can't always anticipate how you'll use an image. If you've simply flipped an image horizontally or vertically in a page layout, don't worry about it. If you've rotated an image by increments of 90 degrees, don't worry about that. But, if you rotate an image in a page layout by anything other than 90-degree increments, or if you scale—or both—you'll see some slight softening of detail in the final output.

- **Filenames.** Avoid using periods, asterisks, and other characters to flag filenames (see Chapter 7, "Cross-Platform Issues"). Even if you and your print service provider are both using Macintosh computers, remember that your files will probably be copied to a server that may be based on another platform such as Unix or Windows.

Checking Vector Artwork

Since illustration programs such as Illustrator and FreeHand allow you to place raster images as content, you have to consider some of the same issues that you encounter in page layout applications. Don't forget to check the following:

- **Correct colors.** If you'll be placing vector art into a page-layout program, try to avoid multiple instances of what should be a single spot color. If the job uses Pantone 384, for example, make sure that the color isn't Pantone 384C in your illustration program and PMS 384CVC in the final page-layout document. Ensure that color naming is consistent across all constituent files.

- **Images.** Most illustration programs offer the choice of embedding or linking placed images. While embedding increases the file size, it ensures that all the pieces are in place. However, it may limit editing if the print service provider needs to modify the image. If you anticipate the need to color-correct or retouch images placed in illustrations, send the image along just to be safe.

- **Fonts.** Embed fonts or outline text (the font EULA permitting). Note that while Illustrator and FreeHand enable the embedding of fonts with proper permissions, this only facilitates correct imaging. The fonts are not available for text editing unless the user (in this case, the printer) also has the fonts active on their system. If you're tempted to convert text to outlines, be advised that some text effects such as underlining or strikethrough may be lost when you outline the text. Another consequence of outlining text to consider: Fonts contain special information called *hinting*, which is lost when text is converted to outlines. As a result, outlined text will not be as crisp as the original text when printed on a desktop printer. However, on a high-resolution output device such as an imagesetter or platesetter, outlined text should be satisfactory.

- **Text.** Spell-check content, and check for pesky little empty remnants of text where you unintentionally clicked with the Type tool (it happens to all of us sooner or later). Those empty instances may result in preflight reports of a font being needed, resulting in time wasted troubleshooting something that isn't truly a problem if the font isn't used anywhere else.

- **Bleed.** If the vector artwork file is your final artwork (that is, you're not going to place it in a page layout file for further assembly), ensure that you've included adequate bleed. Even though you create bleed artwork correctly, the export format that you choose in Illustrator and FreeHand determine whether that artwork is correctly retained during file export. Refer to Chapter 10, "Illustrator Production Tips" and Chapter 11, "FreeHand Production Tips," for some clarification of how Illustrator and FreeHand handle bleed, depending on the version and export format.

Checking Page Layout Files

Once you've determined that your raster images and vector artwork pieces are healthy, you still need to examine any page-layout file that combines that content to make sure that additional errors are not introduced. Don't forget to do the following:

- **Spell check.** It's important to weed out typing errors, but be particularly careful with product names and proper names. You also need to check for mistakes that spellcheckers don't catch, such as grammatical errors and words that are spelled correctly but aren't what you intend. You don't want to go to press with a headline that reads "The Clam Before the Storm."

- **Delete extra junk.** Clean off the pasteboard, and eliminate empty elements.

- **Avoid styled text.** Rather than clicking the *B* or *I* button, choose the genuine bold or italic font.

- **Delete double spaces.** If you were still setting type with a typewriter, double spaces would be fine. But you're not. Double spaces in computer typesetting are large, airy gaps. Perform a find-and-replace to replace double spaces with single spaces. And quit hitting that spacebar.

- **Check for scaling and rotation.** While a few rotations here and there aren't a problem, and it's permissible to scale within a reasonable range (70–125 percent), an image-heavy document with lots of such transformations can be challenging to RIP. Especially if you are transforming large images, consider doing those transformations in Photoshop, and then updating the images in the page layout so they can be handled without rotation.

- **Provide printouts of your job.** They're really helpful to CSRs, planners, estimators, and prepress operators at the print service provider for quick visual aids. It's best if printouts are actual size, but if the piece is too large to print at final size (or you don't feel like tiling output and taping pieces of paper together), mark the printout prominently with the scale factor. This is especially important if the print service provider will be scanning transparencies or other artwork for you. The scanner operator will need to measure your transparencies, measure your printouts, and then determine the proper scale factor for each image. If you indicate the scale factor used in your printout, you reduce the chance for error by alerting the scanner operator and by providing an important factor in his scaling equation.

- **Preflight your job.** The term preflight comes from the aviation industry. If you are about to become airborne in a 150,000-pound metal tube, you check all the operating systems before you pull back on the stick. If you want to minimize problems in a print job, you check all the contents. The preceding sections have provided some guidance for manually checking your job, but you'd do well to consider using dedicated preflight software to do the job for you. The FlightCheck family of products from Markzware — FlightCheck Studio, FlightCheck Designer, and FlightCheck Professional — automate the process of preflighting by allowing you to set up test parameters for checking documents.

Have realistic expectations. Your monitor and your desktop printer's approximation of the final printed piece may be fairly good if you calibrate your monitor and you're using a high-end printer with careful color management. Otherwise, you have to wait for contract proofs from the print service provider to have a good idea of the appearance of the final output.

SENDING JOB FILES

The print service provider should give you some guidelines for submitting job files. Some prefer PDF files, while some would rather have application files such as QuarkXPress, InDesign, or Illustrator. Usually, you'll be asked to provide multipage documents in *reader's spreads*, which is how you normally build such documents: Page two facing page three, and so on. If you're asked to provide *printer's spreads* — imposed for plating — you should be suspicious that the printer doesn't have dedicated software to perform imposition. This may be a sign that the printer lacks other important capabilities.

Submitting PDF Files

If the print service provider requests that you submit PDF files, they should give you specifications for creating PDF files. While PDF creation has been discussed in other chapters, be sure to address these crucial issues:

- **Preflight PDFs before submitting.** Even if you have performed a preflight on the application files that generated the PDF files, it's a good idea to preflight the PDF files themselves. Markzware's FlightCheck Designer and FlightCheck Professional products can preflight PDF files. The print production tools in Acrobat 7.0 Professional offer extensive preflighting features as well.

- **Follow print service provider specifications.** Faithfully replicate the specifications that are provided for creating PDF files. Restrict your PDF to the version your printer requests. That is, don't send them an Acrobat 7.0 file if they've asked for an Acrobat 4.0 file. Ask the print service provider to send you Acrobat Distiller job options if you're distilling PostScript or using Adobe CS2 applications to create your files. CS2 applications share a common repository of PDF-creation settings, and dragging a job options file into Distiller makes those settings available to other CS2 applications.

- **Embed fonts.** Use the correct settings as you export PDFs from your final application, or when you distill PostScript files. If you've used fonts whose vendor forbids embedding, you must either request that the print service provider purchase the same fonts, or you'll have to substitute fonts that *can* be embedded.

- **Ensure safe transit.** Even though it's easy to think of PDF files as being hermetically sealed, they can be corrupted when sent as e-mail attachments unless they're first compressed with a utility like StuffIt on the Macintosh or WinZip on Windows. Encasing the PDF files in a compressed archive protects them in transit. If you are submitting the job on disk, this isn't an issue, and you don't need to compress the PDF files.

Submitting Application Files

It isn't sufficient to send only your finished page-layout file to the print service provider. The page-layout file is like a recipe for the printed piece. And a recipe is not much good without all the necessary ingredients. The fonts and images used in your page layout are the ingredients, and you must supply all those constituent parts for the print service provider to complete your job. While you're working on your project, you may be using graphics stored in multiple locations on your hard drive or on a server. Graphics are simply *referenced* by your page-layout file, as are the fonts you've used. They're not embedded in the page-layout file, so the graphics and fonts must be gathered up to constitute a complete kit for your project. Fortunately, your page-layout programs provide methods for rounding up all the necessary images, vector artwork files, and fonts.

When you're sure all your work is in good shape, the *Collect for Output* feature in QuarkXPress, the *Package* function in InDesign, and PageMaker's *Save for Service Provider* make it easy to gather up all the pieces necessary for printing a page-layout file, including support art and necessary fonts. In QuarkXPress, choose File > Collect for Output. In InDesign, choose File > Package. In PageMaker, choose Utilities > Plug-ins > Save for Service Provider.

Before you exercise your layout program's collection feature, make sure that all necessary fonts are active, and that support art links are current. Make sure that no graphics are missing or in need of updating. The final package for a page-layout file should contain the following components:

- The layout file.

- All support art, including all raster images and all vector artwork. Also include any raster images that have been placed in vector drawings from FreeHand or Illustrator (unless you embedded the images).

- All necessary fonts, including those needed by support art such as Illustrator or Photoshop files. Be mindful of the end-user licensing agreements (EULAs) for the fonts you've used—some forbid supplying fonts to print service providers (see Chapter 6, "Fonts"). Carefully examine the collected job. QuarkXPress 4.0 does not collect fonts, and you must remember to check the Copy Fonts option in PageMaker's Package dialog to package fonts.

Additionally, if you have created any elaborate compositions with multilayered Photoshop files, you should consider including those working files with your support art, even if you have used a flattened, simplified version of the image in your page-layout file. The flattened image may be your final file, but if the print service provider needs to make any corrections to the image, it may be easier to modify your working, layered Photoshop file than to work with the flattened image. If you are using InDesign, you can place the layered Photoshop file in the page layout without flattening it, so the print service provider would make any necessary corrections to that file.

Since software is constantly being updated, make sure the print service provider knows which version of the page-layout application you are using. If you're using QuarkXPress 7.0, for example, alert them that you're using the most current version, in case they haven't yet purchased the update. You might think that print service providers would be the first to buy new software, but they're just like the rest of us—they don't buy new software until they have to.

This leads to another important thought. If you are using an *earlier* version of software than the print service provider, this may present problems if the printer needs to perform any corrections to your files, and then returns them to you for future use. Most print service providers maintain earlier versions of software so they can keep client files in their original version. But not all printers are so conscientious, so it's worthwhile to mention that you're using an earlier version than the current release in the marketplace. If you're one version behind them in QuarkXPress or InDesign, they can usually save your files to your earlier version. Don't forget that, while it's possible to save an InDesign CS2 file to InDesign CS, there's no provision for saving back from InDesign CS to InDesign 2.0. That bridge doesn't exist. And if you are two or more versions behind your printer, regardless of the application you're using, they may not be able to go back that far. If you have no intentions of upgrading, this may become an issue for you. Discuss this with your print service provider. You may have to perform any corrections on your own files using your own, earlier version of the software, and then submit new, corrected files.

Platform Issues

Generally speaking, it's preferable to keep a job on one platform throughout its lifespan. While sending files across platforms is not the major undertaking it once was, fonts remain an issue. If you're using all OpenType fonts, there's no need to worry. But if you are using PostScript or TrueType fonts on Windows, and your print service provider is Macintosh-only, you should insist on submitting your job in PDF format. While there may be Macintosh fonts with the same names as your Windows fonts, they aren't necessarily identical in terms of font metrics, and there may be text reflow as a result of opening the job on a Mac (see Chapter 7, "Cross-Platform Issues"). Most print service providers sensibly keep Windows files in their native habitat for this reason, but if you're using Windows, it's worth mentioning this concern early in your discussions with the CSR.

Sending Files

Ask the print service provider about their preferred method of file submission. If they provide a way of submitting files online via FTP (File Transfer Protocol), they'll give you directions for accessing the correct target directory and any needed passwords. Use a file-compression program such as StuffIt (Macintosh and PC), ZipMagic (PC), or WinZip (PC) to consolidate the job into a single archive and to reduce the amount of data you're uploading. Additionally, both the Macintosh OS X operating system and Windows XP have built-in file compression utilities. On the Mac, select a file or folder, and then control-click it (or right-click with a two-button mouse) to select Create Archive from the context menu that appears. In Windows XP, select a folder, and then right-click and select Send To > Compressed (zipped) Folder. Windows will then create a compressed archive of the folder and its contents.

While CDs and DVDs are probably the most commonly used physical methods of transporting files, many print service providers still support removable media such as Iomega® JAZ® and Zip disks. It's also not uncommon for extremely large jobs to be submitted on large-capacity portable external drives that connect via FireWire or USB connections.

In addition to the files themselves, it's helpful if you provide these collateral materials to the print service provider:

- Contact information for you, along with any alternate contacts such as other members of your design team, or appropriate contacts at your client if you're acting as an intermediary.

- Comprehensive assembled printouts of the job (*comps*) if there's anything tricky about the final piece, such as inserts or foldout panels.

PREPARING FOR PROOFING CYCLES

Depending on the workflow of your print service provider and the nature of the job you are submitting, you may be asked to check proofs at several points during the life of the job. You've probably been looking at the same content for so long that it all starts to look alike, and it's easy to develop blind spots when you're in a hurry to approve a proof. Here are some checklists to help you remember key issues at each stage.

Checking Image Proofs

Image proofs are sometimes referred to as *random proofs* or *scatter proofs*, since they are proofs of just the images without any page-layout context. If you're unsure of how your own scans or digital photos will reproduce, or if the print service provider has performed the scans, you may want to proof images before going ahead with the remaining print production steps. Check these issues:

- **Size.** Are images the correct size? If some images are used multiple times at different sizes within the project, are there separate images for wide variations in scale factor?

- **Crop.** Is there sufficient image to fill the intended area when you place it in the page layout? Make sure nothing's been cropped out incorrectly. Also, if you need only a small portion of a large image, it's OK to crop out unused image area to save storage space and processing time.

- **Orientation.** Does the image need to be flipped vertically or horizontally for use in the final layout?

- **Angle.** Is the image at the same angle at which it will be used in the final piece?

- **Matching the original artwork.** Is the proof a fair rendering of the transparency, reflective art, or digital photo? Matching the art is sometimes a subjective evaluation but, given the limitations of CMYK pigments, is it a reasonable match to the original?

- **Color.** Is it too dark? Too light? Does it lack contrast? Are neutral areas such as whites, grays, and blacks free of any tinge of unwanted color? For example, check gray areas such as concrete or paved road and make sure there's no reddish, bluish, or greenish tinge (called a color cast).

- **Detail.** Is there discernible detail in the highlight and shadow areas? If the original image or original artwork lacks detail, it can't be manufactured, but any existing detail should be maintained.

- **Moiré.** Especially when photographing or scanning patterned originals such as woven fabric or geometric patterns, it may be necessary to give special treatment to all or part of an image. Sometimes slight blurring may be used in Photoshop to subdue the moiré. You may have to decide which is more objectionable—the unwanted pattern or the loss of detail due to blurring.

- **Silhouettes.** This is a good opportunity to check the edges of any silhouettes, whether you've created them or asked the print service provider to create them. An edge that looks acceptable onscreen may need some cleanup once you see a proof of it.

- **Retouching.** If you've requested retouching, does the proof show that it's been done? Does it need additional work to accomplish what you wish? Are there problems that weren't apparent before, that now should be retouched?

Checking Page Proofs

Not every print service provider creates proofs of individual pages. Some may show you imposed proofs, which serve a dual purpose: You can check page content and color, and you and the print service provider can check for correct pagination (page position as a result of imposition). When viewing page proofs, you should check for the following:

- **Correct size.** Make sure the page dimensions are correct.

- **Bleed.** Make sure there is adequate bleed. If images must bleed, make sure they don't fall short.

- **Image area.** Make sure no artwork or text falls too close to the trim edge or interior spine. Such artwork will be at risk of trimming out or disappearing into a fold.

- **Correct fonts.** Check to make sure text intended to be bold or italic really is bold or italic. Look for the Courier font being used instead of your intended font (some RIPs use Courier to call attention to font substitution).

- **Overset text.** Check the end of text flows to make sure the last line is intact. It's helpful if you hold your own printout over the proof and flip it up to check for disparities between your prints and the service provider's proof.

- **Text reflow.** Using the same technique as above, flip between your printout and the service provider's proof to check for changes in line breaks. Reflow could be caused by font substitution or incorrect hyphenation settings.

- **Correct images.** Make sure incorrect images have not been used, especially if intermediate retouching or color corrections have been performed.

- **Crop.** Make sure images fill their frames, and that they are cropped as you intended.

- **Special effects.** If you are using drop shadows or transparency effects created in InDesign, Illustrator, or QuarkXPress 7.0, make sure the effects are correctly rendered, especially where they interact with spot-color content.

- **Rules and other strokes**. Make sure rules are unbroken and uniform in weight.

- **Trapping.** While there should be no misregistration on proofs, look for any unattractive dark lines where trapping has been performed. Some darkening may be unavoidable, but it's possible to mitigate the effect by changing trap settings, especially where light colors interact with each other.

- **Overprint.** Make sure black text and art don't knock out of underlying areas if they're not intended to do so.

- **Rich blacks.** Check that rich blacks have been created for large black coverage areas, or ask the print service provider to assure you that such areas will not be anemic or mottled when printed. The same cautions apply to large single-color areas other than black, such as spot color areas.

- **Moiré in screen tints or images.** While patterns and woven pieces are prone to moiré, the effect can also occur in some combinations of flat-color screen tints, such as combinations of yellow and black. Moiré in an image can occur when a patterned original, such as fabric, is scanned, but it may not be apparent when you view the scanned image on your monitor. When such an image is rendered as a halftone, the combination of fabric pattern and the halftone pattern can produce an unattractive moiré. If you notice the effect at the proofing stage, don't ignore it. Consult with the print service provider to determine if additional work such as rescanning, softening the pattern, or perhaps even changing the screen angles might improve the outcome.

- **Crossover art.** Check the alignment and color match for artwork that crosses from one page to another. Make sure that crossover text isn't awkwardly divided and that any art that should stop at the spine *does* stop at the spine without falling over onto the facing page.

- **Spot colors.** Make sure there are no unnecessary spot colors.

Checking Corrections

By now, you're probably tired of looking at this job. It's particularly hard to focus on corrections because they tend to consist of small details such as typographical errors. It's helpful to place a marked-up intermediate proof on top of a later proof, and then flip it back and forth to look for the corrected areas.

Checking Imposed Bluelines

- **Crossover art.** Make sure that no text or artwork is incorrectly cropped at the spine where pages meet. Make sure that nothing falls short of the spine if it's intended to go all the way to the center of the spread.

- **Correct pagination.** Refer to the folding dummy created by the print service provider's planner or imposition department.

- **Changes from page proof stage.** Make sure nothing has moved or disappeared, especially if corrections have been made since an earlier stage.

Signing Off on Proofs

When you sign off on a proof, you're indicating that you are satisfied with the work. This places responsibility on both you and the print service provider. If the print service provider fails to match the signed proof in subsequent steps, those mistakes should be fixed at no cost to you. However, if you fail to notice problems before you sign off on the proof, you will incur costs when you ask the print service provider to make changes.

ATTENDING A PRESS CHECK

Not all jobs warrant a press check. If all the intermediate proofs have been satisfactory, and the job doesn't involve exotic stock or ink effects, there's no need for the printer to invite a customer to sign off on a live press run. However, there are numerous reasons for holding a press check: There may be concerns about printing on challenging stock, or there may be a desire to ensure the successful outcome of a high-profile job such as an annual report. Don't be intimidated by the atmosphere of a press check. The roar and bustle of a pressroom can be overwhelming, but just take a deep breath—a good whiff of all those solvents may have a calming effect.

Note that since printing plants often run around the clock, a press check may be held at any hour of the day or night. The print service provider will attempt to give you an idea of the time, but problems with other jobs may change the schedule for your job. You may find yourself camping out at the printer or waiting for a call.

During a press check, these are the things you should watch for:

- **Accuracy.** Make sure the press sheet matches the approved intermediate proofs (page proofs and bluelines). Check images, text, content, and color.

- **Ink on paper.** Watch for flaws in registration, color, and ink coverage. Look for smearing, and watch small details for distortion. Small text (especially white text reversed out of multiple colors) may close up. Look for color consistency in elements that are repeated on separate pages. Check that crossover art matches from page to page—you may need to fold up printed sheets to lay the pages side by side to check the match.

  Minor adjustments can be made on press, but major problems—such as the need for a second hit of a solid color or the creation of a rich black—will require pulling the job off press, reworking some portion of it, replating, and going through makeready again.

- **Stock behavior.** Watch for flaking or *picking* (small fibers of paper breaking off after printing, leaving unprinted areas), especially with heavily textured stock. Watch for wrinkling in thin stock. Check for showthrough from the other side of the sheet. To some extent, the pressman can compensate for stock behavior, but if the stock proves unwieldy, you may have to reconsider your choice of paper. Such a drastic change will result in the job being pulled off press. New stock will have to be located (or ordered), and your job will have to be rescheduled. An ink draw-down sample might have established that the inks would look satisfactory when applied to the stock manually, but the combined effects of multiple ink impressions over large areas of the paper and the mechanical actions of paper being pulled through the press may result in unexpected results when the job is actually printed.

- **Debris and scratches.** Keep an eye out for hickeys—small white halos in solid color areas that are caused by a foreign particle stuck to the plate or blanket. Hickeys are fairly easily fixed by wiping the particle away. Watch for scratches in text or large areas of color coverage.

While the prospect of stopping a press and juggling the complexities of corrections and rescheduling may seem distasteful, the costs incurred at this stage may still pale in comparison to the expense of completely reprinting a job if the printed outcome is not satisfactory to your own customer.

At each step of the process, through your design stages and the successive proofing stages at the print service provider, there are multiple opportunities for things to go awry.

While you're focused on kerning an important headline on the cover, it's easy for you to overlook a typographical error on the last page of the publication. While a harried prepress operator at the printer is replacing an image with a color-corrected version, he might err in positioning the new image.

Tiny errors can lead to expensive problems. Tunnel vision is unavoidable, especially in complex projects. That's why proofing is so important. It's also helpful to solicit input from someone who hasn't been staring at the job as long as you have. An innocent bystander can often spot errors you've missed: "Hey, this looks great, but shouldn't there be a picture in this big empty white box?"

CHAPTER NINE

Photoshop Production Tips

There are numerous books and Web sites devoted to using Adobe Photoshop for the entire spectrum of skill levels from beginner to Master of the Pixel-Based Universe. (See the Appendix for a selection of Photoshop resources.) We're assuming you know how to handle the basics of Photoshop, so you won't find any basic how-to instructions here. Nor is this a Hot Tips & Tricks compendium. What you *will* find are tips to help you create print-ready files and some heads-up warnings regarding tricks that the software can play on you. Because Photoshop is used for a wide variety of purposes, from Web to print and video, it provides multiple methods for accomplishing what you want to do to an image. The method that might be ideal for Web is not necessarily appropriate in an image intended for print.

OFF TO A GOOD START

Before you start slinging pixels around, do a bit of planning. You may just be stuck with a supplied image, with no control over how it began life. In that case, you may have to make some compromises for print. But if you have some control over the birth of an image, you can better prepare for a better outcome. You might glance at Chapter 4, "Preparing Raster Images," for some general image guidelines.

Know the Fate of the Image

Before you scan an image, or photograph a subject with a digital camera, it's helpful to know how the image will ultimately be used. Consider some important issues:

- **At what scale factor will the image will be used?** Scan the image to that size rather than scaling the image in Photoshop or a page-layout application.

- **Will the image be used at multiple sizes?** If the scale factors are fairly close—the image is used at 150 percent and at 140 percent, for example—scan for the larger size and just use scaling tools in the page layout for the smaller size. But if there is a substantial difference in scale factors—an image used at 150 percent and 25 percent, for example—it's worth making a separate scan for each use. Alternatively, scan the image for the larger scale factor, and then scale it down in Photoshop (Image > Image Size), using the *Bicubic Sharper* resampling option (**Figure 9.1**). Why have two images, when you could just place the same image twice in your page layout and scale it there? You have a bit more control over the resampling and scaling if you perform the scaling yourself in Photoshop. And you slightly reduce the processing burden on the raster image processor (RIP) that ultimately handles your job by using images that are already the correct size.

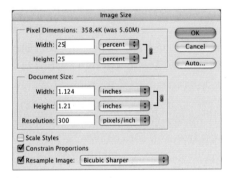

Figure 9.1 When reducing the size of an image in Photoshop, you'll achieve better results by using the Bicubic sharper Resampling method.

- **Will the image be rotated in its final use?** Scan the image at the correct angle. Photographing a subject at an angle, however, may be more challenging ("Can you stand on your head just a little bit longer?"). As with scaling, you'll achieve better results by performing the rotation in Photoshop rather than in a page-layout program. And if you don't hit the correct angle with your first try, don't perform an additional rotation. Multiple transformations (whether scaling, rotation, or distortion) can erode image detail unnecessarily. Figure out what the correct final angle should be, then undo your attempts or revert to the original version of the image and perform the rotation in one step.

- **What are the important elements in the image?** If the image is a product shot, concentrate your efforts on maintaining the best detail and most faithful color rendition in the product, even if that means slightly hurting the incidental contents of the image. Worry about the red in the product package, rather than agonizing over the color of the two partial tulips accenting the upper-right corner of the shot.

- **Will the image be used on the Web, as well as for print?** Consider keeping the image in RGB as you perform color corrections and retouching work. Then save an RGB version of the image to be used as the source file for Web work. Save another copy of the image as CMYK. You should also keep your RGB working file in case you need to do additional work, so that you can regenerate the Web and print images from a new parent image if necessary.

Image Resolution

The rules for image resolution are the same as for image size, because the concepts are intertwined. Start with as much image information as you can. You can always *discard* information, but you can't convincingly *create* it out of nothing. Once you've determined the correct final dimensions for your image, scan the artwork or transparency to those dimensions at the appropriate resolution. What's the appropriate resolution? Generally speaking, 300 ppi at final size is sufficient for printing at 133–150 line screen (see Chapter 4, "Preparing Raster Images," for a discussion of resolution, and Chapter 2, "Ink on Paper," for information about line screen). If your project will be printed at a very high line screen (175 lpi or above), and it is important to maintain a high level of detail in the content—images of jewelry, fine art, or antiques, for example—it may be beneficial to scan at a resolution greater than 300 ppi. If you are doing your own scans for such a projects, consult with the print service provider to determine the proper resolution to use. If the print service provider is doing the scanning, they will take care of the resolution issue.

Color Space

Our eyes see in RGB, yet we print (usually) with CMYK. As mentioned in Chapter 4, "Preparing Raster Images," RGB is the native tongue for scanners and digital cameras as well. Even though an image may be fated to printing in CMYK, there are advantages to keeping the image in RGB as you perform color correction, retouching, and compositing. The wider color gamut of RGB gives you more to work with as you make color corrections, and some interesting Photoshop effects, such as the Vanishing Point, Texturizer, and Artistic filters, are not available in CMYK images.

Converting RGB to CMYK

Unless you and your print service provider are working in a color-managed workflow, you'll be expected to provide CMYK images (except, of course, those images intended to print as grayscale or duotone). Ideally, you'll be given conversion settings customized for their presses, as well as instructions on applying those settings. Lacking that, you should find that Photoshop's built-in conversion settings are serviceable. Choose Edit > Color Settings and then select North America Prepress 2, or use the custom settings provided by your print service provider.

Photoshop invokes these settings when you select Image > Mode > CMYK Color or Image > Mode > Grayscale. Keep this in mind if your print service provider gives you high-resolution scans to incorporate in your design. If you convert those images to RGB to perform a color correction, or apply a filter that's only available in RGB mode, your conversion back to CMYK will result in color values that differ from the original image supplied to you, although the change may not be apparent in your onscreen display. As long as your color settings are not extreme, this will probably not result in a drastic alteration of the printed piece, but it's something you should consider before you begin jumping between color spaces.

WORKING IN LAYERS

While the intricacies of creating and editing Photoshop layers are beyond the scope of this chapter, it's worth mentioning some of the benefits of working with layered files. Layers can keep the individual components of a complicated composition from being glued together prematurely, giving you a safety net in case you change your mind. Multiple undo capabilities are great during a working session, but they don't help if you've saved a file and realize—days later—that you've inadvertently cropped out something crucial, or performed a color correction that doesn't look so great.

Layers offer the advantage of providing nondestructive methods for combining images, for creating silhouette and soft-edged effects, and for doing color corrections without permanently altering pixels.

Don't Erase that Pixel!

When you need to eliminate part of an image, it's tempting to just choose the Eraser tool from the Tools palette in Photoshop, and get rid of it. When you permanently delete pixels, they're gone forever (**Figure 9.2**). If you accidentally erased the CEO's left ear in his portrait for the prestigious annual report, I hope you remember where you backed up the original image. I'll wait while you frantically search through that pile of CDs.

Figure 9.2 Nice seashore! Well, it *was*. Too bad you accidentally erased the ocean and some of the scenic rocks (right). But you still have the original image somewhere. Don't you?

There's a safer and more flexible way to eliminate pixels. Use the Layer Mask feature in Photoshop to selectively *hide* pixels without *destroying* them. If you can create a silhouette, you can create a layer mask.

1. Create a selection by using your favorite method, and make sure it's still an active selection. An active selection appears as a black-and-white dashed shape, often referred to by the highly technical term "marching ants."

2. The layer must be a floating layer to use a layer mask. If the layer is named *Background* (and its name is italicized), it needs to first be converted to a floating layer. To do this, double-click the layer name. In the dialog box that follows, you can enter a new name for the layer or accept Photoshop's default name for the newly floating layer.

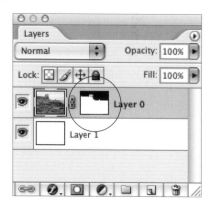

3. Make sure your ants are still marching, and then select Layer > Layer Mask > Reveal Selection. You should see the selected part of the image floating on a transparent background, and a mask icon will be added to the layer in the Layers palette (**Figure 9.3**).

Figure 9.3 A layer mask reveals content rather than erasing pixels. You can always modify the layer mask later, to reveal or hide image contents in a nondestructive way.

Color Corrections with a Safety Net

Some of the color-correction options in Photoshop, including Shadow/Highlight, Match Color, and Replace Color, can only be applied directly to pixels in the image, which alters them permanently. But some of the most commonly used color corrections can be stored in Adjustment layers, which are nondestructive. No pixels are harmed in this type of color correction, and you can always change your mind later. To use an Adjustment layer, click the circular "Create new fill or adjustment layer" icon ( ) at the bottom of the Layers palette, and then select the desired type of correction you wish to make. You can also choose Layer > New Adjustment Layer, and then select a color-correction option from the menu that is displayed. You can choose from a wide assortment of color-correction options, including Curves, Levels, Color Balance, and Brightness/Contrast. When you complete your corrections and click OK in the dialog box, you'll see a new entry in the Layers palette (**Figure 9.4**).

Figure 9.4 An Adjustment layer performs a color correction without actually altering pixels. Don't like it? Delete it or click the eyeball to hide the correction.

Note that the Adjustment layer automatically creates a layer mask for itself. Initially, it's all open (that is, it isn't hiding anything). But if you'd like to prevent the color correction from affecting some areas of the underlying image, use the Paintbrush tool to paint those areas of the mask with black. If you want to rework the color correction, double-click the leftmost icon in the Adjustment layer to display a dialog box. To disable the correction, click the eyeball to turn off the visibility of the Adjustment layer. To permanently delete the Adjustment layer, select the layer in the Layers palette, and then choose Delete Layer from the Layers palette menu.

Should You Flatten a Layered File?

Native Photoshop files offer the benefits of layers and transparency—what's not to love? Admittedly, if a Photoshop file has grown to hundreds of megabytes, it might be more efficient to use a flattened file for placement into a page layout. But you'd be wise to keep a copy of the original, layered, working Photoshop file in case you need to do additional edits. To flatten a layered file, choose Flatten Image from the Layers palette menu.

TRANSPARENCY

Adding effects such as ghosted areas or drop shadows is an easy way to add visual interest to images. Such effects are no longer limited to Photoshop, but as you step outside Photoshop to incorporate those effects, you'll encounter some challenges. Since you can incorporate Photoshop files into Illustrator drawings and Adobe InDesign or QuarkXPress pages, it's important to realize that you're governed by the limitations of those programs. Just because Photoshop can handle an effect doesn't mean that other programs can interpret that content correctly.

For example, Illustrator and InDesign both honor *transparency* in placed Photoshop files, but neither program correctly handles Photoshop *blending modes*. Transparency and blending may sound like interchangeable terms, but they're not.

Transparency is expressed in percentage opacity. For example, a white square with 20-percent opacity allows what's underneath to show through at 80-percent strength. Opacity settings in a Photoshop file are honored by InDesign and Illustrator, which is why the dandelion in **Figure 9.15** appears silhouetted when placed in an InDesign layout.

However, blending modes involve much more complicated math. For example, drop shadows created in Photoshop by selecting Layer > Layer Style > Drop Shadow are set to use the Multiply blend mode with anything they encounter in Photoshop. This results in a realistic darkening of underlying image areas, but only within Photoshop.

Unfortunately, neither Illustrator, QuarkXPress, nor InDesign can understand blending modes within a Photoshop file. So drop shadows created in Photoshop do not interact correctly with elements underneath when they're placed in Illustrator or InDesign (**Figure 9.5**). Instead of darkening underlying elements, Photoshop shadows knock out the shadow area.

Figure 9.5 A Photoshop shadow behaves correctly within Photoshop (left). But when the image is placed in another application, its shadow incorrectly knocks out underlying color rather than darkening it (shown on the right without the black plate).

One solution is to do what we've done for years—combine the elements by placing them on various layers in a Photoshop file. After combining the objects, shadows, and underlying elements in Photoshop, save a layered working file for editing, and then place a flattened image in your final document. Although any changes will require you to go back two generations to the working file (and will require keeping track of both the working file and its descendant), this workflow has been used for years.

If an element requires a simple, soft-edged drop shadow, don't create the shadow in Photoshop. Instead, wait until the image is placed in Illustrator or InDesign and create it there, since both applications handle their own shadows correctly. If you're doing your final layout in QuarkXPress up through version 6.5, you can use a third-party XTension to create the shadow, such as ShadowCaster from Quark, Inc. In QuarkXPress 7.0, use the built-in Drop Shadow feature (Item > Drop Shadow).

SILHOUETTES AND MASKING

The traditional method of silhouetting an object to knock out its background involves using the dreaded Pen tool to create a path, earmarking that path as an official clipping path, and then saving the file as an EPS. However, since few people have any actual fondness for the Pen tool in Photoshop, they have instead become adept at avoiding the issue in several ways:

- Deciding that a square-cut image is much more tasteful

- Bribing someone else to draw the path

- Making a selection with the Magic Wand tool, and then converting the selection to a path

The first two options are adequate, but using the Magic Wand will result in a lousy path. The Magic Wand is not truly magic (sorry). It's acceptable for creating some selections to be used in Photoshop or as a starting point for a mask, but it's not the way to make a suitable path. Let's use the strawberry in **Figure 9.6** as an example of what *not* to do.

Figure 9.6 You could silhouette this strawberry with the Pen tool. (Or perhaps you could persuade someone else to do it.)

Creating a Path: Right and Wrong

Photoshop's attempts to convert an active selection ("marching ants") to a clipping path are valiant, but the results are usually less than stellar. Because a Magic Wand selection follows the rectangular edges of pixels, it's not a very good basis for a smooth clipping path.

In some instances, noodling with the Make Work Path tolerance setting on the Paths palette (Window > Paths) can soften the granularity of the generated path (**Figure 9.7**), but you'll have to keep reloading the selection and experimenting with the tolerance settings, since this function doesn't offer any preview of the outcome.

Figure 9.8 shows the unsavory result of taking the easy way out by converting a selection to a path with the tightest tolerance setting, 0.5 pixels.

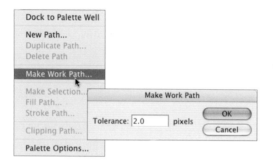

Figure 9.7 The Make Work Path tolerance setting smooths a path that's generated from an active selection.

Figure 9.8 The result of converting a selection to a path by using a 0.5 pixel tolerance. The Wand doesn't seem so magic now, does it?

Using a 10-pixel tolerance setting (**Figure 9.9**) cures the granular look of the path, but note that the smoothness results in a looser clipping path, which lops off some of the strawberry and shows some background.

Figure 9.9 Selection converted to a path, using a 10-pixel tolerance. Smoother than Figure 9.8, but at the expense of fidelity.

It's far better to bite the bullet and draw the path with the Pen tool (**Figure 9.10**). There's no need to obsessively follow every annoying little wiggle. Your goal is a reasonably faithful but smooth rendition of the object's edge, and it's perfectly legal to take a bit of artistic license to improve the edge of the silhouetted image.

Figure 9.10 Clipping path drawn the way nature intended—with the Pen tool.

A dedicated tutorial on using the Pen tool is outside the scope of this book, but check the Appendix for some excellent references and tutorial resources.

Path Flatness Settings

In the olden days of anemic RIPs, users were encouraged to set a high *flatness* value for paths to ease the burden on the RIP. Think of the RIP as constructing curved lines as a series of tiny straight segments. The fewer of those segments the RIP had to chisel—the flatter it could render curves—the faster the job would process. **Figure 9.11** shows a circle imaged with a high flatness setting. It might be easy on the RIP, but it's not easy on the eye.

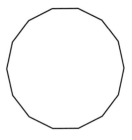

Figure 9.11 A high flatness setting makes things easier for the RIP, but it results in a chiseled appearance for what should be curved lines.

In reaction to seeing such clunky output, some people adopted the unfortunate habit of specifying very *low* flatness values in the Clipping Path dialog (Window > Paths > Clipping Path), such as 0.2 device pixels, in the hopes that this would encourage the RIP to carve more petite segments. Forcing the RIP to chew this finely had the unpleasant side effect of slowing job processing and in some cases, completely preventing the job from being processed by a RIP. When you choose Clipping Path from the Paths palette menu, you have the option to select the correct path and to enter a Flatness value. While RIPs are more robust now, it's actually best to leave the Flatness field *blank* (**Figure 9.12**), which allows the RIP to use its optimal flatness setting without additional calculations. So stop agonizing over what to put in the Flatness field. Just leave it empty, and the RIP will do what it knows is best.

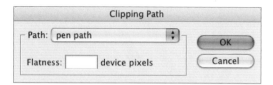

Figure 9.12 When specifying a clipping path, resist the urge to put a microscopic value in the Flatness field. Leaving it blank allows the imaging device to handle curves with its own optimal setting.

Paths that Aren't Clipping Paths

Besides being challenging to draw, clipping paths are bullies. When placed in a page-layout application, an image with an official clipping path can only display what's within the area of the clipping path—that's the whole point of a clipping path. But paths aren't *official* clipping paths until you designate them as such via the Paths palette menu.

Consider an image that contains several elements that you'd like to use selectively in a page layout. If you're planning to use the clipping path approach to silhouetting those elements, you'd have to save multiple versions of the image, resulting in a separate image for each element you plan to use.

But there's a more flexible approach available to you. Both InDesign and QuarkXPress 4.0 and above recognize *any* paths in EPS and TIFF files, and both applications provide the option of choosing which path you'd like to use to silhouette the image (**Figure 9.13**). The paths don't have to be official clipping paths—they just have to be named paths. This trick also works with PSD files in InDesign, as well as QuarkXPress 6.5 and above.

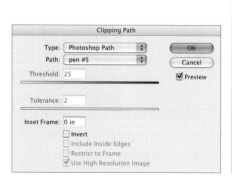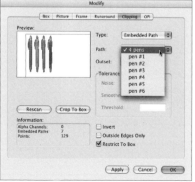

Figure 9.13 Choose a path in InDesign (left) or QuarkXPress (right, version 6.5).

Taking this approach allows you to use the same image in multiple ways without saving multiple versions. In **Figure 9.14**, the same image provides seven uses—a square-cut version and the six, individual silhouetted pens. The only limit is the number of named paths in the image. Note that an unsaved work path isn't recognized by InDesign or QuarkXPress. Unsaved, unnamed paths don't appear as options in either application.

Figure 9.14 Six pens, six paths, one single image used in multiple ways.

Alternative Silhouetting Methods

Here's some good news for those who loathe the Pen tool. Beginning with InDesign 2.0, InDesign has honored transparency in Photoshop images, and QuarkXPress 7.0 follows suit. In addition to providing liberation from the dreaded Pen tool, this means that you can perform the equivalent of photocomposition within a page layout (**Figure 9.15**), if you know how to create realistic masks.

Figure 9.15 The dandelion (left) can be extracted from its background by using a density-based mask (center). Since InDesign honors transparency, the dandelion can then be composited with other elements in a page layout (right).

If the subject was photographed on a fairly consistent background (by which we don't mean *plaid*), you can create a density-based mask similar to that of the dandelion by starting with one of the channels of the image. Open the Channels palette in Photoshop (Window > Channels) to inspect the channels. Click the name of each channel, one by one, until you find the channel with the most contrast between the subject and the background. It doesn't have to be perfect. It just has to provide a good start. In the case of the dandelion, the cyan channel is the most promising. The black channel is a close second choice, but the cyan has finer detail, so it's the winner (**Figure 9.16**).

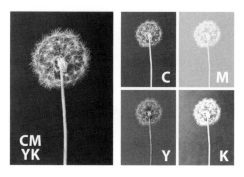

Figure 9.16 Shopping for a channel to provide a starting point for a mask. Either the cyan or black channel might work, but the cyan has more detail.

Once you've decided on the channel that provides the best start for a mask, duplicate it. Select the channel in the Channels palette and, from the Channels palette menu, choose Duplicate Channel. You can name it something memorable in the dialog that follows, or just accept the default name — in this case, *Cyan copy*.

The next step is to manipulate the contrast in the Cyan copy channel so that it becomes solid black and white. Use Levels (Image > Adjustments > Levels) or Curves (Image > Adjustments > Curves) to exaggerate the contrast in the mask channel. The goal in our dandelion image is a white dandelion-shaped hole in a black background. Since each image is different, you'll have to experiment with the values in your images, but you can see the approach (and the results) in **Figure 9.17**.

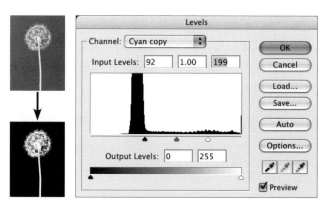

Figure 9.17 Using a Levels adjustment to increase the contrast of the mask channel. Your values will be dependent on your image.

You'll probably have to use your paintbrush to edit the mask to your satisfaction. Paint with white to open up areas of the mask (which will reveal those parts of the image when you're finished). Paint with black to fill in the mask where you wish to hide areas of the image. The mask is stored in what's called an alpha channel (**Figure 9.18**). It doesn't function as a mask until you load it as an active selection. For the rest of the recipe, refer to Figure 9.2, and the instructions in the section, "Don't Erase That Pixel!" earlier in this chapter.

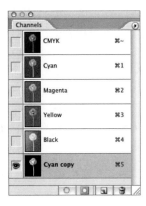

Figure 9.18 When you create and save a mask, it's stored in an alpha channel. But it's just waiting there. It isn't an active mask until you load it as an active selection.

Since the mask is derived from image contents, it's possible to create a much more natural silhouette without the hard-edged cutout appearance that usually results from using a clipping path.

BEYOND CMYK

You're not limited to just cyan, magenta, yellow, and black inks when you print a color image. You can create images that consist of combinations of CMYK and spot color, or even images that print only in spot colors.

Creating Duotones

A *duotone* image is composed of two colors, usually black and a spot color. Such images are a great way to add visual interest to a job with a limited color palette. There are variations on this theme, such as *tritones* (three colors), *quadtones* (four colors), and so on. Since these images usually contain spot-color components, it's important to create them correctly to ensure that they print as intended. Note that these images may be composed of all spot colors or a combination of spot colors and process colors. Start with a grayscale image, and then choose Image > Mode > Duotone (which is the starting point, even if you intend to create a tritone or quadtone image).

In creating a basic spot-plus-black duotone image, designers may make the understandable mistake of thinking that the Black ink listed in the Duotone Options dialog is a spot color (**Figure 9.19**). Don't worry: It's really just the plain, old-fashioned process black of CMYK fame, and there's no need to change it.

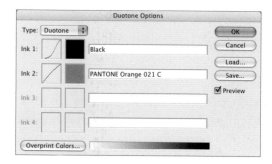

Figure 9.19 The Black ink chosen by Photoshop in the Duotone Options dialog is plain old process black. Don't alter it.

In fact, if you get ambitious and change the name of Black in the Duotone Options dialog to, say, Pantone Process Black C, for example, you actually *cause* what you're trying to *prevent*: You create an extraneous spot color when you import the image into a page layout, as shown in the QuarkXPress Colors palette (**Figure 9.20**). So just leave it alone, and Photoshop will do the right thing.

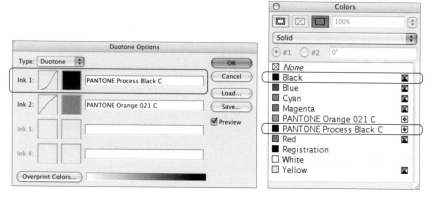

Figure 9.20 Changing the definition of Black in Photoshop's Duotone Options creates an extra black ink when you place the image in a page layout program such as QuarkXPress (right). Not what you had in mind.

Adding Spot Color to a CMYK Image

Occasionally, special handling is needed to accentuate portions of an image or to ensure faithful rendering of a color that falls outside the CMYK gamut. Adding spot ink on top of an image of flowers might allow the printed piece to better render the true color of the actual flowers, if process color falls short of doing so. In this approach—variously called *bump plate*, *touch plate,* or *kiss plate*—the image contains additional colors beyond the standard cyan, magenta, yellow, and black.

The trick is to contain the extra color plates in an image format that's well digested by page-layout software. The most common format for this amalgam of colors is a special flavor of EPS called DCS 2.0, for Desktop Color Separations. Under the hood, these special images consist of all the individual color plates plus a low-resolution representation image for display. Both QuarkXPress and InDesign can handle DCS 2.0 files created by Photoshop, although there are some catches. QuarkXPress does not correctly generate a composite PDF of the DCS 2.0 content. Instead, QuarkXPress produces a PDF containing just the low-resolution component of the DCS file. Because of this issue, QuarkXPress documents containing DCS 2.0 files must be given special handling by the print service provider. InDesign handles DCS 2.0 content more intelligently and produces a correct PDF containing all the high-resolution data for all plates. But neither InDesign nor QuarkXPress correctly image DCS 2.0 files containing vector elements or text. You must add text in the page layout or in an illustration program, then place it on top of the DCS 2.0 file.

The DCS 2.0 format is getting a bit outdated, largely because of the special handling it requires. If you are creating specialized images containing spot color content, consider saving them as Photoshop PDF rather than DCS 2.0. Both QuarkXPress and InDesign accept Photoshop PDFs. Using Photoshop PDF rather than DCS 2.0 also ensures that PDFs exported from QuarkXPress will contain high-resolution content and spot colors.

BEYOND PIXELS

Pixels and vectors can live together in graphic harmony, enabling you to combine smooth, sharp text with images for interesting results. But it's important to save such constructions correctly so that other programs produce expected output.

Vector Elements

While Photoshop is primarily devoted to pixels, it is possible to add text and other vector elements to a Photoshop image. It's not appropriate to create body text in Photoshop, and most text should be created in an illustration or page-layout application. But if you want to bevel and emboss text (**Figure 9.21**), or give a special treatment to a vector logo, you may be compelled to handle it in Photoshop.

Figure 9.21 Vector or text elements are an interesting (although not necessarily tasteful) addition to an image.

Vector elements in Photoshop do not have any inherent resolution, although any shading applied through effects such as embossing must be accomplished with pixels. Those pixels are just part of the effect, and they don't become literal pixels until the file is printed. Consequently, you can scale vector elements within the Photoshop image and the effects will be recalculated, growing new pixels of the appropriate resolution. Since the edges of vector elements are vector, not pixels, they remain crisp.

It's important to save such hybrid files in a way that ensures that the vector edges print sharply, and this is where we encounter an alphabet soup of acronyms.

The ideal file format for cohabiting pixels and vectors is one that retains the crisp edges of vectors when the file is placed in an illustration or page-layout file, and allows round-tripping back to Photoshop for any needed editing. There are several file-format options for this type of image, of which only one is truly satisfactory (**Figure 9.22**).

Figure 9.22 A Photoshop file containing vector elements can be saved in several formats. The sharp vector edges in a native PSD file become rasterized when placed in a page-layout program (left). An EPS retains the desired crisp edges when placed in a page layout (middle), but will lose the vector content if reopened in Photoshop for editing. Only a Photoshop PDF (right) retains vector information for placement in a page layout *and* allows round-tripping back into Photoshop.

A native Photoshop file (PSD) keeps the text and vector elements live in Photoshop and allows round-tripping. You can reopen the file at any time to correct misspelled text or edit anchor points on vector shapes. But PSDs are not treated so kindly when they're placed in an illustration or page-layout file. The vector edges are rendered as pixels during output, taking on the resolution of the underlying image. Consequently, PSDs containing vector elements may serve as working files, but they will not print ideally when placed into other applications.

Saving such an image as an EPS preserves sharp vector edges, even when placed in an illustration or page-layout file. However, while the EPS format ensures good output, it prevents the file from being safely reopened in Photoshop. Photoshop can open it, but the vector content will be rasterized in the process, thus ruining the integrity of the image.

For this special type of image, only a Photoshop PDF provides full functionality. A Photoshop PDF can be reopened by Photoshop without rasterizing, and the vector content is correctly displayed and imaged when a Photoshop PDF is placed into documents created by Illustrator, InDesign, and QuarkXPress. Think of it as two files in one: Photoshop sees the original PSD, with its editable text and vector content; and other applications see the public face of the PDF file, with its nice, crisp edges.

Saving as a Photoshop PDF

To save a PDF that can be reopened by Photoshop, choose File > Save As, and then in the Format list, select Photoshop PDF. When the Save Adobe PDF dialog is displayed, make sure that the Preserve Photoshop Editing Capabilities check box is selected (**Figure 9.23**). This is the default setting for Photoshop PDF files.

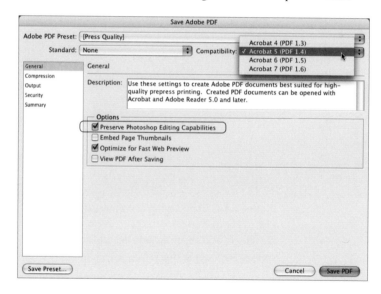

Figure 9.23 To ensure that you can reopen a Photoshop PDF, select the Preserve Photoshop Editing Capabilities check box. For maximum portability, choose Acrobat 4 (PDF 1.3). To maintain transparency, choose Acrobat 5 (PDF 1.4).

If you want to maintain transparency in the image when it is placed into Illustrator or InDesign, you must save with Acrobat 5.0 or above compatibility. If you plan to place the Photoshop PDF into QuarkXPress, choose the PDF/X-1a preset from the list at the top of the dialog. You'll lose the transparency, but the file will print more predictably. For more information on Acrobat and PDF files, see Chapter 14, "Acrobat Production Tips."

Photoshop versions prior to CS2 require you to be mindful of vector settings in the PDF Options dialog that is displayed when you choose File > Save As and choose the Photoshop PDF format (**Figure 9.24**). If you don't select Include Vector Data, the edges of vector and text content will appear rasterized in other applications and will be output as raster content. For maximum portability, also select Use Outlines for Text in the PDF Options dialog so that there are no embedded fonts that might be mishandled by subsequent processes that affect the PDF file. The Use Outlines for Text option has *no* effect on content when the PDF is reopened in Photoshop. The PDF part of the file is perceived by other applications, which will see only the outlined text.

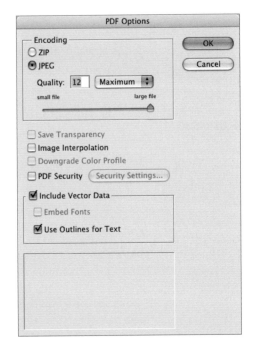

Figure 9.24 When saving as a Photoshop PDF in Photoshop prior to CS2, choose JPEG Maximum, and check Include Vector Data, as well as Use Outlines for Text.

In the PSD part of the saved Photoshop PDF, everything is still "live," so when you reopen the file in Photoshop, the text is still true text, and the necessary fonts must be active on your system to edit the text. By default, Photoshop CS2 includes vector data and outlines the text for use in other applications. It does the right thing without presenting you with confusing options.

SAVING FOR OTHER APPLICATIONS

The old recommendations to save as TIFF or EPS were solid in their day, and you still can't go wrong by adhering to the old ways. But native, layered Photoshop files offer appealing features such as transparency, editable vector elements, and nondestructive color corrections. TIFF files can contain layers, but offer no support for vector elements, so Photoshop native files still trump TIFF files for flexibility.

It's now acceptable to loosen up a bit. InDesign and Illustrator accept layered Photoshop files in all their glory, including transparency effects. QuarkXPress 6.5 allows placement of native PSDs, although it doesn't recognize transparency. QuarkXPress 7.0 offers expanded support for native Photoshop features, recognizing transparency and even allowing you to use alpha channels as soft-edged masks. There's no need to squeeze the fun out of your images before you place them into a page layout. But it's worthwhile to do some house-cleaning before you save and close your Photoshop file.

- Delete unused layers. Select an unwanted layer (or Shift-click to select multiple layers), and then choose Delete Layer from the Layers palette menu.

- Delete unused alpha channels. Select an unwanted channel (or Shift-click to select multiple channels), and then choose Delete Channel from the Channels palette menu.

- Delete unused paths. Select the unwanted path and then choose Delete Path from the Paths palette menu. You'll have to delete paths one by one—Shift-clicking doesn't work when selecting paths.

- Make sure the image is in the correct color space for its final use.

- If you're certain about the final use of the image, crop out any unnecessary image content. But leave a rind of extra image around the outside, just in case you need a bit of elbow room when the image is placed in a page layout.

- If you've created multiple, experimental files on your way to the final image, name the final image in a way that makes it clear It's The One, and put the older, obsolete files in a quarantine folder. Don't send a job to the print service provider with a folder full of images with names like *Final.tif, Final2.tif, NewFinal.tif, Newfinal2.tif, NewerFinal3.tif, NewestFinal.tif, FinalButDon'tUse.tif*, and so on. If *you're* confused, think how *they'll* feel.

CHAPTER TEN

Illustrator Production Tips

As Adobe Illustrator has evolved over the years, it has morphed from a relatively simple vector drawing program into a full-featured graphic arts tool. The addition of flexible effects has blurred the line between drawing and painting. But some effects require special handling to ensure that they behave as expected when the files are imaged or placed in other applications for imaging.

WHY VERSIONS MATTER

With the release of the first version of Creative Suite (CS), Adobe was perhaps too subtle about mentioning version numbers. Witness the countless questions from clients, students, and coworkers: "What's the difference between Illustrator CS and regular Illustrator?" and "Where's Venus?!" Only a careful inspection of splash screens reveals that Illustrator CS is version 11.0, and CS2 is version 12.0.

For many years, a new version of Illustrator just meant the addition of new drawing toys. The file architecture and text composition engine remained fairly static, so there was little danger of adversely affecting a file by bouncing it between users with different versions of the program. Saving to an earlier Illustrator format for someone using an earlier version of the application didn't threaten the integrity of a logo.

However, there can be disappointing results when you attempt to go back in time with content produced by using features such as transparency (introduced in Illustrator 9.0), envelope distortion (Illustrator 10.0), 3D effects (Illustrator CS) or Live Paint (Illustrator CS2). Illustrator does a valiant job of digesting newer content so that older versions can handle it, but this process is often a one-way street. For example, a dimensional effect created in Illustrator CS2 will display and print correctly in Illustrator 10, but the dimensional controls will be gone when the file is reopened in Illustrator CS2. If you're working in a mixed environment with users who have multiple vintages of Illustrator, be mindful of these speed bumps. The ideal solution is to move all members of a workgroup to the same version, but that isn't always feasible. In self-defense, keep a current working version of your Illustrator document when it's necessary to save nostalgic versions for collaborators in case something's munged by saving to an earlier version.

Purely vector components have nothing to fear, but text is a cause for concern. Illustrator CS and CS2 provide support for the extended character sets in OpenType fonts. They also share typographic niceties such as optical kerning, which was borrowed from InDesign in a bit of cross-pollination between applications.

These enhancements to Illustrator opened the door for fine typographic controls and elegant composition. But because the text composition engine was revamped in Illustrator CS to allow these improvements, text in older files from previous versions undergoes conversion when those files are opened in Illustrator CS or CS2. This change in direction may cause some aggravation when you upgrade from earlier versions, but the long-term typographic benefits far outweigh the hiccups.

Text conversion is unavoidable, but at least you're warned when you open a file from an earlier version of Illustrator in Illustrator CS2 (**Figure 10.1**). The yellow triangle of terror is looming behind the Illustrator icon, and you're presented with three confusing options, none of which seems like a safe choice. Illustrator CS offers only Update and OK, with no Cancel.

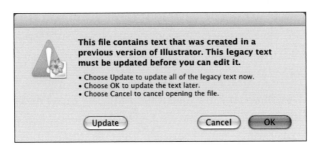

Figure 10.1 In Illustrator CS and CS2, when you open a file created by Illustrator 10 or earlier, you're faced with this alert. Don't panic. And don't choose Update! The correct option is to choose OK.

- **Update** will revamp the text according to the newer CS/CS2 composition rules, but you won't be watching while it happens. If there's text reflow, you may not catch it. One could argue that this shouldn't even be an option. Don't choose this.

- **Cancel** is the coward's way out and prevents the file from opening. You'll have to face this file eventually, so don't chicken out now.

- **OK** opens the file without modifying the text. If you're not planning to edit text in the file, this is the correct choice because it leaves the text untouched. And if you are planning to edit text, this ensures that you'll be watching when the text is translated, so you can make the necessary adjustments. It's understandable that this is the default choice. If you press the Enter key out of habit, you've accidentally done the right thing.

When you choose OK in the opening alert box, you postpone the recomposing of text. As long as the correct fonts are active when you open the file, no harm is done to text by just opening and resaving the file, although resaving does label the file as having been created by the newer version of Illustrator. Performing edits to other elements of the file won't adversely affect the text. Text is protected until you attempt to edit it (**Figure 10.2**).

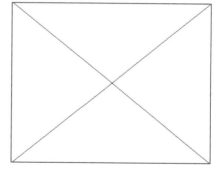

This is text created in Illustrator 10. What happens when we open it in Illustrator CS2?

Figure 10.2 After opening an earlier-version file in Illustrator CS or CS2, you'll wonder what all the fuss is about. It looks like perfectly healthy text (left). But switch to Outline view (right), and you'll see that the text isn't quite as you'd expect. The cross-hatched frame might make you think that the text is behaving like a placed graphic, but the appearance actually indicates that the text is protected from editing until you select it with the Type tool.

When you attempt to edit legacy text, you encounter another alert and another decision (**Figure 10.3**). Choosing Cancel just delays the inevitable. The real choice is between Update and Copy Text Object.

- As in the opening alert, **Update** will recompose the text by the new rules of Illustrator CS/CS2. Unless you have hard copy or a photographic memory as reference, this option may result in unpleasant text reflow that you might not notice.

- **Copy Text Object** preserves an unchanged copy of the text as it appeared in the original file, while creating a duplicate block of text that plays by the new rules. Most importantly, you now can compare the two versions, see what really happened, and repair as necessary. Once again this default choice is the safe choice.

Figure 10.3 When you start to edit text in an earlier-version file opened in Illustrator CS/CS2, you face yet another alert. Lucky you! The default choice is the correct one: Copy Text Object.

When you choose Copy Text Object, Illustrator creates a ghosted replica of the text as it appeared in the original file (**Figure 10.4**). Use the reference text as a guide as you make any edits necessary to match the appearance of the text in the original Illustrator file.

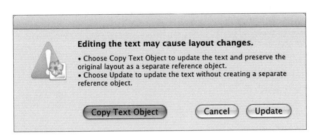

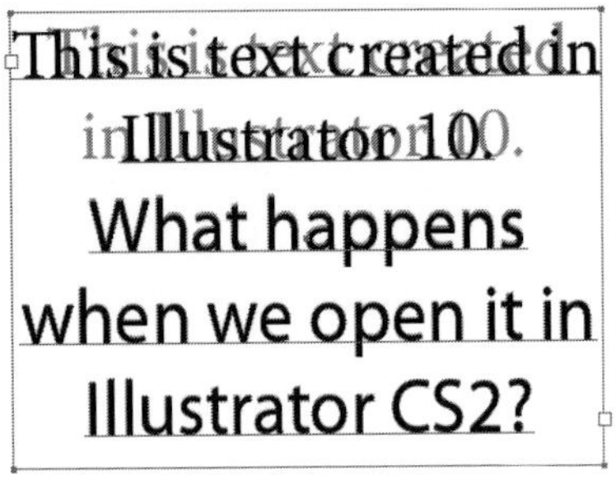

Figure 10.4 The black text is live text being composed by the newer composition rules of Illustrator CS/CS2. In this instance, one line break must be changed to match the original flow of text (ghosted).

After completing the edits, delete the reference text sublayer so that it doesn't ruin output (**Figure 10.5**). You could just hide the layer, but you run the risk that some well-meaning but misguided person might reawaken it.

Figure 10.5 After correcting the converted text, delete the reference layer (indicated by a padlock) to ensure correct output.

The cross-version issues with text don't just occur in one direction. Since the composition engine is so different beginning with Illustrator CS, backsaving for earlier versions of Illustrator will result in text being converted to *point text* (little clumps of letters) or to outlines (**Figure 10.6**).

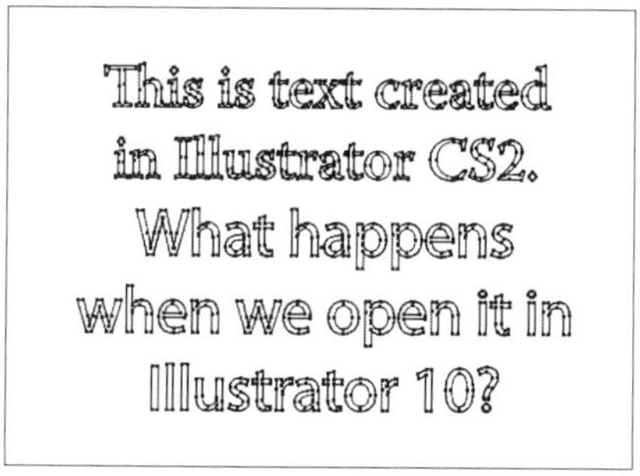

This is text created in Illustrator CS2. What happens when we open it in Illustrator 10?

Figure 10.6 (Shown in Outline view) Check your spelling before trying this at home. Saving for earlier versions of Illustrator is even scarier than *opening* files created by earlier versions. Appearance is maintained, but you can kiss your ability to edit goodbye because text is converted to outlines.

Happily, Illustrator CS and CS2 share the same text composition engine, so opening an Illustrator CS file in CS2 does not wreck text formatting, and backsaving from Illustrator CS2 to CS does not cause text to be outlined.

SAVING FOR EARLIER VERSIONS

The release of Illustrator CS caused a bit of panic: "Hey! How do I save for earlier versions?!" The Save dialog offered only Illustrator CS-flavored options. It took many users some time to divine that the backsave function was lurking under the Export menu as Illustrator Legacy EPS or AI file. Moving backsave controls to the Export menu may have been intended to highlight the fact that backsaves weren't so simple any more. The conversion of text to outlines is a hint that there's a major difference under the hood.

Under Illustrator CS, choose File > Export. For Format, choose Illustrator Legacy for native files, or Illustrator Legacy EPS for EPS files. The available options are Illustrator 10, 9, 8, 3, and Japanese Illustrator 3 (since versions 4 through 7 shared fundamentally the same internal file format). The version you select depends on what your recipient has requested. Don't go any lower than you need to.

Saving to earlier versions is more straightforward in Illustrator CS2, and no longer requires a trip to the Export menu. It's now simply File > Save, and then choose Adobe Illustrator Document or Illustrator EPS. In the subsequent dialog, you can select versions CS, 10, 9, 8, 3, and Japanese Illustrator 3.

When saving or exporting to Illustrator native (AI) format, you may notice that the option Create PDF Compatible File is selected by default. This doesn't mean that it's turning your Illustrator file into a PDF. Leave this option selected to provide compatibility with other Adobe applications. For example, if you clear the check box, you won't be able to place the Illustrator file into an InDesign layout.

Quirks in Save Dialogs

File format issues aside, there are some oddities in the File > Save dialogs that may give you pause. They're harmless, but it might be comforting to know that it's not something you're doing wrong.

- When you're saving an Illustrator 10 native file under Macintosh OS X up through OS 10.3.9, the Format menu contains Text File instead of Adobe Illustrator Document. Just laugh it off. The file will be saved correctly as an AI file, not a text file.

- When you're saving an Illustrator 10 native file under Macintosh OS X 10.4+ (Tiger), the Format menu reads Adobe PDF instead of Adobe Illustrator Document. Again, it's just kidding and will correctly save the document as a native AI file.

- Illustrator CS and CS2 under Macintosh OS X up through 10.3.9 both show the correct choice of Adobe Illustrator Document, but the fix is short-lived. Under OS X 10.4+ (Tiger), the Format menu choice is Adobe PDF instead of Adobe Illustrator Document. Files are saved as native Illustrator files nonetheless.

Now that you have a decoder for the errant Save dialog choices, just ignore the confusion, and go on with your life. (When you consider that the underlying file format for Illustrator 10, CS, and CS2 actually *is* PDF, the behavior of the Save dialogs is understandable.)

Document Color Mode

As you begin a new Illustrator file, you're allowed to specify the Color Mode (**Figure 10.7**). Understandably, a file intended for print should be set up as CMYK color. But what does this do to non-CMYK content?

Figure 10.7 Document Color Mode can be specified as you create a document or after the fact while the document is open.

Within a CMYK Illustrator file, you are allowed to specify colors as CMYK, RGB, or HSB (Hue-Saturation-Brightness), but those colors take on the color mode governing the document. For example, in a document with a CMYK color mode, an object set to an RGB value of R200-G40-B30 still ends up as C2-M98-Y100-K0 in the final file. While this may initially be confusing, the net effect is that it keeps you out of trouble for the most part, as long as you establish the correct color mode to begin with. And if you didn't make the correct choice as you began the document, you can rectify that by choosing File > Document Color Mode. All content created within Illustrator and all embedded images change to the new color mode. That is, a CMYK image becomes an RGB image when embedded in an Illustrator file whose color mode is RGB. Linked images, however, are not affected and remain in their original color mode, regardless of the color mode of the Illustrator file.

SIMPLIFYING COMPLEX ARTWORK

Even though today's computers and current RIPs are significantly faster than their ancestors, there are still some benefits to eliminating complexity where possible. Paths with too many points are rough-looking. And extraneous points can result in incorrect boundaries for artwork, since the bounding box of an Illustrator file is determined by the outermost points in the file. Fortunately, Illustrator offers some tools for polishing your drawing. Choose Object > Path > Clean Up to delete those little stray points that you create with inadvertent pen clicks, as well as objects with no fill and stroke, and those pesky empty text paths that spring up when you *swear* you didn't really click anywhere with the Type tool (**Figure 10.8**).

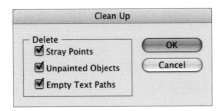

Figure 10.8 Illustrator's Clean Up dialog provides controls for eliminating common junk for a much cleaner drawing.

Given their names, it's easy to confuse Clean Up with another function, Simplify. Clean Up *deletes* unnecessary objects in the drawing. By contrast, Simplify (Object > Path > Simplify) *modifies* objects by reducing the number of points in those objects (**Figure 10.9**).

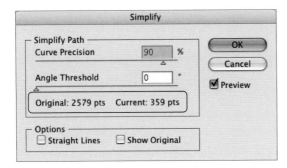

Figure 10.9 Simplify, indeed. Note the striking reduction in number of points from 2579 to 359!

When using Simplify, select the Preview check box so you can immediately see the effect of your settings before you commit to the change. In general, keeping the Curve Precision value around 90–95 percent will achieve a satisfactory smoothing without significantly degrading detail (**Figure 10.10**).

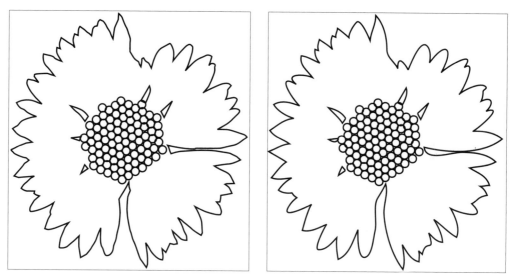

Figure 10.10 Using Object > Path > Simplify reduces the total number of paths in the document. Used judiciously, it can smooth a drawing without adversely affecting it. Reducing the number of points from 2579 (left) to 359 (right) does alter some subtle segments in the process, but it does not substantially degrade the overall look of the drawing.

However, it's possible to overdo things with the Simplify function. Dipping much below 95 percent for the Curve Precision value will quickly erode detail in the drawing by deleting too many points (**Figure 10.11**).

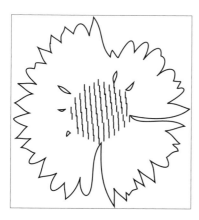

Figure 10.11 Going too far: The result of using a Curve Precision value of 70 percent.

USING FILTERS AND EFFECTS

Illustrator offers a number of filters and effects that are easy to apply, but it's perhaps not obvious how these features can get you in trouble when it comes time to actually image your artwork.

Filter versus Effect: Vector Shapes

Exploring the menus in Illustrator, you'll find two ways to distort an object: Filter > Distort and Effect > Distort. Your first impression is probably that this is sloppy redundancy and that the two menu entries do the same thing. But no, that's not the case (insert evil laugh here). The Distort menu option under Filter produces *literal content*. That is, paths are actually altered. When you use the Effect menu, however, you change the object's *appearance* without changing the object itself (**Figure 10.12**). While not all controls are available as Effects, you will usually want to choose the Effect menu over Filter if possible because of the flexibility it affords.

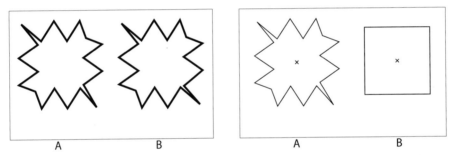

Figure 10.12 In Preview mode (left), objects **A** and **B** appear identical. Both began life as simple rectangles. However, Outline display (right) shows an important difference: Shape **A** was distorted with the Zig Zag Filter, and is permanently altered as a result. Shape **B** was distorted with the Zig Zag Effect. But under the hood, it's still the same old rectangle. This allows you to experiment more freely, or return to the original shape with no penalty.

If modifications made by using the Effect menu are nondestructive, why does Illustrator offer Filters when an effect will give the same visual result? Because there are times when you'll want to tweak the actual anchor points in an object such as Shape A in Figure 10.12, and for that you'll be glad that the Filter menu generates those points. And sometimes you'll appreciate the flexible safety net offered by nondestructive effects.

> **NOTE:** If you want best of both worlds, use an Effect and leave the appearance live. Then, if you need to edit the appearance, use the Expand feature to convert the live appearance to literal points for editing. There's no impact on RIP processing time (or success) either way. So make it easy on yourself.

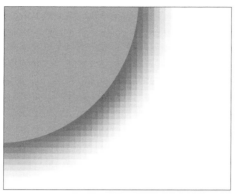 

Figure 10.18 The default setting of 72 ppi for raster shadows (left) doesn't matter if you use Effects. Change the Document Raster Effects value to 300 ppi, and your shadow resolution changes immediately (right).

Despite the name, Document Raster Effects Settings are actually *not* document-specific. They're *sticky* (persistent) settings. If you select 300 ppi while in one document, even quit and relaunch Illustrator, and then create a new document, you'll see that 300 ppi is still in effect. However, if you reset Illustrator preferences to factory defaults, the setting returns to 72 ppi. By the way, there's no way to specify the raster effects settings without a document open.

> **NOTE:** *To reset Illustrator to the original default preferences, get two hands ready. Press three keys a millisecond after launching the application: On the Macintosh, hold down Command (⌘)+Option+Shift. On Windows, hold down Control+Alt+Shift. Keep pressing the key combination until the application is fully launched. Your only confirmation that preferences have been reset will be the appearance of the Illustrator Welcome screen.*

CREATING 3D ARTWORK

If you need an excuse to buy a faster computer, you may find your excuse in the 3D effects that made their debut in Illustrator CS. Similar to the old Adobe application Dimensions,® the 3D effects in CS and CS2 don't rival genuine 3D programs, but they do allow you to add dimensionality to shapes through revolving or extruding operations. Such effects can generate very complex files. Since the illusion of dimensionality depends on realistic shading, 3D effects rely on the Document Raster Effects Settings dialog to determine the resolution of that shading. To speed up processing and display, use the default setting of 72 ppi while you're working on the file. When you're finished, change the setting to 300 ppi.

One of the unfortunate limitations of the 3D effects is Illustrator's inability to perform the necessary complex shading while still maintaining spot colors. No matter how simple the initial shape might be, performing any kind of 3D operation on it—whether extruding, revolving, or rotating—will result in the object's spot color being converted to the document's color mode, whether that's RGB or CMYK. At least Illustrator warns you of this in the 3D dialog boxes, but it's so subtle as to be almost pointless (**Figure 10.19**).

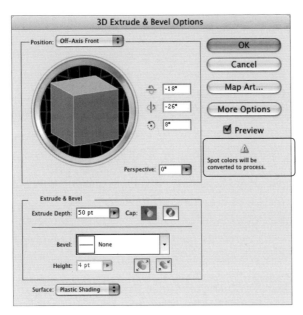

Figure 10.19 Even if you start with a spot-color object, performing a 3D operation on it will convert it to four-color process. Illustrator does warn you, but the alert is rather subtle.

TRANSPARENCY

Other operations may result in undesirable results when spot colors are involved. For example, the blending modes Difference and Exclusion will cause overlapping spot color areas to be converted to CMYK (or RGB if that's the document's working color mode). You may also have undesirable results if you create spot-color objects, apply blending modes to them in Illustrator, and then place the files into another application such as InDesign. If you convert spot colors to CMYK in InDesign by using the Ink Manager or by editing swatches, the output may not show the same color interactions as the original Illustrator file. Illustrator provides a warning as you save the file (**Figure 10.20**).

Figure 10.20 Spot-color objects using transparency may not fare well when other applications render the Illustrator file as CMYK. At least Illustrator warns you. Don't check the Don't Show Again option — it's good to keep this warning in mind.

Even if you don't intend to convert spot colors to CMYK, Illustrator's display can mislead you about the final outcome. The most you can have of any given single ink is 100 percent—solid ink coverage. For example, you can't fill an object with 200 percent cyan. But if you fill two objects with a solid ink, and then apply a blending mode of Multiply, Illustrator will darken the overlapping area (**Figure 10.21**). It's an unfortunate display error. If you turn on Overprint Preview (View > Overprint Preview), the display is correct. Overprint Preview is a great forensic tool to help you diagnose numerous problems, but it does slow down performance. Use it when you need it, and then deactivate it.

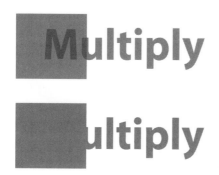

Figure 10.21 The word and the rectangle are both filled with 100–percent Pantone 415. The word uses the Multiply blend mode. The Illustrator display (top) falsely implies that there will be 200–percent coverage of Pantone 415 in the overlap area, which is impossible without a second ink. However, if you turn on Overprint Preview (View > Overprint Preview), you'll see the true story (bottom).

FLATTENING TRANSPARENCY

Transparency in Illustrator is a wonderful feature first bestowed on designers with the release of Illustrator 9.0. This was followed by several years of printers screaming and hiding under desks because of early imaging difficulties. Some printers are still traumatized by their initial experiences and may not realize that transparency is really not that scary these days, as long as everyone plays by some simple rules.

Effects like transparency and blending modes enhance the design flexibility of Illustrator, but those effects go beyond the imaging model of Adobe PostScript, which is the native language of imagesetters (devices that output film for printing plates), platesetters (which directly output printing plates), and many desktop printers.

How can we possibly output transparency if PostScript doesn't understand it? We cheat.

Illustrator, InDesign, and Acrobat all support transparency. If you're creating artwork in Illustrator with the intention of later placing it as a native AI file in InDesign, you don't have to worry about any special handling for transparent objects while you're working in Illustrator.

But if your Illustrator file is going to land somewhere else as a file format such as EPS or PDF/X-1a (a subset of PDF that doesn't support live transparency), then you must face the mysteries of *transparency flattening* (**Figure 10.22**). Don't worry—the Illustrator file itself won't be flattened. Your layers are untouched, your shadows are intact, and everything remains editable. The flattening process affects only output and export and takes place on the fly during export or printing. The purpose is to replace transparent elements with opaque elements, mimicking the colors created in transparent overlaps by creating new colors and invoking PostScript overprint. If images interact with text, flattening may even create letter-shaped clipping paths to contain image material. It's a fairly impressive engineering feat. And the results are much more sophisticated and well-behaved than when they made their debut in Illustrator 9.0.

Figure 10.22 Native transparency (left) involves opacity settings and blending modes. For output or export to PostScript-based formats, all the fun stuff is replaced with opaque, jigsaw puzzle pieces (right), hence the term *flattening*.

For the most part, if you save a file as an EPS earmarked for CS and CS2, the resulting EPS is perfectly editable in Illustrator and still behaves well in other applications such as QuarkXPress. Think of the file as an Illustrator native file with an EPS disguise.

However, if you're requested to submit a file saved to, say, an Illustrator 8.0 EPS for someone using an earlier version of Illustrator, you should also keep a native version of the file for future edits. As you see in Figure 10.22, ancient formats require such extensive conversion that they are altered permanently. This is necessary because file formats have changed substantially since these earlier versions. Be amazed that it works at all!

The rules used for cooking transparency down for earlier versions are contained in the Transparency Flattener Presets dialog. If the recipient of your file gives you any guidance, follow their lead. Lacking that, you should create a widely applicable recipe for flattening. Choose Edit > Transparency Flattener Presets (**Figure 10.23**). Select High Resolution, and then click New. In the Custom Transparency Flattener Options dialog, set Line Art and Text Resolution to the resolution of the final imaging device. If you don't know that, use 2400 ppi. And 300 ppi is a safe bet for the Gradient and Mesh Resolution.

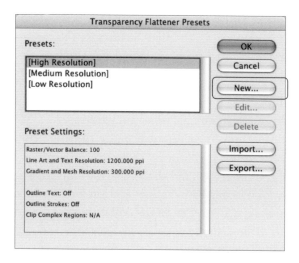

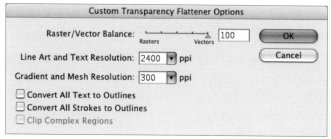

Figure 10.23 Creating a custom transparency flattener preset. Select High Resolution, and then click New. Ideally, the Line Art and Text Resolution setting should be in keeping with the ultimate device resolution. The Gradient and Mesh Resolution can usually remain at 300 ppi.

LINKED AND EMBEDDED IMAGES

When you place raster images in an Illustrator file, you can choose to link or embed those images. Each method has its advantages and disadvantages.

Linking an image results in a smaller Illustrator file than embedding. Additionally, since images are externally stored, they are easily color corrected or retouched. To open an image linked in an Illustrator file, hold down the Option (Mac) or Alt (Windows) key, and then double-click the image. The image opens in Photoshop, where you can make your edits and save the file. When you return to Illustrator, you'll receive an alert asking if you'd like to update modified images. Click Yes to update the image.

As you might expect, *embedding* an image increases the Illustrator file size, since the size of the image is added to the file. While embedding makes it easier to keep track of all components of a file, it complicates image editing. If the original image is still available, you can choose Relink from the Links palette menu, and then navigate to the external image. Edit the newly linked image as necessary, update the link, and then embed the image if you wish.

However, if you've inherited an Illustrator file containing an embedded image and have no access to the original image, Illustrator doesn't provide a straightforward way to extract it for editing. Don't panic. If you can't obtain the original image from the content creator, you can still cheat your way out of this predicament. Select the embedded image in Illustrator with the Selection tool (black arrow), and then copy it to the clipboard. Start Photoshop and choose File > New. A new, blank document is created that's the same size as the clipboard contents. Note that you will need to set the color mode of the new image to the correct setting (CMYK or RGB) in keeping with the image you're extracting. Paste the image, and you're in business.

Saving an Illustrator file in EPS format automatically embeds images and fonts, so you'd be wise to save the external images as insurance against future editing needs.

Image resolution rules and restrictions still apply to images placed in Illustrator, of course. That is, scaling up or down beyond reasonable limits (roughly 75 to 125 percent) has repercussions in terms of degradation of detail and increased processing time. As in page-layout applications, it's best if the image is the correct final size to begin with and is placed at 100 percent into Illustrator.

BLENDED OBJECTS

Illustrator allows you to select two different objects and then use the Blend tool (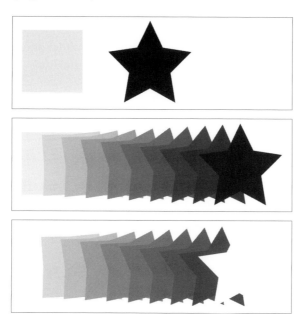)
to create transitional shapes between them. It's an interesting effect, but if the starting
objects are filled with spot colors, the intermediate shapes are generated as CMYK objects
(**Figure 10.24**).

Figure 10.24 Start with two spot-color objects (top). The Blend tool allows you to create discrete intermediate shapes (middle) or a smooth gradient-like transition between the objects. But there's bad news: All the intermediate shapes (bottom) are rendered as CMYK, which is probably not what you want.

If the blend effect is crucial to your design and the job must be printed in spot colors, you
might create each starting shape as a single process color, but let the process color represent
a spot color. For example, use cyan in lieu of Pantone 294 and yellow instead of Pantone
128. Then inform the print service provider that the cyan plate should be used to print
Pantone 294 and the yellow plate for Pantone 128. If you also have four-color images in
the job, this approach won't work for you. Of course, as long as the start and end objects
are CMYK, the final effect is perfectly fine.

CHANGES IN PANTONE RECIPES

In 2000, Pantone revised the recipes for process simulations of the Pantone spot inks. This was done in response to the industry improvements in plating and press controls that made it possible to more closely approximate spot colors with CMYK simulations. The spot-to-process recipes in desktop publishing programs followed suit. This all sounds wonderful, but there is a little kink in the plumbing as a result. Files created in earlier versions of Illustrator, QuarkXPress, InDesign, and Photoshop use the older recipes. The newer recipes start with Illustrator 10.0, QuarkXPress 5.0, InDesign 2.0, and Photoshop 7.0. If your goal is to come closer to Pantone colors with CMYK approximations, great. But if you're using old artwork that uses the old recipes, output may differ from what you expect. For example, consider an Illustrator 8.0 EPS with spot elements that is placed into a QuarkXPress 6.5 page and output as CMYK. Since the Pantone-to-CMYK conversion is performed with the new recipe, the output may not match a previously printed piece that was generated by placing the same EPS into a QuarkXPress 4.11 page.

If it's important to replicate the old appearance of artwork, open the file in the original version of Illustrator and then convert the spot-color swatches to CMYK so they won't be reinterpreted by other applications (**Figure 10.25**).

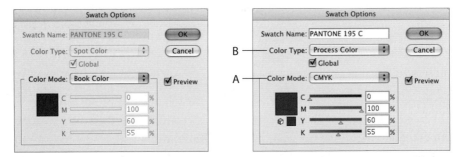

Figure 10.25 In Illustrator CS2, the Swatch Options dialog initially displays Book Color for the Color Mode of a spot-color swatch (left). To convert the swatch to process (right), first change the color mode to CMYK (A). Then you'll be allowed to change the Color Type to Process Color (B).

Double-click a swatch, and then change its color mode to CMYK and its color type to process. Then your artwork will display and print as it did in previous instances.

Going through this might convince you of the wisdom of picking from an all-CMYK color source such as the Pantone 4-color process guide. If you need additional motivation, consider the error you receive if you attempt to print an Illustrator file containing transparency and a surplus of spot colors (**Figure 10.26**).

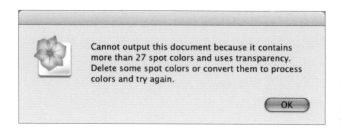

Cannot output this document because it contains more than 27 spot colors and uses transparency. Delete some spot colors or convert them to process colors and try again.

OK

Figure 10.26 Chances are you really didn't intend to budget for 27 spot-color plates.

Saving For Other Applications

Whereas the undisputed choice of file format once was EPS, there are now more interesting possibilities for saving Illustrator files.

If your file's ultimate fate is placement in a QuarkXPress layout, the right answer is still EPS. But you don't have to reach back in time to export a legacy EPS. Even the venerable QuarkXPress 4.11 can handle a CS2-flavored EPS that was generated by an Illustrator file containing all sorts of transparency and the requisite soft drop shadows.

If you're sending your artwork into the void and have no idea where it's headed, consider keeping your native working file intact, but saving a copy of it as a legacy Illustrator 8.0 EPS file.

If your Illustrator file is destined for InDesign, there are some significant benefits to keeping it a native file with live transparency. Since version 2.0, InDesign has supported the blending modes and transparency effects in AI files, allowing such attributes to interact with other elements in an InDesign page.

Finally, the Object Layer Options introduced in InDesign CS2 allows you to selectively reveal or hide layers of Photoshop files or PDFs. Acrobat 6.0 marked the inclusion of layers in PDFs. While this may seem unrelated to Illustrator, saving as a PDF is the only way to allow selective visibility of layers in an Illustrator file from within an InDesign CS2 page. Choose Acrobat 6.0 or higher, and then check the option to create Acrobat layers from top-level layers in the Illustrator file.

CHAPTER ELEVEN
FreeHand Production Tips

In many ways, Macromedia FreeHand's features match those of Adobe Illustrator, even down to some of the shortcuts. After years of being competitors, they're now stable mates since Adobe's acquisition of Macromedia. Will their feature sets be crossbred? We can't foretell the future. We *are* pretty sure there's no truth to the widespread rumor that FreeHand and Illustrator will be combined into a single program called FrusTrator.

FONTS AND GRAPHICS

Like other vector drawing programs, FreeHand enables designers and graphic artists to go far beyond lines, circles, and squares by allowing the inclusion of raster images created in image-manipulation programs such as Adobe Photoshop. Factor in FreeHand's text features, and you'll discover that your FreeHand file must play by some of the same rules that govern page-layout applications. Since you can't place a native FreeHand file into other applications such as page-layout files, you need to save or export to another format, such as Encapsulated PostScript (EPS).

Keeping It All Together

If there's a good chance that your FreeHand EPS file will be reopened for editing, be sure to select the Include FreeHand document option in the EPS Setup dialog (**Figure 11.1**) which is available when you choose File > Export and then select one of the EPS options. While this creates a larger EPS file (because it's also carrying around the original, editable FreeHand file in its pocket), it eliminates the need to save both a working native FreeHand file and an EPS.

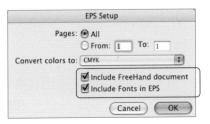

Figure 11.1 If you plan to reopen a FreeHand EPS, select the option to Include FreeHand document.

Font Handling

Within the EPS export setup dialog (File > Export and then select one of the EPS formats), the option to include fonts only makes those included fonts available to external applications for display and printing. If you select the option to include fonts, and then send a FreeHand file to someone who doesn't own the necessary fonts in EPS, FreeHand warns them about missing fonts (**Figure 11.2**). But they can still edit the file—even change content that uses the font they're missing—and then resave the file without causing FreeHand to lose track of which fonts it requires. When the file is reopened with the correct fonts activated, all is well.

Figure 11.2 Embedded fonts in an EPS file are for display and print, not for editing. If the fonts aren't available when you open the file, you're asked if you want to find a replacement. Just click OK. FreeHand retains the original font *information* even if you edit text without the font *active*. Activate it later, and then resave the file.

NOTE: *It's important to conscientiously follow the End User Licensing Agreement (EULA) for the fonts you intend to embed in a FreeHand EPS. Some font vendors place restrictions on embedding fonts in EPS and PDF files—including prohibitions on outlining text. While it may be mechanically possible to do so, you may discover that it's not allowed by the EULA. What's the truly legal solution? Use fonts from vendors whose EULAs don't forbid embedding or outlining.*

Images: Link or Embed?

By default, FreeHand creates *links* to imported images. This allows you to avoid the increase in FreeHand file size that an embedded image would cause and allows you to easily update the image content if it's modified by an external application such as Photoshop. But it also means that you have to keep track of all those supporting performers. How you organize your support artwork is up to you, although it's easier to keep things straight if you avoid deeply nested folders inside other folders. However, as long as you don't move the images to another directory, FreeHand remembers the original directory paths, up to ten folders deep. You probably don't need to be *that* organized.

If you elect to maintain imported images as linked external files, you have two choices as you prepare to send your artwork to a print service provider. Choose File > Collect for Output to gather up the native FreeHand file, images, and fonts. FreeHand will display an alert instructing you to make sure that your font license allows you to collect and send fonts with your FreeHand file. Alternatively, you can save or export the file to a single FreeHand EPS, which incorporates the images and fonts into the EPS file.

If you do use FreeHand's option to embed images, you still have the ability to edit the image in an external photo editor such as Photoshop. To do this, you must first extract the embedded image. Choose Edit > Links (**Figure 11.3**), and then click the Extract button. You can even give a new name to the extracted file, and FreeHand creates a new link to the file wherever you save it and however you name it.

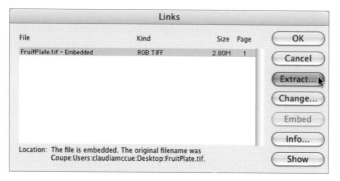

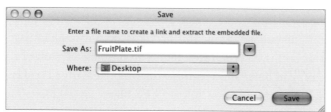

Figure 11.3 Embedded images can be extracted from a FreeHand file for editing. In the Links dialog, select the Extract option (top). FreeHand prompts you for a name and location (bottom), and then automatically establishes a new link to the extracted file.

Modifying Linked Images

While you're working on a project, you or a colleague may modify and resave an image that's linked to a FreeHand native file or editable FreeHand EPS. But when you reopen the FreeHand or editable EPS file, you won't receive any warning that the image has been modified. This could lead to surprises, and not in a good way. You might consider adopting a habit of changing the names of modified linked images. This forces FreeHand to alert you when you open a file, since it can't find the file whose name it's looking for. For example, if you're color correcting a linked image named *FruitPlate.tif*, rename the modified image *FruitPlate_r1.tif*, with the *r* standing for *revision*. If you wish to keep the original image, rename it *FruitPlate_orig.tif*, or some such, to "hide" it from FreeHand. Then FreeHand will squawk when you open a file containing the image, so you can update it consciously.

There are two circumstances, however, in which images are immune to automatic updating. Of course, this may or may not be good news, depending on what you'd prefer. First, you can embed images in a native FreeHand file by choosing Edit > Links, choosing images in the Links list, and then selecting the Embed option (**Figure 11.4**).

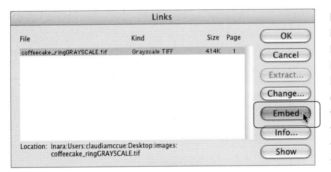

Figure 11.4 To embed an image in a native FreeHand file, choose Edit > Links, and then select the Embed option. While you no longer have to keep separate track of imported images, this increases file size. Additionally, if you modify the original externally stored image, the embedded image won't reflect those changes.

A second way to protect images from automatic updating is to export an EPS without selecting the Include FreeHand document option. Choose File > Export, select an EPS-flavored format, and then click the Setup button (**Figure 11.5**). If you unselect the Include FreeHand document check box in the EPS Setup dialog, images are automatically embedded in the exported EPS file. Therefore, images in the EPS file will not change when you modify the externally stored versions of the images, because the EPS file is self-contained with its own copy of the original image. While this prevents any unwanted image replacement, the flip side of this option is that the file contains an obsolete version of the image. If this is not what you want, you'll need to return to the original, native FreeHand file to update the image content, and then re-export it to an EPS file.

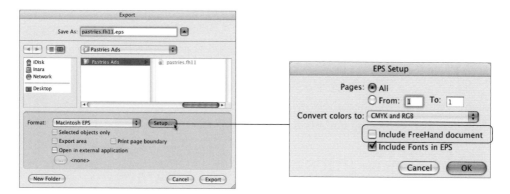

Figure 11.5 When you export an EPS file from FreeHand, choosing to *not* include the FreeHand document will embed images in the EPS file. This makes the EPS file ignore any edits made to the external versions of any imported images.

Importing Images

While FreeHand allows you to copy and paste image content from applications such as Photoshop, try to resist the temptation. There's no link to the original image file, which prevents automatic updating if the original image is modified. On the bright side, this process does deposit full-resolution image content into FreeHand. While there's no link to the original Photoshop file, the Extract option available in the Links dialog (Edit > Links) allows you to extract the pasted image content for editing if necessary. Why the caution about avoiding pasting from Photoshop into FreeHand? There is potential for mishandling of the content later in the process if it becomes necessary to color-correct or retouch the image. Prepress operators who are unfamiliar with FreeHand may freak out unnecessarily because they think the image is not accessible. So it's best—and most predictable—to stick to the old-fashioned method of choosing File > Import and maintaining external image file links.

Importing Multiple Images Simultaneously

When you choose File > Import, you're allowed to select multiple images from a directory, and then place them in succession into a FreeHand document. Press Shift and then click to select multiple files in the Import dialog. Then click repeatedly in the FreeHand document where you want the images to be placed, continuing until they're all deposited.

Surprisingly, dragging and dropping images from the desktop or other directory onto a FreeHand page is a perfectly legitimate alternative to using File > Import. It's a fast way to get multiple images into a document at once, and FreeHand does create a link for each dragged file. So go ahead—have some fun.

Suitable Image Formats

FreeHand accepts traditional TIFF and EPS images, as well as the usual assortment of JPEG and BMP files. But you can also import Photoshop native (PSD) files, even those containing soft-edged transparency. However, Photoshop blending modes are not honored by FreeHand. A Photoshop shadow, for example, is opaque when placed in FreeHand, rather than darkening underlying objects.

Special Handling: DCS Images

FreeHand also allows import of Desktop Color Separation (DCS) images. DCS is a specialized EPS format left over from (relatively) ancient times. DCS images contain associated but separate files for the individual cyan, magenta, yellow, and black plates, which are represented by a low-resolution composite preview file. The purpose of the DCS format was to speed printing from the desktop, since the image was already preseparated into color plates. A DCS image consisted of five separate files—the C, M, Y, and K plus the low-resolution preview. DCS images tend to be a bit fragile. If one of the constituent files is deleted or becomes corrupt, the image is unusable. The later DCS 2.0 flavor improved the breed by allowing storage of all the pieces in a single file and adding support for spot-color plates.

If you have old CMYK DCS files intended for use in FreeHand, it's advisable to resave them in TIFF format or just a plain old Photoshop EPS. We're no longer at the mercy of 80 MB hard drives (yes, that's an *M* for *mega*byte) and slow networks that inspired the DCS approach. If you resave a DCS file as a TIFF or regular EPS, you'll no longer run the risk of losing one plate and corrupting the image. If you import DCS 2.0 images containing spot-color channels into FreeHand MX, printing color separations *directly* from FreeHand MX yields correct results. However, exporting or saving EPS files from such FreeHand documents produces files that do not retain the spot-color image content from imported DCS 2.0 images. You should alert your print service provider if you have placed DCS 2.0 images with spot-color content into your FreeHand file so they can perform any special handling necessary to maintain the spot-color component. They may be accustomed to exporting EPS files or PDFs from applications for their workflow. But they may need to generate PostScript directly from FreeHand to achieve correct output of DCS 2.0 content.

Scaling Imported Images

Raster images imported into FreeHand are subject to the same scaling limitations that govern images placed in page layouts. Enlarging over 120–125 percent softens detail, and scaling down below 75 percent means that you're storing and processing unnecessary amounts of image information. Going outside those rough guidelines isn't illegal of course, but you should be prepared for the consequences.

Importing or Opening Adobe PDF Files

FreeHand's comprehension of Portable Document Format files (PDFs) is limited. It can handle simple PDFs as content, but it fails to correctly translate many PDF files generated from more current programs such as Adobe InDesign or recent versions of Illustrator. If you're not familiar with the original file, you may overlook missing or incorrectly translated objects. If you're working collaboratively, you should request that contributors send EPS files rather than PDF files if possible.

Opening PDF files in FreeHand—in any program other than Adobe Acrobat, really—is asking for trouble. You may get away with opening very simple PDF files for editing, but you truly can't count on maintaining file fidelity. Instead, you should use a dedicated PDF-editing program, such as the PitStop Professional plug-in for Acrobat, marketed by Enfocus.

SPECIAL EFFECTS

FreeHand allows you to apply live vector and raster effects to selected objects by choosing Window > Object, and then using the Add Effects controls in the Object panel (**Figure 11.6**). The vector effects, such as Ragged and Sketch, enliven the *appearance* of a vector object without actually altering the underlying object itself. *Vector* effects are safe to use because the appearance of the object remains vector in nature. The *raster* effects, however, may rasterize some vector content, eroding sharp detail, and should be used with some reservations.

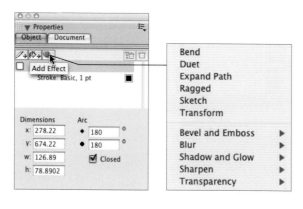

Figure 11.6 The Add Effect menu in the Object panel offers both vector and raster effects. Click and hold down your mouse button on the Add Effect button. *Vector* effects are listed above the dividing line. *Raster* effects are below the dividing line, and should be used with caution.

Live Vector Effects

Multiple vector effects can be applied to a single object to transform its appearance from a staid geometric to something that looks much more, well, freehand. In **Figure 11.7**, despite its punk hairdo, the vector shape is still a circle at heart. If the Ragged and Sketch effects are removed by using the controls in the Object panel, the shape will revert to its original bland appearance. That's why these effects are referred to as *live* effects. They can be changed or removed at any time. If you wish to permanently alter a vector shape that bears a live effect so that the effects becomes literal, choose Modify > Separate Attributes. (Admittedly, the name of the menu item doesn't give any clue what it does.)

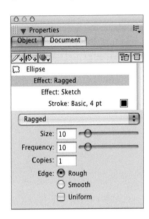
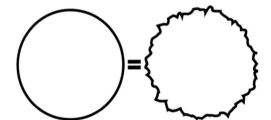

Figure 11.7 The Object panel shows that two live vector effects — Ragged and Sketch — have been applied to the circle, resulting in the roughened version on the right. Under the hood, it's still a circle.

Live Raster Effects

While FreeHand's live raster effects, such as drop shadows and glows, leave the underlying object's *shape* unchanged, the effects can noticeably erode the appearance of the object (**Figure 11.8**). The shape carrying the effect remains vector in nature and can be edited with the vector selection and vector drawing tools, but its appearance becomes pixelated. Portions of underlying objects that interact with the raster effects are also rendered as pixels. Setting the Raster Effects value higher (File > Document Settings > Raster Effects Settings) may improve the appearance of objects, but it still isn't hard to see a demarcation at the edge of raster effects.

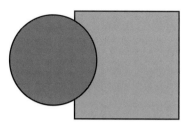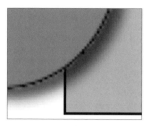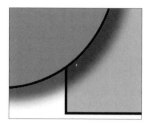

Figure 11.8 A nice, sharp vector shape (left) loses its smooth definition when a live raster effect such as a drop shadow is applied to it (center). Increasing the Raster Effects Settings helps somewhat (right), but the edge is still rendered as pixels, not vector information.

Warning: You'll be misled by the appearance of the effect when it's viewed within FreeHand—things are actually worse than they appear. When you apply a raster effect to an object, you'll see the object change—its appearance becomes pixelated. But FreeHand neglects to indicate that all underlying objects become pixelated as well (**Figure 11.9**).

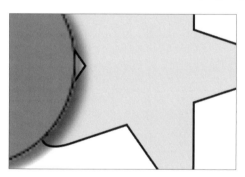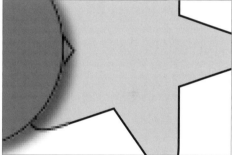

Figure 11.9 It may appear that raster effects alter only the object to which they're applied (left), but an exported EPS (right) tells the true story—underlying objects are also pixelated by the effects.

The problems with raster effects extend beyond their erosion of sharp vector appearance. Applying raster effects to a spot-color object results in that object becoming a CMYK object. And portions of any underlying spot-color objects are converted to CMYK as well. There's really no way to have a happy ending.

If you just can't live without applying raster effects to objects in FreeHand, increase the Raster Effects Settings to a high value to camouflage the rasterization of vector edges. Avoid using raster effects on (or touching) spot-color objects to prevent converting spot-color objects to CMYK.

Lens Effects

FreeHand allows you to create a unique sort of fill called a Lens fill. Lens fill controls are accessed through the Fill control, which is a little bucket icon at the top of the Object panel (**Figure 11.10**). Click on the bucket, and the default Basic color fill is applied to the selected object in the FreeHand drawing. If you wish to get fancier, click on the *Basic* entry near the bottom of the Object panel, and fill choices appear in a drop-down menu. Choose Lens from the drop-down menu, and then you'll see the types of Lens fills available. An object with a Lens fill can perform interesting tricks such as ghosting or magnifying what's underneath it. Lens fills are great creative toys, but there are some pitfalls with spot-color content.

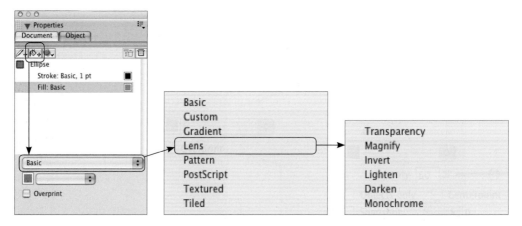

Figure 11.10 Choosing the Fill button in the Object panel allows you to start with a basic fill. Click Fill in the Object panel (left), and then see the types of fills available (center). Choose the Lens option to see the types of Lens fills available (right).

The *Magnify* lens effect (**Figure 11.11**) is fairly safe, leaving vector content unrasterized as well as preserving spot-color objects. However, it's the only lens effect that doesn't convert spot-color content to CMYK. All the remaining lens effects — Transparency, Invert, Lighten, Darken, Monochrome — convert underlying spot-color content to CMYK. But at least they don't rasterize vector objects.

Figure 11.11 The Magnify lens effect is *very* convincing if you're drawing a magnifying glass.

Special Fills and Strokes

FreeHand offers an assortment of decorative fills and strokes for objects. The solid fills are straightforward and don't provide any surprises in output. But the other fill options require some preparation, and some can cause complications (or disappointment) during output. The same cautions apply to the fanciful strokes. Experiment to get a feel for the resulting output. Create a test file, and ask your print service provider to RIP and proof the effects. Then you can decide if such fills and strokes are appropriate for what you're trying to achieve.

Gradient Fills

FreeHand's gradient fills can maintain spot colors, and you can even create gradients that have multiple changes of color across the gradient. However, you'll find that gradient fills are prone to banding (obvious strips of color), and gradients may display hairline gaps between color steps (**Figure 11.12**). You might do well to consider manufacturing a gradient in Photoshop, which is smoother to begin with and will allow you to introduce a small amount of noise (usually a setting between two and three in the Photoshop Add Noise dialog) to minimize the appearance of banding. Then, save the gradient image as a TIFF file and import it into FreeHand. It's a workaround, but unless you want striations in your gradients, it's the most sensible solution.

Figure 11.12 Freehand's gradient fills are prone to banding and hairline gaps.

Pattern Fills

Pattern fills are bitmap in nature and are based on a repeating eight-by-eight grid of pixels. They were originally intended to be printed on a desktop device with a resolution of 300 dpi or lower, and they haven't evolved since those days. Acknowledging this, FreeHand even pops up an apologetic alert when you choose the Pattern fill option (**Figure 11.13**).

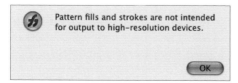

Pattern fills and strokes are not intended for output to high-resolution devices.

OK

Figure 11.13 When you select the Pattern fill option, FreeHand alerts you to its limitations. It's not kidding — Pattern fills are primitive and fairly limited.

FreeHand's Pattern fills are built by turning on and off pixels in the pattern tile area of the Object panel (**Figure 11.14**), which can be found under Window > Object if it's not already visible. If you stick to purely vertical and horizontal patterns, this works quite well. But if you attempt a diagonal motif, the crude, bitmapped nature of the pattern becomes obvious. (Of course, if you *want* that effect, you're in luck.) Just know that sending a Pattern fill to a high-resolution imagesetter will not improve its appearance. It's going to look crunchy no matter what output device is used.

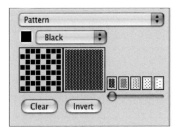 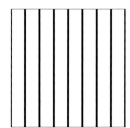 

Figure 11.14 Pattern fills are built pixel-by-pixel (left). Vertical or horizontal patterns (center) work best. Angled patterns (right) betray their bitmapped nature. If you want smooth lines, this is not the way to get them.

PostScript Fills

Here's an option if you're a geek at heart: Write your own PostScript fill! When you select PostScript from the Fill list in the Object panel, you're presented with an empty field for PostScript code. Type or paste the code in the empty field (**Figure 11.15**), and press Enter when you're finished.

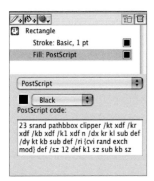 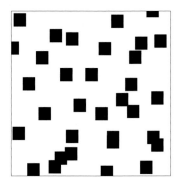

Figure 11.15 Do you speak fluent PostScript? Then you can create PostScript fills from scratch by typing (or copying-and-pasting) PostScript code into the Object panel (left). FreeHand will only display a field of the letters *PS* to indicate a PostScript fill (center). You'll have to print the file or place it in a page layout to see the final results (right). *(PostScript code courtesy of Olav Martin Kvern.)*

Extrude, Smudge, and Shadow

The Extrude, Smudge and Shadow tools allow you to add dimensionality or relatively simple motion effects to objects. These tools are all available under one control in the Tool palette (**Figure 11.19**).

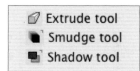

Figure 11.19 The Extrude, Smudge, and Shadow tools available in the Tool palette behave in similar ways. Position the cursor over the Extrude tool, and then click and drag to select an alternate tool from the group.

The issue of cheesiness aside, use this group of tools cautiously if you have spot-color content. Almost every permutation of these tools will cause conversion of spot-color content to CMYK (**Figure 11.20**).

Figure 11.20 Using the Extrude tool (left) converts a spot-color original shape and its extrusion to CMYK. The Smudge tool (center) leaves the original shape as spot color, but the trail of smudged shapes is rendered as CMYK. The results of the Shadow tool (right) depend on its settings. The Hard Edge Tint setting yields all spot-color components. The Soft Edge and Zoom settings for the Shadow tool, however, convert at least part of the resulting shapes to CMYK.

The Extrude tool converts the parent object and its extruded sides to CMYK. The Smudge tool leaves the parent shape's spot color intact, but the trailing shapes are CMYK. The Shadow tool leaves the parent shape as spot color, but the shadow elements are composed of CMYK. There is one exception: The Hard Edge Tint setting for the Shadow tool just creates a duplicate of the parent shape, offsets the shadow shape, and screens back the content while maintaining the spot-color definition. It's hardly a shadow—you could achieve the same effect by duplicating the parent shape and applying a tint of the spot color.

SIMPLIFYING COMPLEX ARTWORK

As you prepare to print or export a FreeHand file, you can minimize potential imaging issues by removing unnecessary objects and simplifying content.

Clean House

Check for extraneous objects by toggling between Preview and Keyline mode. To do this quickly on the Macintosh, press ⌘+K. On Windows, press Control+K. Keep an eye out for objects that disappear in Preview mode, and then hunt them down in Keyline mode and delete them. Even if they're not visible, such objects are still processed during print and export.

FreeHand makes it easy to eliminate empty text blocks and unused swatches. Choose Xtras > Delete, and then select Empty Text Blocks or Unused Named Colors and let FreeHand hunt them down for you (**Figure 11.21**).

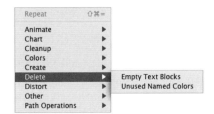

Figure 11.21 Let FreeHand help you eliminate clutter from your file by deleting empty text blocks and unused colors. Choose Xtras > Delete to access these options.

Smooth and Simplify

It's easy to overdo the number of points in a path as you're straining to make sure you capture as much detail as possible. But lots of points don't necessarily mean a better path. In fact, fewer points usually result in a smoother path. If you were overly ambitious while creating a path, FreeHand can smooth things out for you. Select the path and then choose Xtras > Cleanup > Simplify (**Figure 11.22**). This feature is also available under Modify > Alter Path. Experiment with the sliders, clicking the Apply button to see the results before committing the changes by clicking OK.

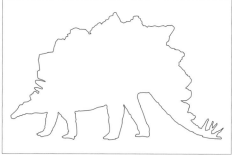

Figure 11.22 Too much caffeine can lead to creating a path with 936 points (left). Choose Xtras > Cleanup > Simplify, and FreeHand can reduce that to 406 points (right) without adversely affecting the path's appearance. But maybe you should cut back on the caffeine anyway.

Trim Off the Fat

Extra image content adds to file size, which increases the amount of information that's processed during print or export. If you've pasted a large image into an object in FreeHand, revealing only a portion of the image, use an image-editing program such as Photoshop to crop out what isn't going to show in the final piece, and then reimport the cropped image.

EXPORTING FREEHAND FILES

When you choose File > Export, you'll discover that FreeHand offers a dizzying list of export formats—most of which you will probably never need for print production (**Figure 11.23**). How can you choose the correct format? It depends on how you intend to use the file.

If you need to export a FreeHand file so that someone else can open it in Illustrator, choose the most recent version of Illustrator from the list, rather than one of the EPS options. Think of the EPS option as a format for placement in other applications, such as page-layout applications, rather than as a way to share artwork that will be further edited by someone else. So if you're collaborating with someone who is using Illustrator, it's better to send them a file that's intended for Illustrator editing, rather than an EPS file. In truth, it's ideal for all collaborators to use the same version of the same application throughout a project, but that isn't always possible.

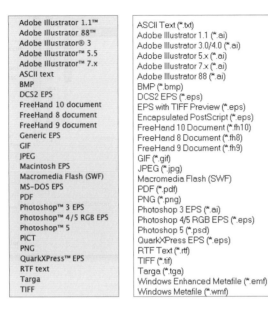

Figure 11.23 Something for everyone — 27 export formats on the Macintosh (left) and on Windows (right).

Exporting Raster Formats

Besides losing the sharp detail inherent in a vector format, exporting FreeHand files with complex fills to a raster format such as TIFF may result in loss of content. PostScript fills manifest themselves in the exported image the same as they appear in FreeHand: as rows and rows of letters. What is the preferred solution if you truly need a raster image? You'll have more control if you export the file as Generic EPS (Mac), and then open the file in Photoshop to rasterize the content at an appropriate resolution (usually 300 ppi at final size). In Windows, export to EPS, and then open the EPS file in Photoshop to rasterize it appropriately.

Exporting Vector Formats

The most reliable export format for print is vector EPS. FreeHand offers two methods of creating vector EPS files: File > Save and File > Export.

Choose File > Export on the Macintosh, and you can select from a long list of formats, including Generic EPS, Macintosh EPS, and MS-DOS EPS. On a PC with Windows, you'll see EPS with TIFF Preview and Encapsulated PostScript. While the internal content of an EPS is the same regardless of the choice you make, the file's appearance when imported or placed into other applications depends on the type of EPS you make (**Figure 11.24**).

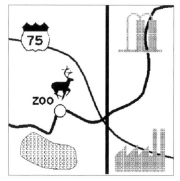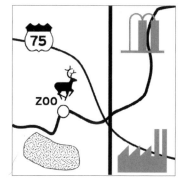

Figure 11.24 When generating EPS files, you'll find that some previews are more realistic than others. Selecting the Generic EPS format on the Macintosh or the plain Encapsulated PostScript option on Windows displays as a gray block in other applications (left). Choosing MS-DOS EPS yields a rough bitmap preview (center). The Macintosh EPS provides the best preview on the Macintosh, matched by the quality of the EPS with TIFF Preview option on Windows (right).

The **MS-DOS EPS** option produces an EPS that displays a coarse black-and-white bitmap preview when imported into other applications such as QuarkXPress and PageMaker, although InDesign creates its own color preview. Despite its appearance, the file's content should image correctly to a PostScript printer.

The **Generic EPS** option creates a file that provides no preview when placed in QuarkXPress. You'll just see a gray rectangle with the text *PostScript Picture*. However, PageMaker and InDesign automatically generate a color preview for such files. Regardless of the application, though, the file should output correctly on a PostScript printer.

The **Macintosh EPS** option creates a file that displays and prints correctly with most common Macintosh graphic arts programs, but displays the gray *PostScript Picture* rectangle when placed into the Windows version of QuarkXPress. In Windows, PageMaker generates a color preview. Again, the preview isn't the whole story. When it is output, the artwork should be correct.

Using FreeHand on Windows, the **Encapsulated PostScript** option gives you the gray rectangle appearance in QuarkXPress but a color preview in PageMaker and InDesign. Choosing **EPS with TIFF Preview** provides a color preview in all applications.

Conclusion? While there's no single, cross-platform, one-size-fits-all flavor of EPS, Macintosh users can create good previews by choosing the **Macintosh EPS** format, and Windows users will achieve the same results by selecting **EPS with TIFF Preview**.

Regardless of the format you select, click the Setup button in the Export dialog, so you can check the appropriate options. Select the Include FreeHand document option so you can place the EPS in other applications and still reopen in FreeHand for editing. Select the Include Fonts in EPS option to ensure correct imaging of text from other applications (**Figure 11.25**).

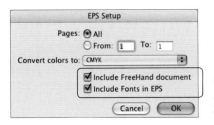

Figure 11.25 Be sure to select the option to Include Fonts in EPS to ensure that the file will image correctly.

If you select File > Save As > Editable EPS, FreeHand automatically includes the native FreeHand document in the resulting EPS. This may seem nonsensical: Isn't the EPS file the same thing as the FreeHand document? Well, strangely, no. FreeHand's native format is for use in FreeHand only. It's not understood by other applications such as Illustrator, QuarkXPress, or InDesign. Therefore, to place this artwork into a QuarkXPress page, for example, you have to send it out of FreeHand as an EPS file. Including the FreeHand document within the EPS file creates a two-for-one file: To other applications, it's an EPS file. But if you wish to edit the file, FreeHand sees the original FreeHand document inside. This sleight of hand is possible both when *saving* and when *exporting* to EPS files. But there is a very important difference between exported and saved EPS files. When placed in other applications, *exported* EPS files are cropped at the visible edge of the FreeHand page, eliminating any artwork that extends outside the document edge. *Saved* EPS files, however, display artwork in its entirety within other applications, even if the artwork extends beyond the page limits of the FreeHand file. Keep this in mind as you choose between Save and Export for generating EPS files from FreeHand documents.

Providing Correct Bleed for Export

When building a FreeHand document that requires bleed, you have two choices. Either build your artwork inside an oversized page and include sufficient bleed within the page, or create the document to the correct final trim size, create sufficient bleed outside the document bounds, and specify the desired bleed value in the Document panel (**Figure 11.26**). The bleed value entered in the Document panel doesn't inspire FreeHand to magically create bleed artwork for you. Instead, it allows FreeHand to earmark a designated bleed area so that its content is honored when it is printed or exported, even though artwork in that bleed area may fall outside the document bounds. And you don't have to be concise as you yank on selection handles to create bleed. The bleed value in the Document panel will see to it that any artwork *outside* the bleed zone is lopped off during export, provided you select the correct export settings.

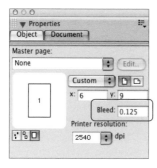

Figure 11.26 Specifying a bleed value in the Document panel allows FreeHand to give special handling to artwork that bleeds.

For example, if you've created a business card with bleed in the center of a letter-sized page rather than setting the document dimensions to the correct measurements, the edges of the FreeHand document don't matter. Just the artwork itself is important. Such a file can be either exported to EPS or saved to EPS with the same results. All the artwork is maintained, and empty space outside the artwork is not included. You must carefully create exactly the depth of bleed you want. Don't just add an arbitrary amount of extra art rather than a uniform eighth of an inch, for example. If you've created a FreeHand document whose dimensions equal the final trim size (for example, an 8.5-by-11 inch letterhead created on an 8.5-by-11 inch FreeHand page), and then you've specified a bleed value in the Document panel, you should *export* it as an EPS, rather than choosing File > Save. *Saving* the document as an editable EPS allows all visible artwork to appear in the saved EPS. If you were a bit sloppy in adding bleed artwork, your page will be off-center in the saved EPS, which would throw off subsequent processes such as imposition. However, if you use File > Export, FreeHand uses the document bleed setting to determine the boundaries of the exported EPS, ensuring that it will be correct when placed into other applications.

Exporting Documents Containing Multiple Pages

If you have created a multipage document in FreeHand, you'll discover that the option to save it as an EPS is not available. Instead, you must use File > Export. Multiple EPS files will be generated—one for each page in the FreeHand document, and named *filename_1.eps*, *filename_2.eps*, and so forth. If you select the Include FreeHand Document option, each single-page EPS will still contain the complete, original multipage FreeHand file. While this facilitates editability, since each EPS file provides access to the complete originating FreeHand file, it also adds to the file size of the exported EPS files.

Exporting PDF Files

The highest level of PDF that FreeHand can generate is Acrobat 4.0 (PDF 1.3). That in itself is actually not a serious limitation. But the built-in PDF export features in FreeHand are inadequate for correctly handling anything but the most basic artwork. If your FreeHand file is fairly simple, the PDF export feature may be adequate for successfully generating PDF files. But to create acceptable PDF files from some FreeHand documents, you may have to use other methods of creating PDF files. First, it's important to know the limitations of the built-in PDF export function.

Exporting Directly to PDF

To export a PDF directly from FreeHand, choose File > Export, and then select PDF from the Format menu. If your document contains Textured, PostScript, or Custom fills, FreeHand displays an alert to warn you that such content may not be maintained (**Figure 11.27**). It's not kidding, and it's referring to a very serious limitation in FreeHand's ability to render your document to PDF.

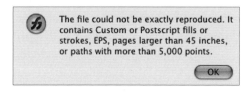

Figure 11.27 FreeHand warns you during PDF export that certain content may not be correctly expressed in the PDF.

Any Custom, Textured, or PostScript fills will not be present in an exported PDF, rendering it useless as a representative of your FreeHand document. But even if you have not used custom fills, you'll be greatly disappointed to discover that all spot-color content is converted to CMYK during PDF export. And if you're using OpenType fonts under OS 9 on the Macintosh, those fonts will not be embedded in the exported PDF, requiring you to convert text to outlines (Text > Convert to Path) before exporting to PDF, provided the font vendor's license allows this. At least TrueType and PostScript fonts should embed as expected. In addition, PDF export does not correctly handle bleeds. If you've specified a dedicated bleed value in the Document panel, FreeHand ignores that during PDF export and crops out any artwork outside the document bounds. If you've built bleed inside the document by creating an oversize page, the PDF page size will match the oversized page. If you've built the FreeHand document to exactly the bleed size (say, 8.75 by 11.25 inches for a letter-sized page), this is fine. But if you've just slapped artwork in the middle of an arbitrary page, the oversized PDF will complicate subsequent steps, such as imposition.

This is starting to sound fairly grim, isn't it? Clearly, if you need to provide a print-ready PDF of a document containing spot-colors or custom fills, you'll have to use another method of PDF creation. And to do that, you'll have to install Adobe Acrobat Standard or Professional so you have access to Acrobat Distiller. (Downloading the free Adobe Reader application won't give you the ability to create PDF files.)

Print to Adobe PDF

When you install Acrobat, you'll see a new entry in your list of printers—Adobe PDF (or Adobe Distiller, or Adobe PDF 7.0, depending on which version of Acrobat you've installed). The mechanics of printing to the imaginary PDF printer are much like those of printing to an actual printer: Choose File > Print, and then wade through the options. Since you're printing directly to PDF, you must choose the correct PDF setting under PDF Options in the Print dialog box (**Figure 11.28**) to ensure that font embedding and image compression and resampling are performed correctly. If you keep the setting at Use Default, you're at the mercy of the settings last used by Acrobat Distiller. Ideally, your print service provider should provide specifications for correct PDF settings. But if they don't, PDF/X-1a is a safe choice. If you have installed Acrobat 7.0, and choose it as the target printer, you will see this listed as PDF/X-1a:2001.

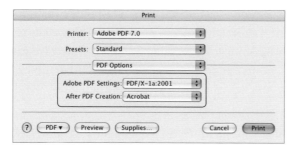

Figure 11.28 Printing to the PDF printer. Don't forget to check the Adobe PDF Settings to ensure correct conversion.

Stepping through the print dialogs, choose FreeHand MX from the menu (**Figure 11.29**) so you can select Quality PS Level 2. Then click the Advanced button in that same dialog so you can select options for crop and registration marks if your print service provider requires them in the supplied PDF.

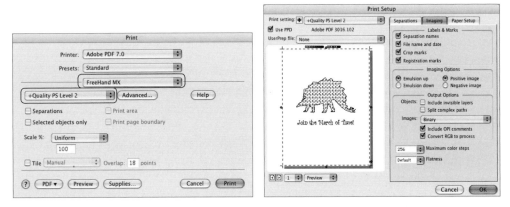

Figure 11.29 When printing to PDF, select the FreeHand MX option, and then select Quality PS Level 2 (left). Then, click the Advanced button for more imaging options (right).

The PDF page size will be equal to the page size of the FreeHand document. Printing to PDF will maintain spot-color content, and it will correctly render custom fills. You may find, however, that it does not correctly embed some fonts. How will you know? You can visually check PDF files in Acrobat by toggling on and off the Use Local Fonts option (Advanced > Use Local Fonts) and watching for changes. For quick toggling, use the keyboard shortcut: On the Macintosh, it's ⌘+Shift+Y. On Windows, use Control+Shift+Y.

However, if you must maintain bleed on the PDF you're generating, don't select the Print to PDF option. Any bleed setting specified in the Document panel will not be honored. And if the document was built on an oversized page, the entire page is rendered, which may interfere with correct imposition.

Distill PostScript or EPS for Best Results

The most reliable method of creating PDF files from FreeHand is to export an EPS file or generate a PostScript file, and then process the file through Acrobat Distiller. This method embeds fonts, crops the PDF to the correct bounding box of art, honors bleed settings, and maintains spot-colors. Why not just tell you this and be done with it? It's helpful to know the pitfalls of other methods, so you know *why* this is the best way to make PDF files from FreeHand.

Macintosh OS X: Save As PDF

Just don't do it.

In every print dialog in Macintosh OS X, you'll see the Macintosh system's built-in option to save as PDF (**Figure 11.30**). This option is quick and painless, so you might already suspect that it's inadequate for print production. But if you need convincing, note that this method of PDF creation provides no control over image compression or resampling, breaks FreeHand artwork into little separate slices in the resulting PDF, converts all CMYK and spot-color content to RGB, and ignores bleed settings in the Document panel. The OS X PDF-creation function is great for capturing Web pages and text files, but it's not appropriate for producing PDF files from FreeHand.

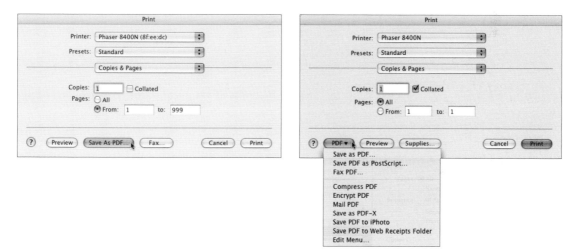

Figure 11.30 The Save As PDF option in Macintosh OS X through 10.3.9 (left) provides no easily accessed options. However, the PDF button in the Print dialogs in OS X 10.4 and above (right) offers an expanded list of options.

CHAPTER TWELVE

InDesign Production Tips

Thanks to its intuitive interface and integration with other Adobe applications, Adobe InDesign is reasonably easy to learn. But like any application, it has some little quirks that can surprise you if you don't know the workarounds.

GRAPHICS

InDesign accepts a wide variety of graphics formats, but that doesn't mean that all those formats are equally well behaved. In addition, while InDesign offers some interesting methods of placing graphics, not all of those methods will yield satisfactory results.

Placing Graphics

If you were raised on QuarkXPress, you're accustomed to making a box before importing graphics. PageMaker users making a switch to QuarkXPress were irked by the need to create a box, and QuarkXPress users regarded it as unnatural that PageMaker allowed you to just plop an image in the page. InDesign gives you the best of both worlds: Both PageMaker and QuarkXPress users can work the way they wish. QuarkXPress users are usually most comfortable making a frame first. It's helpful to know that both the Rectangle Frame tool ([⊠]) and the plain old Rectangle tool ([▢]) can create shapes that accept graphics as content. (Notice that the Rectangle Frame tool looks suspiciously like the Picture Box tool in QuarkXPress.) In fact, any enclosed shape—even one drawn by the Pen tool—will accept graphic content.

But part of the fun of InDesign is that you don't have to select—or even create—a frame before placing a graphic. Just choose File > Place, select a graphic, and then click anywhere in the page. InDesign creates a frame on the fly, positioned at the limits of the image. It's a tremendous timesaver. And it's a relief for PageMaker users making the switch.

One quirk of this frame flexibility is that you may unintentionally put content in the wrong frame. You get a lot of visual feedback in InDesign, so keep your eye on the cursor's appearance. If your loaded-graphics cursor ( ) develops parentheses , you're about to place your graphic in an existing frame. You've been warned. But even if you slip up, you're not stuck. Just undo once, and you're back to a loaded graphics cursor, so you can place the graphic in the correct frame. Click the Selection tool (black arrow), you're relieved of the graphic burden, and you can start over again.

There's *Good* Drag and Drop…

If you need to place multiple graphics and want to just get them all in the page at once, there are some handy methods available to InDesign users.

One method allows you to drag directly from a folder. Position your InDesign application window and a directory window (the Finder on the Macintosh or Windows Explorer on the PC) side by side, and you'll be able to drag images directly in from folder contents. This is the equivalent of File > Place, but much faster, since you can place multiple graphics simultaneously. This method doesn't allow you to position the images exactly—they just fall in a pile on the page. But the idea is to just get them on the page, then position them later.

Perhaps the most elegant way to drag and drop is to use the Adobe Bridge (**Figure 12.1**). If your first exposure to Bridge was underwhelming ("Hmmm… the old Photoshop File Browser. So what?"), that's understandable. The handy nature of the Bridge isn't immediately obvious. But explore it and you'll wonder how you lived without it. Use the Bridge to navigate to the appropriate folder, then select multiple files and drag them on top of the InDesign page. This offers a couple of advantages over just dragging from a folder in the operating system. The Bridge window can more easily be positioned over the InDesign page than directory windows. And the Bridge provides zoomable thumbnails of graphics to make it easier to find the correct files.

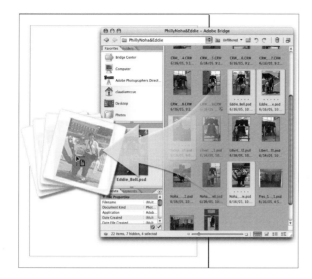

Figure 12.1 Dragging and dropping from Adobe Bridge into an InDesign page. You get a little stack of the same number of slides as the number of images you're dragging into the file. And the topmost slide depicts one of the dragged images. Cute, huh?

… and There's *Bad* Drag and Drop

Once you discover drag and drop, it's tempting to try it with everything. However, not all dragging and dropping will produce the same results. For example, it's possible to drag and drop directly from Adobe Photoshop into InDesign. The software won't prevent you from doing so, and it gives no warning that you might be dissatisfied with the results. But if you drag and drop directly from an open Photoshop file into an InDesign page, there are unpleasant repercussions:

- The size of the image is added to the heft of the InDesign file. If you drag the contents of a 10 MB Photoshop file into an InDesign page, you've added 10 MB to the file size of the InDesign file.

- The dragged image content becomes RGB in InDesign, even if the original Photoshop file is CMYK.

- There is no information about the resolution or color space of the image in the InDesign Info palette.

- A dragged image has no connection to its Photoshop source. There's no entry in the InDesign Links palette, and no direct editability with the Edit Original options. Basically, it's an orphan. If the image later requires retouching or color correction, you (or the print service provider) will have to jump through some hoops to extract an image to work with.

So the time you think you're saving by dragging directly from Photoshop into InDesign isn't really time saved. Bluntly speaking, don't do it.

As for drag and drop from Adobe Illustrator—things are a bit more optimistic. CMYK content is not converted to RGB, and even spot color content is maintained. The addition of dragged vector content doesn't cause a substantial increase in the size of an InDesign file. But the dragged file is also an orphan, with no link back to the original Illustrator file.

It's important to note that if the Illustrator file contains transparency effects such as opacity settings or blending modes, those effects are *not* honored when artwork is dragged and dropped into InDesign. Shadows are surrounded by opaque white boxes, and any transparency effects and blending modes are lost. It's not a pretty sight.

Special circumstances, however, might motivate you to drag and drop from Illustrator into InDesign. If you want to create a complex shape to use as a container in InDesign for text or an image, you may find Illustrator's drawing tools more flexible than those in InDesign. But to use Illustrator content in this fashion, you'll have to change a preference in Illustrator if you're using version CS or earlier.

The File Handling & Clipboard preference in Illustrator governs how dragged or copied Illustrator content behaves in other applications. In version CS or earlier, you'll need to select the AICB (Adobe Illustrator Clipboard) option (**Figure 12.2**). There's no need to clear the PDF check box. Illustrator CS2 already sports this set of options.

As long as you think of this as just allowing you to draw in Illustrator for ultimate use in InDesign, you won't be too disappointed by the loss of transparency and other attributes.

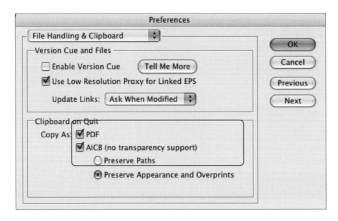

Figure 12.2 To fully utilize dragged or copy-and-pasted Illustrator content in InDesign, change Illustrator's File Handling & Clipboard preferences. Select the AICB check box (clear by default in versions up through CS1).

Copy and Paste

The rules and behavior for copying and pasting from Illustrator and Photoshop into InDesign are essentially the same as those for dragging and dropping. There—that saved you a bunch of reading, didn't it?

To summarize, *don't* copy and paste from Photoshop into InDesign. Period.

Before performing a copy and paste into InDesign from Illustrator CS or earlier, change Illustrator's File Handling & Clipboard preference to AICB as shown in Figure 12.2. And don't forget that there are no family ties between the pasted art and its ancestor in Illustrator. Any changes you make in Illustrator will not be reflected in what's been pasted into InDesign.

Embedding and Unembedding Graphics

While QuarkXPress does not support embedding of graphics in a layout file, InDesign will allow you to cram graphics right into the page-layout file so that they do not need to be externally stored. Fortunately, this is *not* the default behavior. By default, InDesign links to external files and only stores a proxy representation of the graphic in the page.

Perhaps it's a vestige of PageMaker-think that InDesign even allows it, but there's almost nothing to love about embedding graphics. Embedding slows down performance by increasing the size of the InDesign file, and embedded images must be extracted for any color correction or retouching. A change to the original graphic file will have no effect on the embedded version, since it no longer has any relationship with the original. A high wind is not going to blow through your hard drive, peeling graphics out of your InDesign file. So there's absolutely no justification for embedding and some very good reasons *not* to. So if that's your habit, perhaps after years of using PageMaker, please break it now.

To unembed an image for editing, select its name in the Links palette, and then choose Unembed File from the Links palette menu. InDesign will ask how you want to handle the unembedding (**Figure 12.3**).

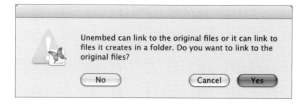

Figure 12.3 In the Unembed Files dialog, selecting Yes allows you to replace the embedded file with a link to an external file. Selecting No gives InDesign permission to extract the embedded images and save them as external files on disk.

The choices might not seem quite clear upon first reading. If you have a copy of the original graphics file, and you wish to link to it rather than use the embedded version of the graphic, select Yes (meaning, "Yes, I have a copy of the graphic, and I want to link to it rather than embedding it."). If you don't have the file, and you want InDesign to extract the embedded image and put it in a folder so you can link to it, select No (meaning, "No, I don't want to link to the original file. Well, I *want* to, but I can't. So please extract it").

Updating Missing or Modified Graphics

The Links palette (**Figure 12.4**) allows you to see which images are up to date, which are modified (marked by a yellow triangle), and which are missing (indicated by a red stop sign). Most of the Links palette controls are fairly straightforward, but there are several little secrets that may make life easier for you.

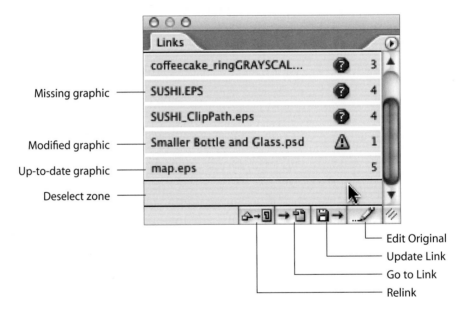

Figure 12.4 The buttons at the bottom of the Links palette offer helpful tool tips if you rest the mouse cursor over them. But one of the most useful areas in the Links palette — the Deselect zone — doesn't advertise itself.

Finding Missing Graphics

If you've switched from QuarkXPress to InDesign, you unavoidably bring some old habits with you. Using the Utilities > Usage > Picture Usage dialog in QuarkXPress, we all learned to select a missing graphic in the list, click the Update button, point QuarkXPress to the right folder, and then let it find all the missing graphics that were also in that folder. Selecting one missing graphic was a form of priming the pump to put QuarkXPress on the trail, like a graphic-seeking bloodhound. If the graphics were unmodified, this was great. QuarkXPress would display an alert: "Additional missing pictures are located in this folder. OK to update these as well?" You'd click the Update button, and all graphics were quickly updated.

When you take this same approach in InDesign, however, you're initially frustrated. Select one missing graphic in the Links palette, point InDesign in the right direction, and it fixes the link. *Only* that one link. Even though all the missing images for the document might be in the same folder, InDesign only updates the image you selected in the Links palette. It's maddening, isn't it?

InDesign actually does give you the option of updating *all* links—or just one—for total control over updating links. It's just what you want, but the implementation is perhaps too subtle. Here's what's really going on….

If you select an image in the Links palette listing, you're telling InDesign you want to update *just that one link*. There's no alert that mentions this. You just have to know it (and now you do).

To update all missing links, no links can be selected in the Links palette. To do this, scroll down in the Links palette list until you see a seemingly pointless empty horizontal space (the deselect zone indicated in Figure 12.4). Click in the deselect zone, and you've just told InDesign, "I'm not picky. Fix everything you can find." Click the Relink button (⟨⤴▪⟩), and then browse to the appropriate folder. InDesign even highlights the first image as if saying, "Is this it?" Click the Open button to accept the selection and, if all missing images are in that folder, they're all updated. If the missing images are located in more than one folder, however, you'll have to do this for each folder.

Updating Modified Graphics

The trick to updating all modified graphics at once is the same trick used for missing graphics. Click first in the deselect zone in the Links palette and then click the Update Link button (![button]) to kick off the hunt. Poof! All modified graphics are immediately updated.

Replacing Current Graphics

The Relink button (![button]) is good for more than just finding missing graphics. It's also an easy way to replace an existing graphic with a new one. For example, if you've applied a special effect to an image in Photoshop and saved the enhanced image as an alternate version, you don't have to hide the previous image to convince InDesign to take the new one. Just click the Relink button and navigate to the replacement image. InDesign will update the image while retaining any transformations (such as cropping, scaling, or rotation) that had been applied to the original image.

Editing Graphics

InDesign offers several quick methods for opening graphics in their originating applications for editing. You can select the graphic in the Links palette, and then click the Edit Original button (![button]) at the bottom of the palette. Or you can select the graphic on the page and right-click (Control-click on the Mac) to display the context menu. The easiest route is to press the Alt key (PC) or the Option key (Mac) while double-clicking the image. Regardless of the method you choose, InDesign awakens the original application and opens the graphic. It's even smart enough to differentiate between an EPS file generated by Illustrator and one created by FreeHand or QuarkXPress and will open the correct application.

Make the necessary changes to the file in the original application, and then choose File > Save. Return to InDesign and the edited graphic is automatically updated, without so much as a click of a button. If you had manually opened the artwork, edited, and then saved it, you'd also have to manually update the graphic through InDesign's Links palette. The Edit Original approach is a great timesaver.

Why Is My Image Opened by OS X Preview?

Macintosh OS X File Association Bug

The first time you try the Edit Original trick on the Macintosh, you may be disappointed that a Photoshop image is opened in Apple's Preview application, which doesn't do you any good at all. This is because the default file associations under OS X are incorrect.

The fix? You'll have to educate the operating system. Select a Photoshop native file (PSD) in any directory, then choose File > Get Info. From the Open with list (initially set to Preview), select Adobe Photoshop instead (**Figure 12.5**). If you have several versions of Photoshop installed, go for the newest version.

Very important: You must click the Change All button for this to take hold. And there's more. You'll have to do this for all the popular graphics formats that you wish to open with Photoshop, including TIFF, raster EPS, and JPEG. Find a vector EPS file and hook it up to Illustrator. And don't forget to fix your PDF files so they'll be opened by Acrobat rather than by Preview.

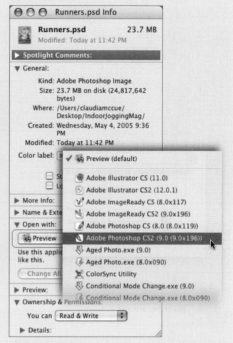

Figure 12.5 To take advantage of the Edit Original feature in InDesign, you have to straighten out the file associations in OS X on the Macintosh.

Transforming Graphics

There are several ways to scale frames containing graphics in InDesign. Select the frame with the Selection tool ( ). Then you can use the Scale tool ( ) or the Free Transform tool ( ) to scale the frame and its contents. Or you can enter values in the X/Y scale fields in the Control palette (**Figure 12.6**). You can also scale interactively by pressing Command+Shift (Control+Shift on the PC) and then dragging on a corner of the frame.

Scale X Percentage
Constrain Proportions
Scale Y Percentage

Figure 12.6 The horizontal and vertical scale fields in the Control palette are linked together. Type a value in the top field, press the Return key, and the bottom field is automatically populated, because of the Constrain Proportions control.

But whichever method you employ to scale a graphic frame, you'll be stunned to see that the X/Y scale fields cheerily insist that the scale factor is still 100 percent. However, if you select the graphic itself with the Direct Selection tool (⬚), the lying-dog fields suddenly tell the truth (**Figure 12.7**). What's going on?

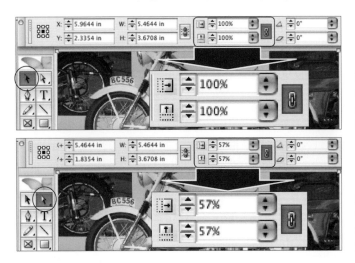

Figure 12.7 Select a graphic frame with the *Selection* tool (top), and the scale fields in the Control palette tell blatant lies.

Select the image with the *Direct Selection* tool (bottom), and you'll get the true story. This image has been scaled to 57 percent of its original scanned size.

It's important to realize that the two InDesign selection tools perform very different functions. InDesign perceives a graphic and its frame as two distinct entities. When you select a frame with the Selection tool, you're addressing the whole shebang—frame and graphic together. When you select a graphic with the Direct Selection tool, you're speaking directly to the graphic itself. This is the only way to find the true scale factor of a graphic.

But if you scale the whole shebang, why don't the X/Y scale fields reflect the new size? Why does it bounce back to 100 percent? That's an unexplained mystery. You'll just have to laugh it off, and ignore the X/Y scale fields unless you're using the Direct Selection tool.

USING NATIVE FILES

One of the joys of InDesign is its ability to use native Photoshop, Illustrator, and PDF files. There's certainly nothing wrong with using old-fashioned TIFF and EPS files, but there are advantages to using native files, including the ability to maintain live transparency and to keep layers aloft.

Photoshop Native Files (PSD)

It's not necessary to flatten Photoshop layered files before placing them in an InDesign page. In fact, unless a Photoshop file has reached an unwieldy size, there are compelling reasons *not* to flatten it because of the flexibility and editability you sacrifice. Maintaining live layers means simplified housekeeping because there's no need to keep a separate working image file. But there are some situations that present challenges.

Drop That Shadow

Both Photoshop and InDesign make it easy to add drop shadows to objects, which is why you see shadows under *everything* these days. Tastefulness aside, InDesign creates perfectly nice drop shadows that interact correctly with other elements in a page (**Figure 12.8**). As long as you want a simple, concentric drop shadow, it's just one click away.

Figure 12.8 If you just need a simple drop shadow, InDesign makes perfectly good ones.

But there's a limitation in the way InDesign perceives shadows from Photoshop. As mentioned in Chapter 9, "Photoshop Production Tips," Photoshop's blending modes are ignored by InDesign. If the shadow falls on empty space, this doesn't matter. However, if the shadow needs to realistically darken other content beneath it in InDesign, it will require some special handling.

To place an image containing a custom shadow on top of other content already in InDesign (**Figure 12.9**), you'll have to perform some surgery to allow the shadow to interact correctly with underlying elements. Since the Multiply blend mode applied to the shadow in Photoshop is not honored by InDesign, it lightens (rather than darkens) underlying elements in the page.

Figure 12.9 Custom shadows created in Photoshop (left) need special handling when placed in an InDesign file, or they will not interact correctly with underlying elements in the page (right).

To force the shadow to darken elements beneath it on the InDesign page, you need to set the blending mode of the shadow to Multiply (**Figure 12.10**). To do that, you'll have to isolate the shadow from its parent object so you can control its blending mode.

Figure 12.10 Select the frame containing the shadow, and then set its blending mode to Multiply in the Transparency palette.

If you're using a version of InDesign prior to CS2, you need to save two separate images to address the shadow issue. You'll need one image for the main object and a separate image for the shadow. Set the shadow's frame to use the Multiply blend mode, and then place the separate object on top of the shadow (**Figure 12.11**). If the images are derived from the same original image, use the Align palette to align the top and left edges of the shadow and object images so that they're positioned correctly relative to each other. If you have InDesign CS2, you can perform this trick with a single image, thanks to the Object Layer Options feature.

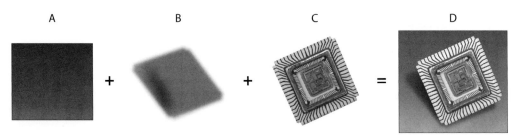

Figure 12.11 Think of this process as creating a shadow sandwich. Start with a background (A). Then place the shadow image (B), and set its frame to Multiply in InDesign. Top it off with the silhouetted object (C), and you have the finished assembly (D).

InDesign CS2: Object Layer Options

The Object Layer Options dialog (Object > Object Layer Options) allows you to selectively hide or display layers within a placed Photoshop file or PDF. Think of the possibilities for versioning and design flexibility. A single, layered Photoshop file can be placed multiple times in an InDesign document, displaying a different combination of layers in each instance. Layered PDF files can be treated the same way, whether they were generated by Illustrator or InDesign. And it just so happens that Object Layer Options are a splendid solution to the Photoshop shadow dilemma.

You can choose to invoke Object Layer Options either when you import an image or after it's placed in the page. During import (File > Place), select the Show Import Options check box to select which layers you wish to display (**Figure 12.12**). To correctly handle the shadow, you'll still have to place the image twice (or duplicate the frame)—once for the shadow and once for the silhouetted object. But at least you only have to keep track of one image on disk with this method.

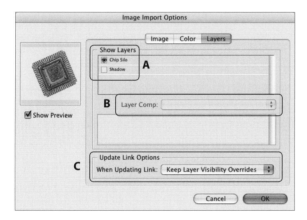

Figure 12.12 Invoked during image import or after an image is placed, Object Layer Options allow you to selectively show or hide layers within a Photoshop or PDF file (A). Extra credit: If you use Layer Comps in Photoshop, InDesign allows you to select them by name (B). The Update Link Options determine what happens if you edit the image in Photoshop after placement.

If you selectively reveal layers, what happens if you edit the image in Photoshop, and then update it? You can choose whether to keep InDesign's layer visibility overrides or start over when updating.

If you've invoked Object Layer Options for a placed graphic, InDesign politely provides an indicator in the Links palette in the form of a staring eyeball icon (**Figure 12.13**).

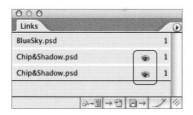

Figure 12.13 If the Object Layer Options feature has been used, InDesign provides a helpful eyeball reminder in the Links palette.

To take advantage of InDesign's Object Layer Options feature, you have to save graphics files appropriately from other applications:

- Photoshop files must be saved as PSD files. Layers in TIFF files or Photoshop PDF files aren't recognized by InDesign.

- Illustrator files must be saved as PDF files, compatible with Acrobat 6.0 or above. You must also select the Create Acrobat Layers from the Top Level Layers option in the Illustrator Save dialog. InDesign does not recognize layers in native Illustrator files—you have to dress them up as PDFs. Note that Illustrator PDF files can be reopened without penalty by Illustrator, since the original Illustrator artwork is contained within the PDF.

- InDesign files must be exported as PDF files, compatible with Acrobat 6.0 or above. You must also select the Create Acrobat Layers option in the InDesign Save dialog.

Illustrator Native Files (AI)

Illustrator native files offer several advantages over the traditional EPS files when placed in InDesign. Transparency and blending modes in Illustrator files are fully honored by InDesign. Drop shadows created in Illustrator with the Effect > Stylize > Drop Shadow method will interact correctly with underlying elements in an InDesign page—unlike Photoshop's drop shadows. Illustrator objects with blending modes such as Multiply, Screen, or Darken will affect InDesign elements as expected. A native file can also be considerably smaller on disk than an EPS version of the same file with no loss of data.

While it's unnecessary to open your vast store of Illustrator EPS files and resave them as native AI files, there is one circumstance that may require you to change the format of an old EPS. If you are adding a drop shadow to an EPS placed in InDesign CS or earlier, you will encounter a quirk in the way the shadow is rendered (**Figure 12.14**). The fix is to resave the art as an AI file or an EPS file with a TIFF preview.

Figure 12.14 Drop shadows created for EPS files placed in InDesign CS1 and earlier have an unfortunate bug. If you add a drop shadow, it will *display* correctly (top), but will *print* as if the shadow is following the containing frame (bottom). The answer? Save the artwork as a native AI file—then the shadow displays and prints correctly. (This was fixed in InDesign CS2.)

PDF Files as Artwork

In general, you'll use PSD, AI, EPS, and TIFF files as graphic content, but there are situations in which only a PDF will do what you need:

- Photoshop PDFs contain transparency and true vector art (including text), whereas vector components in a PSD are rasterized when placed in InDesign.

- Illustrator PDFs contain layers that can be selectively displayed or hidden with InDesign's Object Layer Options feature.

- Multipage PDFs can be placed one page at a time. Select the Show Import Options when placing a PDF, and you can page through a preview thumbnail to choose a single page, a range of pages, or the entire, multipage PDF. If you choose mutiple pages, your placement cursor changes appearance ( ), and each mouse click deposits a separate page of the PDF. To stop placing pages at any time, just click the Selection tool.

SWATCHES

It may seem redundant that InDesign has a Color palette as well as a Swatches palette, but they serve slightly different functions. Think of the Color palette as an informal mixing bowl for creating a color you'll only apply to a selected object. Colors created in the Color palette are not automatically stored in the Swatches palette—they evaporate. In addition, you can only specify CMYK, RGB, or Lab colors with the Colors palette. However, if you select an existing object colored with a spot color, the Colors palette does offer a quick method of creating a tint of the spot color.

In practice, it's best to create swatches rather than informal colors. In addition to allowing you to select from Pantone, Toyo, and TRUMATCH swatchbooks, the Swatches palette ensures that you have global control. Change the recipe for a swatch, and you change every object filled or stroked with the swatch.

If you've applied colors with the Color palette, you can easily turn those colors into official swatches without even hunting for the objects to which those colors have been applied. In the Swatches palette menu, choose Add Unnamed Colors, and InDesign hunts them all down and adds them to the Swatches palette.

The Swatches palette itself can be a bit confusing (**Figure 12.15**). The colorful semaphore flags in its rightmost column do *not* indicate whether a swatch is spot or process. Instead, those icons merely indicate the color mode used to generate the onscreen appearance of the swatch. It's the column with the dull gray icons that answers the question "spot or not?" A gray square indicates a process color (a swatch that will image in CMYK), regardless of the swatch name or the color mode indicated in the far-right column. A white square containing a gray circle—a spot—indicates a spot color.

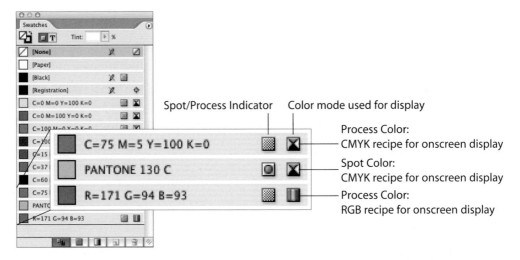

Figure 12.15 The indicators in the Swatches palette can be confusing. Here's a decoder ring.

RGB colors may drastically change appearance when converted to CMYK. If you're in a color-managed workflow, you may wish to retain your RGB swatches, but preview their conversion to CMYK. To do this, first choose the appropriate color profiles in InDesign by choosing Edit > Color Settings, or use the great Synchronize Color Settings function in Adobe Bridge. Then, choose View > Proof Colors to display content using the color profiles in effect.

If you're not in a color-managed workflow, and the print service provider requests that there be no RGB content, double-click the name or an RGB swatch, and then change its color mode to CMYK.

Stubborn Swatches

When you import artwork such as an Illustrator file or a Photoshop duotone containing a spot color, InDesign adds the color to the Swatches palette. As long as that artwork is in the document, you can't delete the spot swatch, nor can you merge it with another swatch—it's protected. If the swatch is used by a paragraph, character, or object style, it will also resist deletion. However, if you delete all artwork and styles related to the swatch, InDesign will allow you to delete the swatch. At least, it *should*.

Occasionally, InDesign develops a fondness for a swatch and will not allow you to delete it or convert it to process, even if you've deleted the artwork or eliminated the styles that inspired it. It's a petty annoyance. If there's truly nothing using the swatch, it won't appear during output or export. If you want to assure yourself that the color is a phantom, pre-flight the document (File > Preflight) and check the Colors and Inks information. If the swatch doesn't show up in Preflight, it won't show up on output or export either.

However, if it just bugs you to see that insolent swatch in the list, exporting the file to InDesign Interchange may be the cure. The true purpose of InDesign Interchange is to allow InDesign CS2 users to save files for individuals using InDesign CS. But it also can often repair a neurotic document. Choose File > Export, and then select InDesign Interchange for the format. InDesign creates an INX file with the file extension *.inx*.

Close the misbehaving document, and then open the Interchange file by using File > Open. You should now be able to edit or delete the offending swatch. You'll also find this feature in InDesign CS, although users of InDesign 2.0 will *not* be able to open an Interchange file—that bridge is out. The curative powers of INX, however, are still useful in InDesign CS.

What to Do About All Those Extra Swatches

Does this sound familiar? You're working on a job that should consist of CMYK plus one spot color, Pantone 130. After importing duotone images created by your team's retouch-ers and placing the vector art provided by another designer, you realize that there are three spot colors in the Swatches palette—Pantone 130 C, PMS 130 CVC, and something named Harvest Gold. Although we easily recognize that PMS 130 CVC and Pantone 130 C refer to the same color (and we suspect that *Harvest Gold* does too), a RIP sees the different names as indicating different inks and faithfully outputs them separately. Consequently, you need to take measures to ensure that only spot-color plate—Pantone 130—is output. And you'll have to perform some detective work to find the culprits responsible for the extra spot colors.

To determine which artwork uses each spot color, you could print out separated prints if your desktop printer supports that feature (some non-PostScript devices don't). But this would require you to endure the printing process, waste half a tree, and get out of your chair and walk over to the printer. There's a much more efficient way to determine where the spot colors are being used. You can use the Separations Preview feature in InDesign. Choose Window > Output Preview > Separations Preview.

Initially, the Separations Preview palette (**Figure 12.16**) doesn't do anything special until you choose Separations from its View menu. When you do, InDesign assumes you want to know as much as possible about your document, so it activates Overprint Preview, which in turn displays all graphics at high resolution. Consequently, in a document containing extensive graphics, you may experience slower performance.

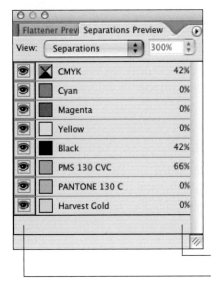

Figure 12.16 The Separations Preview palette lets you selectively display individual or multiple printing plates. As you move your mouse over areas of the page, the percentage value of each ink color is displayed in the right column. There's bad news here: It's a five-color job, so somebody's going to have to fix those two extra spot colors.

Color Percentages
Visibility Controls

Using the visibility controls in the left-most column of the Separations Preview palette, you can hide and display individual plates or combinations of plates. As you move your mouse over the document, the right-most column displays the percentage values of each ink.

NOTE: *If you close the Separations Preview palette while it's set to Separations view, Overprint Preview and High Resolution Display remain in effect, which slows things down a bit. Before closing the Separations Preview palette, choose Off from the View menu. This turns off Overprint Preview and returns display performance to the setting in effect before you activated Separations Preview.*

The Separations Preview feature may show you where most color problems are, but it can't *fix* the problems. To correct the problem, you could open all the images and vector artwork containing the PMS 130 CVC and Harvest Gold components and change them to use Pantone 130 C. Alternatively, if you're under a tight deadline, you could instruct the print service provider to resolve the problem during output. Or you could fix it in seconds by using the Ink Manager.

Ink Manager

The primary purpose of the Ink Manager (**Figure 12.17**) is to fix spot-color errors by remapping extraneous colors to correct inks. In this example, the job should only have one spot color, Pantone 130 C. So the Ink Manager is used to remap the two problematic colors—PMS 130 CVC and Harvest Gold—to the correct Pantone 130 C plate for output.

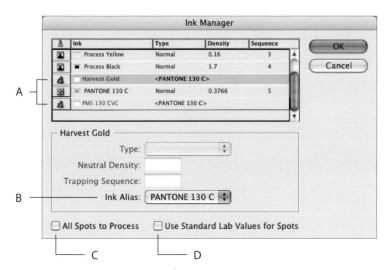

Figure 12.17 The Ink Manager can remap an incorrect spot color (A) to the correct ink (B) by using what InDesign calls Ink Aliasing. With one click, you can designate all spot colors to image as CMYK builds (C). Selecting the Lab option (D) may provide more accurate onscreen approximation of spot colors. In a color-managed workflow, this option may provide more accurate rendering of spot colors in CMYK. However, this may not match output from previous versions of InDesign.

You can launch the Ink Manager in several ways (**Figure 12.18**). The Separations Preview palette menu offers one route. The Swatches palette menu provides another. You will also find the Ink Manager in the Print dialog box (under Output) and in the Export dialogs for both EPS and Adobe PDF.

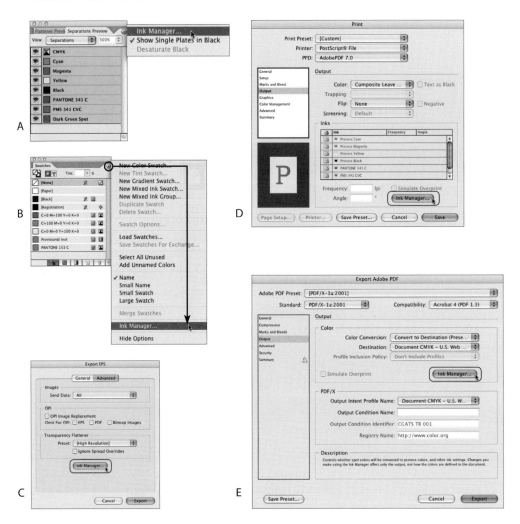

Figure 12.18 The Ink Manager is available from the Separations Preview palette (A), the Swatches palette (B), the Export EPS dialog (C), the Output section of the Print dialog (D), and the Export Adobe PDF dialog (E).

To map one spot color to another spot color with the Ink Manager, select the spot color you wish to remap. The dialog comes to life, offering you the Ink Alias list. Choose the correct color in the Ink Alias list and you're done. You can even remap a spot color to a single process plate—output the Harvest Gold on the magenta plate, for example. You cannot, however, map a process color to a spot color. But you can convert all spot colors to process with one click, by selecting the All Spots to Process check box in the Ink Manager dialog.

The remapping function is nondestructive—the remapping takes place in the output stream, as the file is printed or exported to another format such as EPS or PDF. It doesn't actually change placed artwork or any content created in the InDesign file, so it's easy to undo at any time if you make the wrong choices. Just turn off the Ink Alias for an ink, or unselect the Spots to Process option in the Ink Manager dialog.

Changes made in the Ink Manager are not reflected in the Swatches palette, which may unnerve you. But there's a certain logic to this. Since you haven't actually *changed* content, the Swatches palette doesn't feel compelled to change its display. But rest assured that any output—export to EPS or PDF, or File > Print—will contain only the correct inks. You can confirm this by reopening the Separations Preview palette (Window > Output Preview > Separations Preview) to check for process and spot-color usage.

If you're sending native InDesign files to the print service provider rather than submitting PDF files, it's a good idea to inform them that you have already rectified the spot-color issues with the Ink Manager, lest they freak out unnecessarily. ("There are 15 spot colors in the Swatches palette!")

Colorizing Images

InDesign allows you to colorize grayscale and bilevel (black and white, with no shades of gray) TIFF and PSD files to create simplistic monotone effects. Colorizing is a quick-and-dirty way to apply color to images with the ability to change your mind late in the game.

There are two ways to colorize images in InDesign. Select the image by clicking with the Direct Selection tool (white arrow), and then choose the swatch. Alternatively, you can just drag a swatch on top of the image, and then release the mouse button. The swatch is then applied to the image, not the frame.

If you want to create a true duotone, it's preferable to use Photoshop, where you have complete control over the mixing of inks. But if you're in a hurry or don't care about the refined controls in Photoshop, InDesign allows you to create what's often called a *fake duotone*. First, colorize the image using one of the methods above, and then apply another swatch to the frame itself. The frame color will show through the lighter areas of the image in the frame. (Warning—this has some potential to be truly ugly.) For a somewhat less ugly result, select the image with the Direct Selection tool (white arrow) and then, using the controls in the Transparency palette, apply the Multiply blend mode to the image itself.

Note that grayscale TIFF and PSD files with transparency on the bottom layer cannot be colorized by InDesign. All other layers can contain transparency, but the bottom layer cannot. InDesign does not give you any warning or explanation when you attempt to colorize such an image—it just doesn't do anything.

CONVERTING LEGACY QUARKXPRESS AND PAGEMAKER FILES

InDesign can directly open QuarkXPress 3.x and 4.x files, as well as files created by PageMaker 6.0 and later, thereby converting those files to InDesign documents. InDesign CS2 can also open and convert QuarkXPress Passport files. Note this limitation for QuarkXPress files. On its own, InDesign cannot open and convert QuarkXPress 5.x or 6.x files. However, the Q2ID utility from Markzware can open and convert QuarkXPress 5.x, 6.0, and 6.5 files.

Preparing for Conversion

Even though you only have to choose File > Open to open these legacy files, it's important to realize that this is a *translation* process—you're not simply opening a file. There are some precautions you can take to minimize problems in conversion, but you should be emotionally prepared to massage the resulting InDesign file. You'll achieve the best results if you first ensure the health of the original file you're going to convert.

- Make sure that all the required fonts are active on your system.

- Open the file in the originating application and update all graphics. Skipping this step won't prevent conversion, but it may save you some time hunting for links in the converted file.

- If there are any unnecessary elements in the document, such as extra elements in the pasteboard or unused colors and styles, delete those. It's best to start with a file that's as clean as possible.

- If you're starting with a QuarkXPress 5.x file, save it as a 4.0 file so that InDesign can open it.

- Before closing a PageMaker document, perform a Save As (rather than a File > Save) to streamline the file. The PageMaker Save command is a *fast save*, and there may be vestigial hidden data. Make it easy on InDesign.

- If the document is quite large, consider breaking it into smaller chunks for easier digestion.

- Convert embedded graphics to linked graphics in PageMaker if possible.

- Close the file before you attempt to open it in InDesign.

What to Expect

It's wise to check the results of conversion. You could laboriously compare hard copy to what's displayed onscreen, but here's a suggestion. After you've prepared the file in QuarkXPress or PageMaker, create a PDF from that file. Then, once you've opened the QuarkXPress or PageMaker file in InDesign, create a new topmost layer in the new InDesign file, and then place the pages of the PDF in that layer. Turn on and off the visibility of that layer by using the Layers palette visibility controls, or noodle with the opacity of the placed PDF, and watch for problems.

Expect reflowed or overset text, and keep an eye out for shifting graphics. Watch for subtle changes as you toggle the visibility of the proof PDF.

It's a conversion process, and it's amazing that it works at all. Here's what happens during the process:

- Styles are converted to InDesign styles.

- Swatches survive the trip.

- Master pages are retained, as are master elements in document pages.

- Graphics links are retained.

- Strokes and lines—even paragraph rules—are preserved.

- Groups are preserved (except for nonprinting items within a group).

- Multi-ink colors in QuarkXPress become mixed inks in InDesign. If the multi-ink color does not contain at least one spot color, a process swatch is created instead.

Frankly, you should expect text reflow—then you can be pleasantly surprised if it doesn't happen. InDesign's text composition engine differs from those of QuarkXPress and PageMaker. If line breaks are not crucial, the good news is that text will look smoother in InDesign because of the default composition method, which is called the *Paragraph Composer.* In the Paragraph Composer approach, InDesign considers the entire content of a paragraph as it determines how to break lines. If you switch to the Single-Line Composer, InDesign behaves like other page-layout applications and makes composition choices on a line-by-line basis. Open the Paragraph palette (Window > Type & Tables > Paragraph), and choose Single-Line Composer from the palette menu if you'd prefer to mimic the composition approach used by QuarkXPress or PageMaker. Text may not be as smooth—you'll see more white rivers, as well as tight and loose lines—but you may find that line breaks more closely resemble those in the original document. (Note that the choice of Single-Line or Paragraph Composer applies to text on a paragraph-by-paragraph basis.)

PageMaker Conversion Issues

Choosing File > Open to convert a PageMaker file to an InDesign file is a translation process. Here are some of the issues to consider when you perform the conversion:

- PageMaker's pasteboard contents are stored on the first spread's pasteboard.

- Two layers are created—Master Default (containing all master elements) and Default (containing everything else).

- Hyphenation in InDesign differs from that in PageMaker, which may result in line-break changes.

- PageMaker's Top of Caps and Proportional leading styles become baseline-based leading in InDesign, which contributes to text reflow and occasional overset text.

- InDesign provides no support for OLE (object linking and embedding). Any OLE graphics will be missing.

- PageMaker's Image Control effects are not retained.

- Shadow text becomes plain text.

- Inline graphics may shift vertically.

QuarkXPress Conversion Issues

While InDesign does a remarkable job of opening and converting QuarkXPress files, there are some issues you may encounter:

- InDesign does not have a Superior text style, so text styled as such in QuarkXPress becomes superscript text with a positive (upward) baseline shift (**Figure 12.19**). The Superior style might be described as a version of superscript, and is often used in QuarkXPress for currency symbols such as dollar signs.

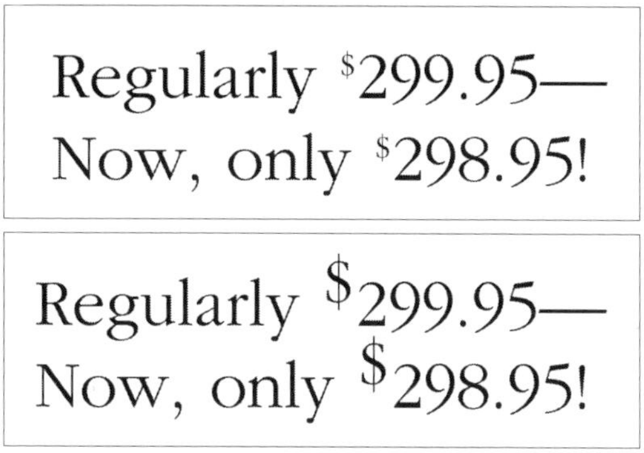

> Regularly $299.95—
> Now, only $298.95!
>
> Regularly $299.95—
> Now, only $298.95!

Figure 12.19 In QuarkXPress, the Superior type style raises the position and reduces the size of text such as dollar signs (top). InDesign doesn't have a Superior type style, so it applies the superscript style instead. While this maintains the raised position of the text, it does not reduce the size (bottom).

- QuarkXPress color profiles are ignored.

- Outlined text takes on a .25-point stroke.

- Line endings such as arrowheads may not match the originals in QuarkXPress.

- Artificially emboldened or italicized text takes on a true bold or italic font if it's available. If the correct font (or style within a font) is not available (for example, bold and italic styling applied to Impact, which can't get any bolder and has no italic face), the text will sport an unattractive pink highlight indicating a missing font or font style.

- Text shadows created by selecting the S in the Measurements palette are deleted.

- By default, text wrap in InDesign is created irrespective of stacking order. A frame carrying text wrap affects text frames above *and* below it in stacking order, even across layers. Modifying text in a converted file makes it subject to InDesign's rules. So if a neighboring frame is set to create text wrap, the text in your just-selected frame will feel compelled to play along and will reflow (or seem to disappear). Select the text frame whose text you don't want responding to text wrap, and then choose Object > Text Frame Options. Select the Ignore Text Wrap option, and then click OK. Note that you can change the InDesign text-wrap preference to behave like QuarkXPress. Select Preferences > Composition, and then choose Text Wrap Only Affects Text Beneath.

- Up through InDesign CS, there were occasional conversion errors resulting in images being set to be nonprinting as a result of the file conversion. A quick way to check for this is to activate Preview mode (press W on your keyboard). Toggle Preview on and off by repeatedly pressing W, and watch for images to disapear. Think of it as a crude video game. If you find any problem images, open the Attributes palette (Window > Attributes), select the images with the Direct Selection tool (white arrow), and then clear the Nonprinting check box in the Attributes palette. This problem seems to have been fixed in InDesign CS2.

Cleaning Up

After you've tuned up your line breaks and massaged any errant images, don't forget to delete the PDF layer you created for checking the conversion. Preflight the file (File > Preflight) to check for missing fonts or images.

To ensure that you're working with a healthy file from this point forward, it's a good idea to export the file as InDesign Interchange (File > Export). Then open up the resulting INX file, save it, and work from that. Think of it as a voodoo ploy to remove any memory of the file's previous incarnations. In fact, InDesign Interchange is a great general remedy for misbehaving files, regardless of their origin.

When *Not* to Convert Legacy Files

If you're simply reprinting an old job, it's saner to just keep it in its original PageMaker or QuarkXPress state. There's no true advantage to converting it and, as you can see, the conversion is likely to engender additional work and the risk of errors that you might not catch.

When creating templates that will be used as the basis for many documents, we strongly recommend building a new template in InDesign rather than working with a converted file. It's the healthiest start you can have. Besides—you need the practice.

GENERAL DOCUMENT ISSUES

IDLK Files

When you have an open InDesign document, there is an additional file with a similar name that magically appears in the same directory as the file you have open. For example, if you have opened a file named Chapter_1.indd, you'll see a companion file named ~chapter_1~p965so.idlk in the directory. The tilde (~) in front of the name and the file extension .idlk tell you that this is an InDesign lock file. Its purpose is to prevent another user from simultaneously opening your InDesign file and thinking they're making progress. Instead, they'll see an alert informing them that they do not have permission to open the document.

Don't delete .idlk files—InDesign cleans up after itself. The files will evaporate when you save and close the open file. If InDesign should crash while a document is open, it won't have time to delete the .idlk file, but just leave it anyway. InDesign will take care of the housekeeping the next time you open, save, and then close the file.

Automatic Recovery

As you work, InDesign keeps track of what you're doing, but not in a creepy way. Without impeding performance, it keeps a private version of your working file. This is the same mechanism that gives you unlimited undo capability.

If your system crashes for any reason—power outage, corrupt font, system crash—let InDesign recover as much of your document as it can. To that end, don't just reopen your original file. Instead, reopen InDesign and marvel as your document reappears. You may lose the last few things you did, but you won't lose everything you did in that session. That's because InDesign keeps your most recent operations in memory so you can quickly undo, and it may not have time to write those to disk as it crashes. But it's better than losing the whole shebang. You can't turn off Automatic Recovery—and why would you want to?

Going Back in Time

If you need to backsave an InDesign CS2 document for use in InDesign CS, you'll find that backsaving is not available through File > Save. Instead, you must export an InDesign Interchange file (File > Export). In order to open this file from the future, the users of InDesign CS must first update their software with a free patch from Adobe. In the Downloads section of the Adobe site, go to the InDesign area and find the heading Adobe InDesign CS 3.0.1 April 2005 (CS2 Compatibility) update.

Reducing File Size

InDesign files are fluffy by nature. Even a simple file is larger on disk than an equivalent QuarkXPress file. It's just a fact of life. But you can economize a bit by performing a File > Save As at the end of the job. When you just choose File > Save, InDesign adds any new data to the existing file on disk. It's faster than rewriting the entire contents of the file, but it adds to file size. However, when you choose File > Save As, InDesign rewrites the file. You should see a reduction in file size, especially in a document with a lot of large graphics. For example, the file for this chapter had ballooned to 3.9 MB. Performing a Save As reduced that to 2.8 MB. Enormous disk capacities have made us lax about taking up space—*I have a 250 GB hard drive. Why should I ever throw anything away?*—but you may find that document performance improves as a result of using Save As instead of Save.

Let It Bleed

When you create a new InDesign document, you're given the option to create a dedicated bleed zone (**Figure 12.20**). In the New Document dialog, click the More Options button and you'll see the Bleed and Slug options. Entering a value in the Bleed fields does more than just provide spiffy red bleed guides. It earmarks a special *bleed area* so you can easily invoke it with one click when you print or export the file.

It's important to note that InDesign makes a distinction between this official bleed area and any bleed you *manually* create by extending frames beyond the trim edge of the page, and this fact can bite you. During print or output, if you select Use Document Bleed Settings, InDesign looks for the dedicated bleed value entered in the Bleed options fields of document setup. If you haven't entered values in these fields, InDesign sees a zero value and obligingly gives you zero bleed (**Figure 12.21**).

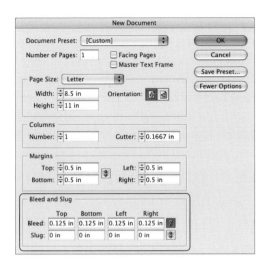

Figure 12.20 Click the More Options button (not shown, because it's already been clicked) and InDesign allows Bleed and Slug entries. Creating a dedicated bleed area in this manner makes it easy to invoke bleed as you print or export.

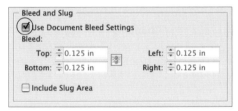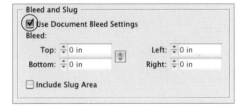

Figure 12.21 If you select Use Document Bleed Settings and see the correct value in all the Bleed fields (left), you're in good shape. But if you see all zeroes (right), you'll have *no* bleed on printed or exported output, regardless of any manual bleed you add.

If you forgot to designate the official bleed area when you created the document, you can still do so at any time by choosing File > Document Setup and then clicking the More Options button in the resulting dialog. You can then create the bleed area. When the Use Document Bleed Settings check box is selected, you will get the desired result during output.

One Size Fits All: Layout Adjustment

If you've (oops) built a document with the incorrect page size or need to change margins, the world has not ended. InDesign's Layout Adjustment can save your proverbial bacon. Choose Layout > Layout Adjustment (**Figure 12.22**), and then change the document size or margin settings. The default settings will do all the right things. Guides will move as will objects snapped to those guides. Text frames created by autoflowing text will expand or contract as necessary, adhering to shifting margins. Radical changes in page size or margin settings may require some massaging after the treatment, but you may be surprised by how good the initial results are.

Figure 12.22 So what if your evil twin built the document the wrong size? Select the Enable Layout Adjustment check box to give InDesign permission to fix it.

Checking Out of the Library

InDesign libraries are a great way to have a ready repository of commonly used elements, including text, graphics, and page geometry. These elements can then be quickly dragged into a page without having to re-create them each time. Libraries can be stored locally or on a server (although they must be locked on a server for multiple users to have access).

As you drag content from a library into an InDesign document, however, there's something the library doesn't tell you. If you're missing graphics that are required by the library content, you get no warning when you open the Library, and none when you drag content from the Library into an InDesign document. You won't make the discovery until you preflight the document. One workaround for this dilemma is to embed the graphic in InDesign before dragging content to the library. In the Links palette, select the link name, and then go to the Links palette menu and select Embed File. Then drag the graphic or a group containing it to the Library palette. When you drag the Library item onto another page, the embedding is maintained, and there's no need to hunt for the original artwork. One caveat: This is most appropriate for small artwork, since embedding increases the InDesign file size by the amount of the graphic. Embed a 2 MB image in an InDesign file, and you have increased the InDesign file size by 2 MB. Do this for 20 images in a document and—well, you get the idea.

TRANSPARENCY

InDesign's ability to create transparent effects has great appeal for designers. It's easy to make objects translucent, feather the edges of vector components, and add drop shadows to *anything*. But the introduction of transparency in InDesign 2.0 caused printers to grumble. The short story is that transparency effects, such as blend modes and opacity settings utilize an imaging model that goes beyond what PostScript understands. And since PostScript is the native tongue of imagesetters, platesetters, and many of our desktop printers, this presents a challenge. But InDesign converts new-fangled transparency content to a form that can be correctly handled by PostScript devices and processes by performing transparency flattening. Flattening occurs during any of the following procedures:

- Choosing File > Print and then selecting a desktop printer or PostScript as the target.

- Choosing File > Export and then selecting the EPS format.

- Choosing File > Export to create a PDF and then selecting Acrobat 4 (PDF 1.3) compatibility.

Transparency Flattening

Nothing *within* InDesign is flattened by Transparency Flattening. Your layers remain intact, and all transparency effects are still live. Instead, it's the output stream that is flattened. Content is cut apart, recreated, and reassembled in a form acceptable to PostScript (**Figure 12.23**). And this jigsaw puzzle will image as you expect—if you provide the correct ingredients and the right recipe.

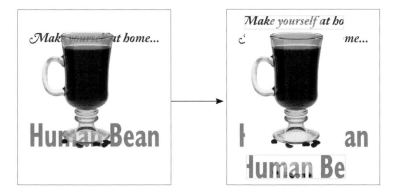

Figure 12.23 During print or export, InDesign starts with transparency involving graphics and text (left), then takes it apart, creating opaque stunt doubles (right) that look like the original effect. Note where the glass cup interacts with text: A text-shaped clipping path is created, which contains a generated image to portray the color interaction of the cup with the text.

Taking some relatively simple precautions when you build a document containing transparency will ensure that it produces predictable results when flattened and processed by the RIP. And there are some changes that print service providers must make to correctly handle transparent content. The following sections present some best practices for handling transparency as you create documents.

Put Text on Top

When text and vector elements fall beneath transparent elements in InDesign, those elements may be rasterized or converted to outlines during printing or exporting. Bring text and vector elements to the top of the pile, and they'll be safe from rasterization (well, until they hit the RIP). Putting such elements at the top of the stacking order should be sufficient. But it's not a bad idea to think in layers, just as a reminder of the issue (**Figure 12.24**).

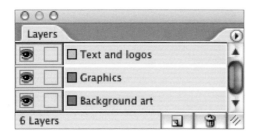

Figure 12.24 Placing text and vector art on a topmost layer ensures that such content will not be rasterized by interaction with any transparent content.

Choose the Appropriate Transparency Blend Space

As InDesign flattens transparent overlapping objects, it must create new objects to replace the overlap area (**Figure 12.25**). While this may sound like extra work, it's necessary as part of creating an output file that PostScript understands. To create the most faithful color in the replacement area, InDesign looks to the Transparency Blend Space setting to determine how it should do the color math. To control the Transparency Blend Space settings, choose Edit > Transparency Blend Space.

The default setting for Transparency Blend Space is CMYK, and you should leave it that way for print. When generating a PDF for the Web or an onscreen presentation, you can reduce file size by choosing a PDF preset such as Smallest File Size, which uses the RGB color space. In that situation, change the Transparency Blend Space to RGB in keeping with the fact that content will become RGB in the outgoing PDF. This will result in a more satisfactory rendering of the color in overlapped areas in the resulting PDF.

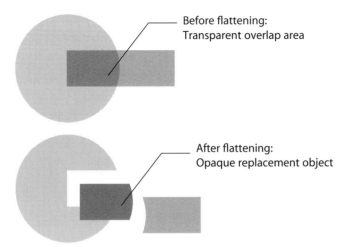

Before flattening:
Transparent overlap area

After flattening:
Opaque replacement object

Figure 12.25 It's easy to create interesting effects by using opacity settings and blend modes (top, before flattening). During the transparency-flattening process, InDesign creates replacement objects for overlapping areas (bottom, after flattening). The Transparency Blend Space needs to match the color space (RGB or CMYK) of the objects so that InDesign can properly match the color of the overlapping areas. It may look messy, but it's easily digested by devices that speak fluent PostScript.

Choose the Appropriate Transparency Flattener Preset

As InDesign performs flattening, it needs a recipe for generating two important components—rasterized text and vector art and soft-edged effects. That recipe is contained in the Transparency Flattener Preset (**Figure 12.26**). Before we discuss appropriate flattener settings, it's helpful to consider some of the functions that take place during flattening.

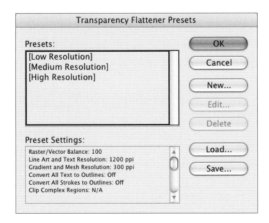

Figure 12.26 Transparency flattener presets are invoked during output or export to govern the generation of shadows and feathered effects. They also govern any necessary rasterizing of text and vector art. The default flattener presets in InDesign are only a starting point. Custom presets are necessary for proper imaging.

Rasterizing Text and Vector Content

The interaction of transparent images with text and vector art is one of the most challenging combinations to image. Text and vector content must sometimes be rasterized during export or output to satisfy PostScript requirements. While it may be disturbing to hear the words *rasterize* and *text* in the same sentence, rasterizing text is not inherently a bad thing (you are no doubt gasping in distaste as you read this).

But consider this: Your text and vector content *will* be rasterized eventually when it is processed by a RIP—a raster image processor. The RIP ultimately converts *everything* to pixels, but at such a high resolution (usually 2400 ppi or above) that pixels are not apparent in the output. So it isn't the rasterization process itself that's problematic. It's the choice of incorrect resolution during rasterization that can lead to undesirable results.

Similarly, when you scan signatures, maps, or drawings, you set the scanning resolution to a high value, such as 1200 ppi, to smoothly render drawn lines. Pixels are not apparent in the final artwork because of the high resolution. See? Pixels aren't a problem, as long as the resolution of an image is sufficient to fool the eye into seeing a smooth line.

Generating Shadows and Feathered Edges

All those festive drop shadows you're tempted to create in InDesign must be expressed in pixels. Similarly, feathering effects (Object > Feather) applied to InDesign objects or placed artwork are also accomplished with pixels. The feather and drop shadow aren't *literal* pixels until you export or print—they're just live effects for display until output makes them real. And the resolution of those effects is determined by the flattener preset chosen at the moment of export or print.

Appropriate Flattener Settings

To create and edit flattener presets, choose Edit > Transparency Flattener Presets. The dialog offers three default flattener presets, but since you're creating content for print, the Low and Medium resolution settings are fairly useless. To create a worthwhile flattener preset for print, select the High Resolution option as a starting point, and then click New (**Figure 12.27**).

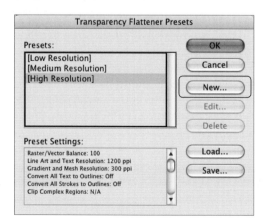

Figure 12.27 The default flattener presets are a bit like the Goldilocks fairy tale, except there's no "just right" setting. Start with High Resolution and then select New to create a custom style.

The two key values in the flattener options dialog are Line Art and Text Resolution and Gradient and Mesh Resolution. There isn't a one-size-fits-all transparency flattener setting. The settings should be dictated by the resolution of the output device.

The Line Art and Text Resolution option governs the rasterization of text and vector content. It should equal the resolution of the output device. For example, if you're printing to a desktop printer with a resolution of 600 ppi, set the Line Art Resolution to 600 ppi. On the other hand, a prepress technician preparing to generate PostScript for a 2400 ppi imagesetter would choose 2400 ppi, and so on. If you're creating PDF/X-1a files to send to a print service provider, ask them to give you specific instructions for creating a flattener preset. Be concerned if your contact responds, "Oh, I don't know. Just make a PDF." Push your way past that person, and ask to speak to a prepress technician for guidance.

The Gradient and Mesh Resolution value governs the generation of drop shadows and soft feathered edges created in InDesign. A prepress technician would usually choose 300 ppi for general output, although lower resolutions might be sufficient for low line-screen jobs such as newspaper work. If you're printing to your 600 ppi desktop printer, 150 ppi is probably a sufficient gradient setting for printing comps. By the way, this setting has no effect on the resolution of placed images — only on the shadows and feathered edges generated by InDesign (**Figure 12.28**).

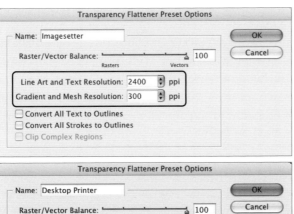

Figure 12.28 Flattener options should be in keeping with the resolution of the output device. For output on an imagesetter (film) or platesetter (plates), a typical setting might be 2400 ppi for line art and 300 ppi for gradients (top).

For a desktop printer with an imaging resolution of 600 ppi (bottom), the line-art resolution should be 600. Setting the gradient resolution to 150 saves a little time in the print process.

Invoking Transparency Flattener Presets

Although you may have created custom flattener presets, they don't actually *do* anything until you invoke them during print or export. You'll need to pick the proper flattener preset when you print, export an EPS, or generate a PDF with Acrobat 4 compatibility (**Figure 12.29**). Flattener presets are located in the Advanced section of print and export dialogs.

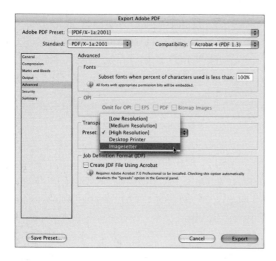

Figure 12.29 When exporting a PDF with Acrobat 4 compatibility, such as PDF/X-1a, select the appropriate flattener preset in the Advanced section of the Print and Export dialogs.

Chances are, you'll be invoking flattener presets in two situations: Printing to your desktop printer and generating PDFs for submission to the print service provider. Revisit Figure 12.28 to see *suggested* settings for both of those situations: Your *actual* settings will depend on output resolution. We'll wait here while you look up your desktop printer resolution. You can do that while you're on hold, waiting to talk to a technician in the print service provider's prepress department so you can inquire about their RIP resolution.

Special Case: Spot Color Content

In addition to performing the jigsaw trickery of flattening during output or export, InDesign instructs some components to *overprint* in order to render such blending modes as Multiply.

What is overprint? Here's a simple example: Create a solid yellow square, and then place a solid cyan circle on top of the yellow square. The cyan circle *knocks out* (covers up) the portion of the yellow square underneath it, because shapes are usually opaque in PostScript reality. Like pieces of construction paper, they completely cover up anything underneath them.

However, if you set the cyan circle to overprint, it's no longer opaque. It allows the yellow square underneath to show through, and the overlap area becomes green (cyan plus yellow, as shown in **Figure 12.30**).

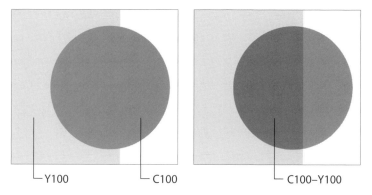

Y100   C100   C100–Y100

Figure 12.30 By default, opaque shapes knock out everything underneath (left). Overprinting allows a shape to intermix with everything underneath (right).

Overprint is not a complicated concept, and it's been part of PostScript forever. InDesign counts on the RIP to understand overprint in order to properly image transparency effects. However, many desktop printers don't implement overprint, which is why you may see ugly white or discolored boxes around drop shadows that fall on spot-color areas when you print on a desktop printer (**Figure 12.31**). It's just One of Those Things. To eliminate (or at least subdue) this problem, make some changes in the Output tab of the Print dialog.

Figure 12.31 To image correctly, a drop shadow on a spot color background (left) requires that the RIP understand how to handle PostScript overprint. A white or discolored box around the shadow (right) indicates that the RIP is not correctly processing PostScript overprint. Many desktop printers suffer from this shortfall, but a print service provider's RIP should handle the shadow correctly.

Choose Composite CMYK and select the Simulate Overprint option (**Figure 12.32**). You may still see some discoloration, but the white box should be eliminated. Don't freak out: This is due to some limitations of many desktop printers, and doesn't foretell how the effect will be processed by your print service provider's RIP.

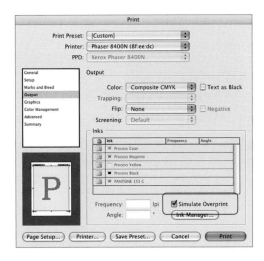

Figure 12.32 To subdue the dreaded white-box-under-a-shadow syndrome on a desktop printer, choose Composite CMYK and select the Simulate Overprint option.

Spot Colors and Transparency: Overprinting at the Print Service Provider

InDesign exploits the overprint capability of PostScript to allow shadows and other transparency effects to interact correctly with spot-color content. If you intend to print spot colors, you certainly don't want to convert spot colors to process on your final print job to avoid the dreaded white box syndrome, and—whew!—you don't have to. To correctly process shadows and other transparency effects that interact with spot color areas, the print service provider will have to enable PostScript overprint on their RIP (in the past, it was usually turned off). This isn't something you can do from within InDesign. It's the responsibility of the prepress department to make this change. But it's helpful for you to know, so that you can communicate with the print service provider. Different RIP vendors label the function slightly differently, but the gist of it is, "Hey! Honor any PostScript overprint instructions!"

Note that, just as correct rendering of overprinting is crucial to imaging transparent effects correctly, being able to *preview* overprinting is necessary for correct display of such content on a monitor. By default, Adobe Acrobat does not show overprinting effects, but you can turn on this feature in Acrobat 6.0 Professional and Acrobat 7.0 Professional by choosing Advanced > Overprint Preview. Adobe Reader 7.0 also offers overprint preview, but the setting is lurking in Preferences > Page Display. Note that the Macintosh OS X application Preview cannot display overprint in PDF files.

Drop Shadows: The Sun Never Moves

In the real world, if you rotate a box sitting on a table, the shadow doesn't rotate with the box because the light source remains stationary. The same rules apply in InDesign. Its imaginary sun doesn't move either. This doesn't seem unreasonable until you begin rotating objects to which you've applied drop shadows in InDesign. If you rotate the objects, their shadows do not rotate with them. While it's logical, it may not produce the effect you want. In home-brewed imposition, for example (**Figure 12.33**), a shadow's relationship with its parent object will change. In the example, the SmithcoMatic logo is supposed to have a drop shadow that's positioned down and to the right of the logo. However, rotating the art 180 degrees causes the shadow to be positioned *up* and to the *left* of the art. Oops.

Figure 12.33 This looks fine, doesn't it? Try standing on your head, and you'll see what's wrong with this picture.

InDesign doesn't offer the option to turn off the global light source position (as Photoshop does). The only cure is to manually change the position of the shadow by choosing Object > Drop Shadow, and then entering a new value for the shadow position (**Figure 12.34**). In the example, the correct shadow position is .04 of an inch for both X and Y offsets. To correct for the rotation, the shadow for the rotated artwork is set to -.04 of an inch for both X and Y offsets (that's a minus sign in front of the number, indicating a negative value).

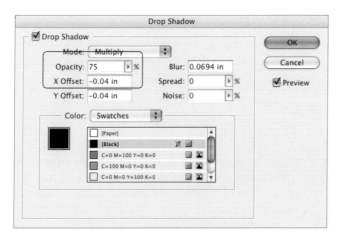

Figure 12.34 To compensate for InDesign's single-sun approach to drop shadows, you may have to alter the X and Y Offset values for rotated objects (for example, during manual imposition).

FINDING & FIXING PROBLEMS

InDesign provides a number of tools that are useful when you're playing "What's wrong with this picture?" before you send your job to the print service provider. Several tools help you spot problems visually, and the Preflight function provides a written report.

Forensic Tools

Preview Mode (View > Screen Mode > Preview) simplifies your view of the document, hiding any nonprinting objects such as guides, frame edges, and hidden text characters so that you can concentrate on content. You can toggle the Preview mode among four states: Normal, Preview, Bleed, and Slug. But you can easily toggle between the two most common states, Normal and Preview, just by pressing the W key on your keyboard. In addition to simplifying your view, Preview mode will hide any images or other elements that have been assigned a nonprinting attribute in the Attributes palette (Window > Attributes). If you've set an object to nonprinting while you experiment with your design, its disappearance in Preview mode serves as a reminder to fix the attribute or delete the object.

Overprint Preview (View > Overprint Preview) can be used to confirm that you've set objects to overprint. But perhaps more importantly, you can use it to catch common problems. For example, white objects set to overprint will disappear during output, and they'll disappear during Overprint Preview as well. Why is this? With rare exceptions, *white* in illustration and page layout just signifies "this is blank paper—no ink prints here." The rare exception would be a literal white ink created for printing on metallic surfaces or clear substrates. What kind of a fiend would set a white object to overprint? Oh, nobody does it intentionally. It's usually the result of creating a black object, such as a logo, in a drawing program and then setting it to overprint. Subsequently changing the object's fill to white does not turn off the overprint attribute.

Overprint preview also provides a more realistic representation of blending modes applied to spot-color objects. The default view mode in InDesign doesn't always correctly represent blending modes other than plain old Normal (**Figure 12.35**).

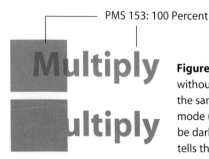

PMS 153: 100 Percent

Figure 12.35 It's impossible to have 200 percent of a single ink without a second printing plate. But if you create two objects with the same 100-percent spot fill, and then apply the Multiply blending mode (top), InDesign's display implies that the overlapping area will be darker. But turn on Overprint Preview (bottom), and the display tells the true story.

Activating Overprint Preview turns on High Resolution Display, so you may experience slower performance in a graphics-heavy document. When you're finished using Overprint Preview, turn it off to speed up performance.

Flattener Preview (Window > Output > Flattener Preview) uses red highlighting for text and vector content that may be rasterized during the output process (**Figure 12.36**). Notice the word *may*. During a direct export to PDF, InDesign CS and CS2 perform engineering feats to avoid rasterizing such content. However, when you select File > Print, both versions may be forced to rasterize vectors and text content that interacts with transparency. The Flattener Preview can't prevent rasterization, but it provides a visual warning. Use it as a guide as you modify stacking order and layering in a file.

Figure 12.36 The Flattener Preview uses red highlighting (here, represented by black) to indicate potential text and vector rasterization.

The **Component Information** dialog (**Figure 12.37**) provides a peek under the hood of your copy of InDesign, as well as a glimpse of a document's life story. In Windows, hold down the Control key as you choose About InDesign from the Help menu. On the Macintosh, hold down the Command key and choose About InDesign from the InDesign menu.

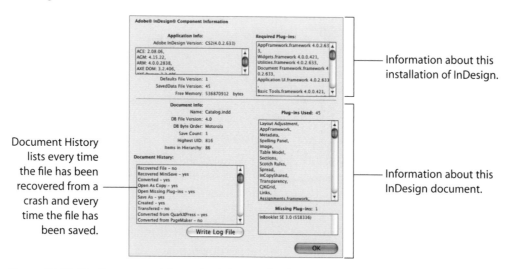

Figure 12.37 The Component Information box provides details about the application itself as well as the currently active open document.

The top part of the dialog shows information about the current version of InDesign (Figure 12.37 shows version 4.0.2.633) and the active plug-ins. This may be useful if you need help from Adobe tech support, since you'll need to provide the current version and other environmental information when you call.

The bottom part of the dialog displays information about the active InDesign document, including the very useful Document History, which constitutes a personal diary of the document. You'll see whether the document was converted from QuarkXPress or PageMaker, whether it's been recovered after a crash, and how many times it's been saved (including the versions and platforms in effect during the saves). Would you ever be this nosy about a file? Well, if it's neurotic—crashing frequently or just plain acting strange—take a look at the Document History. If the file has had a traumatic childhood, it may be worth exporting it to InDesign Interchange as a purification ritual. Then, open the Interchange file and make a new start.

Info Palette

Often overlooked, the Info palette (Window > Info) provides valuable information about image and text content (**Figure 12.38**). Select an image frame, and the Info palette displays color space such as RGB, CMYK, or grayscale, along with the effective resolution in ppi. *Effective* resolution is the *actual* resolution of the placed image, which is a product of the original scanned resolution and any scaling. For example, a 300 ppi image scaled to 200 percent in InDesign has an effective resolution of 150 ppi, which would be inadequate for standard 133–150 lpi printing.

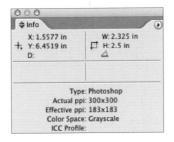 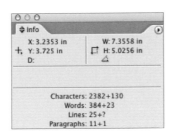

Figure 12.38 The Info palette shows the color space and resolution of a selected image (left) and alerts you if there is overset text for a selected story (right). Numbers after the plus sign indicate overset text.

You can click a text frame, and the Info palette will tell you if there is overset text at the end of the story, even if the end is many pages downstream. In Figure 12.38, the entry "Words: 384+23" indicates that there are 23 words in overset text.

Preflight and Package

The preflight features in InDesign (File > Preflight) aren't quite as intensive as those in dedicated preflight applications such as Markzware's FlightCheck. But using the built-in preflight routine can ensure that you catch problems before sending the job out (**Figure 12.39**).

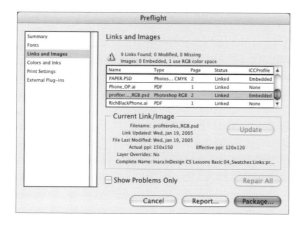

Figure 12.39 Preflight warns you of problems such as missing images and fonts. Here, it highlights an RGB image and also indicates that the image's resolution is only 150 ppi.

InDesign's preflight uses triangular yellow caution icons to alert you to missing images and fonts as well as RGB images. However, it isn't blatant about mentioning image resolution—there are no yellow triangles, and there's no way to set up the preflight process to flag images below a certain resolution. You're on your own there.

If you're concerned that you might overlook problems—or if you need to preflight multiple files—consider using one of the preflight utilities from Markzware, such as FlightCheck Studio or FlightCheck Designer.

InDesign's Package function (File > Package) copies all necessary fonts and art files into a folder for job submission—under most circumstances. However, if you're using Multiple Master fonts, you'll have to manually package any font instances you've created, because InDesign packages only the parent font. For example, if you've created and used Myriad MM 700 BD 600 NO, InDesign packages only the Myriad MM. While Multiple Master fonts were a great concept, this sort of challenge may inspire you to avoid them.

If you've created any text layers in Photoshop and placed the image as a native PSD into InDesign, fonts will not be packaged. It's preferable to save such images as Photoshop PDF files anyway, since fonts can be embedded, and vector edges remain sharp when imaged from Photoshop PDFs placed in InDesign.

PDF CREATION METHODS

There are multiple methods for generating PDF files from InDesign files.

- **Export to PDF:** If you're using InDesign CS2, you'll be happy to know that the easy way is usually the best way—how often does *that* happen? A PDF file generated via InDesign's direct export (File > Export, and choose Adobe PDF as the export format) is as digestible as one created by distilling PostScript. And, most importantly, there's less chance of vector and text content being rasterized during a direct export. Like Illustrator and Photoshop, InDesign contains the necessary resources to create PDF files without invoking Acrobat Distiller. Unless your recipient instructs you otherwise, use File > Export, and then choose the PDF/X-1a setting.

- **Print to Adobe PDF:** By default, this approach uses Distiller as the target printer, following the PDF job options last used by Distiller. However, you can change those settings by clicking the Printer button at the bottom of the Print dialog. In the dialog that follows, change Printer to Adobe PDF, and then click the Copies & Pages list and select PDF Options. Then you'll be able to choose from the full range of Distiller job options from the Adobe PDF Settings list. Vector and text content may be rasterized if it interacts with any transparency effects.

- **Acrobat Distiller:** Generate PostScript by selecting File > Print, and then selecting PostScript File for the printer. For PPD (PostScript Printer Definition), choose Adobe PDF unless instructed otherwise. Use Acrobat Distiller to convert the PostScript to PDF. Whereas this long-winded approach was previously recommended to minimize CID (Character ID) font encoding, you'll achieve equivalent results if you're using InDesign CS2. You may still encounter instances of CID font encoding in a directly exported or distilled PDF, since some glyphs must be CID-encoded regardless of the method of PDF creation.

- **Save As PDF:** The Macintosh operating system offers a built-in approach to creating PDF files. You'll encounter a Save As PDF option in Print dialog boxes in OS X 10.3.9 and below. In 10.4 and above, you'll see just a PDF button. While this method is acceptable for PDF files intended for a quick-and-dirty e-mail attachment, it does not offer appropriate controls for making a print-ready PDF file.

To sum up, direct export from InDesign CS2 is the preferred method unless the file recipient specifically instructs you otherwise. If you're still using InDesign CS, and you need to make a PDF for unknown circumstances, generate PostScript and use Distiller's PDF/X-1a settings to minimize any CID font encoding that might be problematic on older devices. CID font encoding—necessary for Asian fonts and some special characters—has been part of PostScript and PDF specifications for years, but many RIP vendors neglected to allow for it. Earlier versions of InDesign encoded all fonts—even lowly Times Roman—as CID. Distilling PostScript was the common fix to avoid CID font encoding. But with the release of InDesign CS2, this should no longer be necessary.

PDF CREATION SETTINGS

If you're asked to submit PDF files, that request should be accompanied by specifications for creating an appropriate PDF for the recipient's workflow. If you're told, "Uh, I don't know. Just make a PDF," the person on the other end of the phone may not be of any help.

It's important to know that the P in PDF stands for *portable*, not for *perfect*. It's possible to make a bad PDF, so barring any specific guidance, it's good to know that InDesign provides reliable recipes for common circumstances:

- **Smallest File Size** is appropriate for PDFs that are to be e-mailed or posted online. This setting resamples raster images to 100 ppi, applies aggressive compression, and converts all images to RGB while retaining spot colors. This generates a file that is inappropriate for commercial printing and results in color shifts that may adversely alter the appearance of the PDF onscreen. The PDF is compatible with Acrobat 5.0—transparency is not flattened.

- **High Quality Print** is meant for printing on a desktop printer. Images are down-sampled to 300 ppi and compressed with the Maximum quality setting. RGB images are not converted to CMYK, but existing CMYK and spot-color content is maintained, and the PDF is compatible with Acrobat 5.0.

- **Press Quality** is similar to High Quality Print, but it uses InDesign's current color management settings to convert any RGB content to CMYK on the fly, while retaining any spot content. While this setting generates a healthy PDF, its compatibility with Acrobat 5.0 may cause some problems with older devices. It places you at the mercy of someone else's approach to transparency flattening.

- **PDF/X-3:2002** is intended for use in a color-managed workflow. Color profiles are embedded in the PDF, and RGB content is not converted to CMYK. Don't use this setting unless specifically instructed to do so. These PDF files are compatible with Acrobat 4.0—any transparency content is flattened in the process of generating the PDF.

- **PDF/X-1a:2001** is your best choice when you're given no specifications for PDF file creation. Any RGB images are converted to CMYK during PDF generation, spot-color content is maintained, and the compatibility with Acrobat 4.0 will render the PDF well behaved on a wide variety of devices.

CHAPTER THIRTEEN

QuarkXPress Production Tips

In the late 1980s, Quark's flagship product QuarkXPress surpassed PageMaker (then owned by the now-defunct Aldus, later owned by Adobe) as the preferred page-layout program in the desktop publishing universe. As a side note, although industry habit is to say simply "Quark" when referring to the product, *Quark* is the company and *QuarkXPress* is the product.

VERSIONS

Many users upgrade their applications upon release of a newer version. It's a combination of the thrill of ripping off shrink-wrap, coupled with the Christmas-morning sensation of playing with new toys. All of this is disguised as a professional need to keep up with change. But Quark's own upgrade cycle has traditionally been glacial, and QuarkXPress users often lag behind even that pace. It isn't due to stodginess or inattention: Many users are dependent on features provided by XTensions—plug-ins developed to extend the functionality of QuarkXPress. XTensions and scripting-based solutions are often key to the productivity in large production groups, and the lure of new software is tempered by workflow requirements. So, while QuarkXPress 7.0 is the current version as of this writing, many QuarkXPress users are working with version 4.11 or 5.0 because of dependency on version-specific XTensions whose developers have not yet revised their XTensions for later versions of QuarkXPress.

This mix of versions in the page-layout ecosystem presents some challenges. If you are using QuarkXPress 6.0 or 6.5 but sharing files with users of QuarkXPress 5.0, you can save files in the earlier version, but some content, such as support for native Photoshop files, will not survive the trip. And if you need to save down for a user of QuarkXPress 4.11, you'll need to first save it as a QuarkXPress 5.0 file, and then open QuarkXPress 5.0 to save the file to QuarkXPress 4.0, since any version of QuarkXPress allows you to go back only one version. (So don't discard old software!) If you anticipate having to do a lot of these back-saving gymnastics on the Macintosh, you will have to consider keeping an older computer that allows you to boot into OS 9 (or run the Classic environment, which is an emulation of OS 9), since QuarkXPress 4.0 and 5.0 won't run in OS X. Newer Macintosh computers using the Intel chip won't run Classic or boot into OS 9, which will close the door on QuarkXPress 4.0 and 5.0 for those computer users.

Saving QuarkXPress 6.5 Files to Earlier Versions

Saving to earlier versions within *any* application can be risky because of the potential for translation errors. And since saving to earlier versions can modify content extensively, don't count on being able to move everything back and forth between versions. If you save your QuarkXPress 6.5 file to a version 5.0 file, send it to a user of QuarkXPress 5.0, and then reopen their work in QuarkXPress 6.5, it may not be obvious what has changed or been lost during the round trip. So be wary of utilizing some of the late-model features in QuarkXPress 6.5 if your project requires that you collaborate with users of the earlier version. At least be emotionally prepared for the consequences.

About the Versions

While there are no doubt substantial numbers of QuarkXPress 3.32 and 4.0 users out there, we've elected to confine discussion to QuarkXPress 5.0 through 6.5, with an addendum on QuarkXPress 7.0. For in-depth information on all versions of QuarkXPress, consult David Blatner's incomparable series of books. From The QuarkXPress 4 Book (Peachpit Press, 1998) through Real World QuarkXPress 5.0 (Peachpit Press, 2002) and Real World QuarkXPress 6.0 (Peachpit Press, 2003), they're the best available resource. And no, I don't get a kickback.

Synchronized Text

Content marked as synchronized text in QuarkXPress 6.0 through 6.5 will become plain text if the file is saved for QuarkXPress 5.0. Reopening the file in QuarkXPress 6.0 through 6.5 does not restore the special synchronized text tagging, so that functionality is lost as a result.

Projects: Convert to Individual Documents

QuarkXPress 6.0 introduced the concept of *projects*, which can contain multiple individual documents called *layout spaces*. For example, you might choose to build a set of business collateral—letterhead, business card, and envelope—as a single project containing three layout spaces. Layout spaces share synchronized text boxes, colors, and styles, but can be disparate page sizes. Each layout space has a unique name. Saving a project from 6.0 or 6.5

to version 5.0 creates a folder containing individual documents. The family relationship between the documents is lost, as is text synchronization and shared style sheets. There's no way to knit them back together into a single project, QuarkXPress 7.0, however, allows you to append layouts.

> **NOTE:** Once you've saved a QuarkXPress file for an earlier version, the document remembers and will populate the Version field in the Save dialog accordingly. It's meant to give you a head start, but may trip you up if your intention is to save as the current version instead.

Font Issues

In addition to noting the differences between QuarkXPress 5.0 and QuarkXPress 6.0 and above, you must consider that QuarkXPress 6.0 and above on the Macintosh run only under OS X. QuarkXPress 5.0 is an OS 9 application and, even though you may be running it in the Classic environment under OS X, it doesn't recognize the OS X System fonts, referred to as *dfonts* because of their .dfont file extension. Consequently, any dfonts you've used in, say, a QuarkXPress 6.5 file will not be available to users of QuarkXPress 5.0. However, there's some good news: The dfontifier utility from Mark Douma (http://homepage.mac.com/mdouma46/dfont/dfont.html) converts dfonts to conventional fonts understandable by OS 9.

Photoshop Native Files

QuarkXPress 6.5 introduced the PSD Import XTension, which provides support for many of the features of Adobe Photoshop's native format. The PSD Import XTension honors layers, channels, and paths without requiring you to flatten layered files. Provided the Photoshop file doesn't contain transparency on the bottom layer or layer effects such as embossing or drop shadows, the XTension allows you to selectively hide or reveal Photoshop layers. You can even control the opacity and blending mode of individual layers without launching Photoshop. However, as you might expect, QuarkXPress 5.0 has no idea what to do with a Photoshop native file. By the way, users of QuarkXPress 6.0 and 6.1 will have the same difficulty, since the PSD Import XTension works only in version 6.5 and above. The 6.5 upgrade is free for users of versions 6.0 and 6.1.

If you want the advantages of native Photoshop files, but need compatibility with earlier versions of QuarkXPress, save layered images as TIFF files. Like PSD files, TIFF files can contain layers and internal transparency, but they're palatable to QuarkXPress 5.0 and above. However, note that any transparency on the bottom layer of the image will *not* be honored by QuarkXPress: The background of the image will appear opaque white when placed in a page layout.

QuarkVista™ Picture Effects

QuarkXPress 6.5 introduced the QuarkVista XTension, which enables you to apply Photoshop-like effects such as color corrections, unsharp masking, and special-effects filters to images within a layout. The original image remains unchanged, and the effects are only rendered when the layout is exported or printed. Like the PSD Import XTension, QuarkVista is present only in QuarkXPress 6.5. Consequently, Vista Picture Effects will evaporate when you save for version 5.0 or 6.0 (**Figure 13.1**).

Figure 13.1 You're warned that QuarkVista Picture Effects will be lost when you attempt to save from QuarkXPress version 6.5 to version 5.0 *(left)*. The error message in QuarkXPress 6.0 is rather demure *(right)*, but the translation is "all your fancy effects are gone."

Fortunately, there's a built-in solution for this dilemma. During Collect for Output (File > Collect for Output), the Vista tab in the dialog box provides the option to render picture alterations (**Figure 13.2**). Rendering QuarkVista effects creates new, finished images with the Vista effects applied.

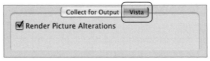

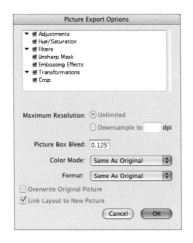

Figure 13.2 Picture Effects created by QuarkVista can translated into finished images during a Collect for Output by clicking the Vista button (above). You're presented with export options (left), including the opportunity to change color mode and image format.

This allows you to share files with users of QuarkXPress 6.0. It's also the first of two steps necessary to save Vista content for QuarkXPress 5.0 users. First, collect for output and click the Vista button. Then select the option to render picture alterations. Then, open the collected QuarkXPress 6.5 file (which is now linked to rendered image content) and save it to QuarkXPress 5.0.

You'd think that it's such a short jaunt from QuarkXPress 6.5 back to QuarkXPress 6.0 that there wouldn't be anything to worry about. Actually, provided you have no content in a QuarkXPress 6.5 file that couldn't have been created by QuarkXPress 6.0, it's an uneventful round trip. It's only the exotic features such as native Photoshop files and QuarkVista content that require special handling.

GENERAL QUARKXPRESS CAUTIONS

Regardless of the version of QuarkXPress you're using, there are some time-honored cautions that apply. Like all software, QuarkXPress provides, at no additional charge, easy ways to get yourself into trouble.

Beware the B*I*OS

The Measurements palette (Window > Show Measurements) offers some quick and easy controls for text. The text styling buttons—*B, I, O, S*—allow you to artificially embolden or italicize text, create stroked outlines, or add cheesy drop shadows (**Figure 13.3**). But the results are not always what you intended.

Figure 13.3 The B, I, O, and S buttons in the Measurements palette should be used with caution.

When you select text and then click the *B* button, QuarkXPress chooses the bold version of the applied font—if it's available. If it's not available, the text is plumped up, creating a faux bold. For example, if the text uses Times, QuarkXPress changes it to Times Bold. But if the text starts as Impact, clicking the *B* button produces fatter text on screen but not truly bold text, since there is no such font as Impact Bold. While the text might look more plump on your monitor, the best you can hope for during output is plain old Impact, which may result in changes in text spacing. But if the RIP substitutes another font—such as Courier—for the imaginary Impact Bold, the appearance of your text will be a disappointment (**Figure 13.4**).

BOLD, *ITALIC* **BOLD ITALIC**	BOLD, *ITALIC* **BOLD ITALIC**	Bold, Italic Bold Italic

Figure 13.4 Text styling in the Measurements palette produces mixed results. While the faux bold looks promising in the QuarkXPress layout (left), it won't image as bold text (center). And there's a possibility that the RIP will perform a type substitution, which often results in the replacement of your text with Courier (right).

By the way, this is why you might be advised to warn the print service provider if you're *intentionally* using Courier, lest it be mistaken for an output problem.

On the Macintosh, the correct approach is to avoid the *B* button and choose a bold or italic font from the font list available in the Measurements palette. On Windows, the list shows only the font family name, which means that the *B* button is the only way to choose a bold font. So it's necessary to know what fonts you've activated on a PC to know whether the *B* button is a legitimate choice.

The *I* button invokes the italic version of a font if it's available on the system. If a true italic font cannot be found, QuarkXPress slants the type and slightly alters the horizontal scale. It's not as attractive as a genuine italic font, but it's serviceable. As with the B button, Macintosh users should traverse the complete font list and select the correct italic font, whereas Windows users must use the I button to select active italic fonts.

The *O* button on the Measurements palette places a 0.25 point stroke on the edge of letter-forms and leaves the interior with a fill of None. While the outline effect may print satisfactorily on your desktop printer, some older RIPs can't trap such text, and some RIPs reject such jobs outright and cannot process them. There is no method for specifying a different weight for the stroke. You're stuck with the .25-point thickness. If you want better-behaved outlined text, plus control over the stroke weight, select the text box and convert the text to outlines (Style > Text to Box), then adjust the stroke weight by using the frame settings (Item > Frame). Note that framing outlined text deforms the letter's shape, since the stroke grows inward. Kerning and tracking may also be altered as a result of converting the text to outlines. To convert only *some* of the text in the box to outlines, select the Content tool () and highlight only that text, and then hold down the Option (Mac) or Alt (PC) key while you choose Style > Text to Box. The text will become polygon boxes, anchored in the flow of text. You can then fill and stroke the polygons as you would any other shape in QuarkXPress. Because the polygon shapes are anchored in the text, they will still flow with the surrounding text.

The *S* button creates a drop shadow composed of 20-percent black for selected text (**Figure 13.5**). You can't control the shadow's offset from the text, nor can you specify a different color or strength for the shadow. Such shadows are not set to overprint, so they don't interact correctly with objects beneath them in the page.

It's safer to skip the Shadow button, and just make your text shadows the old-fashioned way. Duplicate the text frame, move it a bit, apply a color to the text, and then send the new text box to the bottom of the stacking order. It's not the painless fun of clicking a button, but you'll have more control over the appearance and position of the shadow. In QuarkXPress 7.0, you can apply realistic shadows to all the text in a box with the Drop Shadow controls.

Figure 13.5 Text shadows created through the Measurements palette are 20 percent black, which is fine on a white background. But the shadows don't correctly interact with objects underneath, which can result in a lightened area instead of a shadow (right).

Graphics

QuarkXPress allows you some leeway in importing graphics, but some methods produce unsatisfactory results. Why, you're asking, does it allow this? All software contains "just because you *can* doesn't mean you *should*" features. It's just one of the enduring, entertaining mysteries of software.

No Pasting from the Clipboard

QuarkXPress will allow you to paste some Clipboard content into a selected picture box, but don't give in to the temptation. RGB image contents can be copied and pasted from Photoshop, but while the visual results might be initially satisfactory (depending on the zoom factor in effect at the time of copying), the pasted content has no link to the original file. Consequently, any change to the Photoshop file is not reflected in the contents of the QuarkXPress layout. Vector objects can be copied and pasted from Illustrator, but the results are choppy, as if a very high flatness setting had been used (**Figure 13.6**).

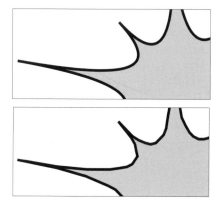

Figure 13.6 Importing vector artwork by selecting File > Get Picture (top) is the right way to go. Copy and pasting from Illustrator (bottom) may be quick and easy, but the results are ugly and there's no link to the original artwork.

Clipping Paths

If it seems too easy, it's probably wrong. It's true in life, and perhaps equally true when dealing with clipping paths. QuarkXPress offers several clipping options (available under Item > Clipping), one of which isn't appropriate for commercial applications. That would be the Non-White Areas option, which uses a density threshold to erode the white background of an image, generating a rough clipping path at the boundary (**Figure 13.7**). It chews away at the edge of an image on a light background, stopping when it hits darker pixels that meet the threshold setting you choose.

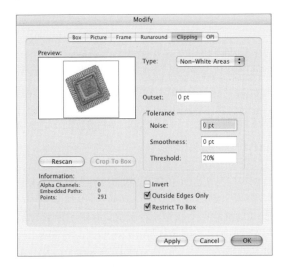

Figure 13.7 The Clipping dialog box includes several options. Don't use *this* one, Non-White Areas. The results are rough, and unacceptable for most images.

Since the path is generated by following the rectangular edges of pixels, and then averaged, it's rough and inexact, and produces an unprofessional silhouette (**Figure 13.8**). You'll achieve much the same lousy result by making a Magic Wand selection in Photoshop, and then converting the selection to a path. Don't do *that*, either!

Figure 13.8 The Non-White Areas option produces rough-edged silhouettes (left). It's preferable to bite the bullet (or the Pen tool) and create a vector path in Photoshop (right).

So, while you may consider it a painful, character-strengthening, tool, the Pen tool in Photoshop is still the most professional way to create a path. And once you get comfortable creating paths, it's helpful to know that multiple paths in an image can provide some interesting flexibility for images imported into QuarkXPress.

QuarkXPress doesn't limit you to using just one path. When you select the Embedded Path option in the Clipping dialog (available by choosing Item > Clipping or choosing Item > Modify and clicking the Clipping button at the top of the dialog), you'll see a list of paths available in the image (**Figure 13.9**). Provided that none of the paths is earmarked as a clipping path by Photoshop, you can pick whichever path you prefer in the QuarkXPress Clipping dialog. This offers the advantage of allowing multiple uses of the image without having to save multiple copies of the image on disk.

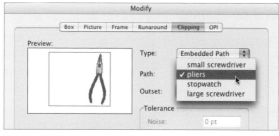

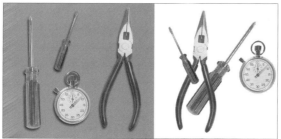

Figure 13.9 The Clipping options are available under Clipping in the Modify dialog (Item > Modify). Alternatively, you can reach it directly by choosing Item > Clipping.

When you select the Embedded Path option (top) you can select from multiple saved paths within a Photoshop file. An image with a separate path for each object (bottom) can be imported multiple times and the components positioned as necessary in the layout. By selecting a different Photoshop path in each case, you can display different parts of the image. The advantage? There's no need to save multiple versions of the image.

The multiple path trick works with TIFF, EPS, and PSD files as long as you follow some simple rules. It's important to note that these paths must be named, saved paths in Photoshop. Temporary, unofficial paths—those labeled *Work Path* in the Photoshop Paths palette—aren't recognized.

If the file contains paths that have been designated as official clipping paths through Photoshop's Paths palette menu, *and* the image has been saved as an EPS, the official clipping path trumps all other paths. In this situation, you don't have the option to select any other paths in the image through the Clipping dialog—you're stuck with the clipping path specified in Photoshop. Thus, if you want maximum flexibility, create multiple paths, but *don't* designate any of them to be an official clipping path. Just let them be plain old, free-range paths.

Portable Document Format Files (PDFs) as Artwork

Most supplied artwork will come to you as TIFF, PSD, or EPS files. However, if you're creating components such as advertising pages, you may receive ads submitted as PDF files. While the *P* in PDF stands for *portable*, some aspects of the file may not survive the import into QuarkXPress. In versions of QuarkXPress prior to version 6.0, for example, spot-color content in PDF files was converted to process color. Version 6.0 and later correctly honors spot-color content in PDF files.

PDF files compatible with Acrobat 4.0 (PDF version 1.3) should be reliable, whereas later-model PDFs such as those compatible with Acrobat 5.0 can contain live transparency, which is flattening during import into QuarkXPress. While the internal appearance of the PDF is retained, it is opaque to objects underneath. And even some Acrobat 4.0 files can be problematic, depending on the originating application's adherence to PDF standards.

Communicate with clients who supply you with PDF files, and gently request that they follow some guidelines:

- Create Acrobat 4.0-compatible PDF files.

- Embed all fonts. If their fonts prohibit embedding, change to another font that allows embedding.

- Convert spot colors to process if they're intended to print as process to prevent unintended spot-color output.

- Ensure that any necessary bleed is present in the finished PDF file they submit.

Do make sure that you have the most current version of the PDF Filter XTension, available from Quark's Web site.

Even if the PDF files you import are perfect, there's some risk of impairing the embedded fonts with incorrect subsequent handling. For example, if you place multiple PDF files in a page, then generate a PostScript file from that page and use Acrobat Distiller to make a new PDF that's then placed in another document, which is exported to PDF…well, it's sort of like those charming Russian nesting dolls. If one of those steps fails to maintain font embedding, the result can be dropped characters in the final output.

If this workflow (and this outcome) sounds familiar, consider asking your clients to submit their artwork as EPS files with text converted to outlines. If there aren't any fonts, there's no risk of wrecking the embedding. It's a bit cheesy and old-fashioned, but it works. The methods for outlining text vary by application, so consult the documentation for the application.

Specifying Colors

A new QuarkXPress document presents you with a Colors palette (Window > Show Colors) containing a fairly simple box of crayons, including cyan, magenta, yellow, and black (**Figure 13.10**). Prior to QuarkXPress 7.0, the red, green, and blue colors were specified as RGB builds, which were festive in the palette but converted to duller CMYK versions during output. QuarkXPress 7.0 deals with this issue by omitting these colors. The *None* color listed in the Colors palette is like clear plastic, whereas *White* signifies "this is empty paper; no ink prints here," as in most graphics programs. *Registration* is a special color that images on all output plates. It's intended for use by the application to print crop and registration marks—hence the name. Don't mistake Registration for a rich black. You should never use it within a page, unless you're manually creating crop marks within the page limits (in which case you're probably building your page the wrong size).

Figure 13.10 The Colors palette provides a basic starting set of colors. It's not obvious, but the Red, Green, and Blue colors are specified as RGB builds. They will be converted to CMYK at some point in the printing process, becoming duller than their onscreen appearance in QuarkXPress.

QuarkXPress allows you to pick from the standard assortment of digital swatchbooks, including Pantone, Toyo, and TRUMATCH. In addition, you can create *multi-ink* colors, which are combinations of spot colors, or combinations of spot and process colors (**Figure 13.11**). You can also create multi-ink colors that are only combinations of process colors, although that's sort of overkill.

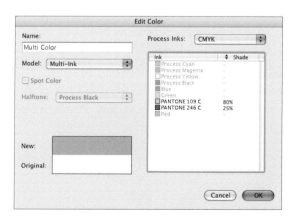

Figure 13.11 Multi-ink colors are a combination of spot colors (or spot and process colors). They may require special handling during output depending on your version of QuarkXPress.

Up through version 6.0 of QuarkXPress, Multi-Ink colors presented a challenge when imaging, producing the intended spot-colors only when printed as separations. Consequently, PDF files exported from QuarkXPress did not contain the correct colors. QuarkXPress 6.0 rectified this by introducing the option to use *DeviceN*, which maintains spot-color definitions even when generating composite output during print or export (**Figure 13.12**).

Figure 13.12 QuarkXPress 6.0 and above allows you to specify DeviceN as the output color space, which maintains spot-color and multi-ink content correctly during printing and output.

If you're using Multi-Ink colors, mention that in your communications with the print service provider so they'll be prepared, especially if you're not using QuarkXPress 6.5.

Creating PDF Files

Through version 5.0, QuarkXPress could only generate PDF files if you had installed Adobe Acrobat, which includes Acrobat Distiller. If you only had the free Adobe Reader, you wouldn't have this capability. Although the PDF export feature was accessed either through Utilities > Export as PDF (QuarkXPress 4.0) or File > Export to PDF (QuarkXPress 5.0), QuarkXPress was actually generating PostScript and then launching Distiller without user intervention and prompting the generation of a PDF.

With the release of QuarkXPress 6.0, Quark collaborated with Global Graphics to provide PDF creation without Acrobat Distiller. It's invisible to the user, but QuarkXPress generates PostScript, which is silently processed by Global Graphics' Jaws PostScript interpreter, which is part of the QuarkXPress 6.0 through 7.0 installation.

If you're asked to provide PDF files, ask for detailed specifications for generating PDFs. If the recipient fails to provide specs, you're safe creating a PDF that meets the PDF/X-1a specification. Unfortunately, QuarkXPress prior to version 7.0 does not provide a one-button PDF/X-1a setting, but here are the important parts of the PDF/X-1a requirements:

- Content must be CMYK and/or spot (no RGB). Version 7.0 converts any RGB content to CMYK on the fly during export to a PDF/X-1a file.

- Fonts must be embedded and subset. While embedding fonts places an entire font in a PDF file, subsetting embeds only the characters used in the PDF file.

- The MediaBox, and *either* TrimBox or ArtBox must be defined by the originating application. BleedBox is optional, but desirable. These aren't settings you can control in most applications. The application developers must build in the ability to define these limits in outgoing PDF files.

  MediaBox corresponds to the paper size necessary to contain all the elements (art, cropmarks, and so on).

  BleedBox corresponds to the exterior edge of the bleed.

  TrimBox corresponds to the final intended trim size of the piece (usually the original document page size, such as 8.5 by 11 inches).

  ArtBox corresponds to the bounding box for artwork.

You can use the great new Job Jacket option in QuarkXPress 7.0 to check for inappropriate image resolution.

You may find it odd that the PDF/X-1a specification does not include a stipulation for minimum image resolution, but that's the case. Understandably, this doesn't relieve you of the obligation to ensure that image content is of sufficient resolution. But you're on your own there. If you've imported images of a healthy resolution, and choose an appropriate resolution setting in the PDF export options, the resulting PDF will be satisfactory. Usually, it's appropriate to use an image resolution of 170–200 ppi for newspaper work, and a resolution of 300 ppi for other work.

There are several methods for generating PDF files, which are described in the following sections.

Export to PDF: QuarkXPress 5.0

If you're still using QuarkXPress 5.0, you're dependent on Acrobat Distiller to generate your PDFs. By default, QuarkXPress uses the settings last used by Distiller, but you can exert remote control over Distiller's behavior by overriding options from within QuarkXPress. In the Export as PDF dialog (File > Export > Document as PDF), click the Options button. Then, in the dialog that follows, click the Job Options tab to display the dialog shown in **Figure 13.13**.

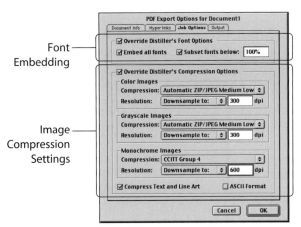

Font Embedding

Image Compression Settings

Figure 13.13 QuarkXPress 5.0 allows you to override Distiller's last settings. Note that the Compression settings refer to the *amount* of compression, not the quality. Lower settings mean lower *compression* and thus higher *quality*. The 100-percent font subsetting threshold ensures that all fonts are fully subset. Subsetting embeds the characters required by the PDF and gives the font a unique name to prevent font substitution during output.

If you've ever used Distiller, the Job Options tab in QuarkXPress looks a bit familiar, but the image compression settings may seem backwards from those in Distiller. Whereas *Low* in Distiller means low *quality*, in QuarkXPress it means low *compression*—high *quality*. Subsetting fonts ensures that subsequent processes will use the font information embedded in the PDF rather than using fonts available on the RIP, since subset fonts are given unique internal identifiers. Setting the threshold to 100 percent forces all fonts to be subset. Since QuarkXPress generates PostScript as part of the PDF creation process, it needs a target printer. Always choose Distiller as the target printer unless you're instructed by your print service provider to use a specialized vendor target (**Figure 13.14**). Using a real world printer as a target limits the page size and resolution choices, whereas the Distiller target printer creates healthy PostScript with a size limit of 200 by 200 inches.

Figure 13.14 Always choose Acrobat Distiller as the target printer in Output options. Don't forget to specify bleed.

Export to PDF: QuarkXPress 6.0 Through 6.5

Since QuarkXPress 6.0 and above do not rely on Acrobat Distiller, it's important to specify the correct PDF creation settings within QuarkXPress. If you set PDF preferences with no document open, you've paved the way for all future documents (**Figure 13.15**). Once you have a document open, choose File > Export > Layout as PDF to export a PDF. If there are multiple layouts in a project, you must export each layout to PDF separately. There's no provision for automatically exporting multiple layouts in a project to PDF.

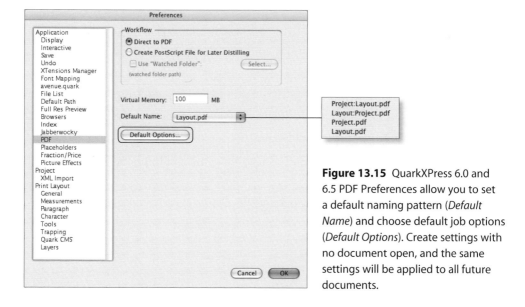

Figure 13.15 QuarkXPress 6.0 and 6.5 PDF Preferences allow you to set a default naming pattern (*Default Name*) and choose default job options (*Default Options*). Create settings with no document open, and the same settings will be applied to all future documents.

There's no need (or opportunity) to specify a target printer. Behind the scenes, QuarkXPress generates PostScript and invokes the built-in PDF creation process using whatever settings you've requested. Note that you're limited to creating only Acrobat 4.0-compatible PDF files through the direct export. There's no way to specify an earlier or later version of PDF. But that's not necessarily bad news. Acrobat 4.0-compatible PDF files are the most widely supported flavor of PDF.

Print to Distiller/PDF Printer (QuarkXPress 5.0 and Above)

If you want more granular control over PDF creation, or if you encounter problems trying to use the PDF export features in QuarkXPress (such as a complex layout that fails to export to PDF), one solution is to print to the Acrobat printer. Think of it as an imaginary printing device that spits out PDF files rather than paper. To use this option, you must have Acrobat Distiller as part of an Acrobat Standard or Professional installation: The free Adobe Reader does not include Distiller.

1. Choose File > Print.

2. Under Setup, choose the appropriate PDF target from the Printer Description menu. Depending on your installed version of Acrobat, you may see Acrobat Distiller, Adobe PDF, or Adobe PDF 7.0.

3. Under Setup, choose the correct page size. Make sure that the page size is large enough to include any printer marks.

4. Click the Printer button, and then click OK to dismiss the subsequent alert.

5. Choose Adobe PDF from the Printer menu, and then switch from Copies & Pages (initial drop-down menu) to PDF Options. For Adobe PDF Settings, select the correct setting for your job. (The available settings depend on the settings that have been previously created in Distiller).

6. Click the Print button, then specify a filename and location. Click Save in the subsequent dialog.

7. Click Print in the Quark XPress print dialog box.

8. Take a deep breath. That's a lot of work. It's much easier and more relaxing to just use File > Export.

Print to PostScript, Distill Manually

To use this option, you must have installed Acrobat Distiller. Choose File > Print, set Acrobat Distiller or Adobe PDF as your target printer, and then save the result as a PostScript file. Then launch Acrobat Distiller, choose the appropriate job option, and Distill to create the PDF file.

Why might you choose this long way around? If you must supply PDF/X-1a files, as many publications require, generating PostScript allows you to use the dedicated PDF/X-1a Distiller setting (available as one of Distiller's default job options) to ensure that you are creating fully compliant files. And the Image Policy option available under the Image controls in Distiller 7.0 allows you filter out images below a user-specified resolution (see Chapter 14, *Acrobat Production Tips*). However, you must be mindful of Distiller licensing restrictions: Under a single-seat Distiller license, you are not allowed to use Distiller to process PostScript files for colleagues who don't have a licensed copy of Distiller. If everyone has a license for Distiller, then go ahead and make some poor intern do all your Distilling.

Save as PDF

Under Macintosh OS X, there are some built-in PDF creation and PDF viewing capabilities, but the operating system doesn't utilize the Adobe engine to create PDFs. (It does use an older version of Adobe's Normalizer to enable the Preview application to view PostScript as PDF.) And unless you dig very deeply into some arcane preferences, you can't specify settings appropriate for commercial printing purposes. The Save As PDF option available in the Print dialog box of all applications activates the system PDF creation, but since the controls for PDF creation are not readily found, it's best to avoid this method if you're creating PDFs for print (**Figure 13.16**).

 **Figure 13.16** The Macintosh system PDF creation tool may not be appropriate for commercial print.

Collect for Output

Despite the increasing use of PDF files for job submission, you're often still required to gather up all the pieces of your job and submit them in their original form. Fortunately, QuarkXPress offers the capability to collect most of the pieces.

Create a new folder to hold all the parts, then choose File > Collect for Output to set things in motion (**Figure 13.17**).

Figure 13.17 The Collect for Output feature in QuarkXPress gathers up all the necessary pieces… in most cases.

QuarkXPress 6.0 and 6.5 collect the pieces for each individual *layout* in a project. In a project containing multiple layouts, you'll have to collect each layout separately. It's helpful to know what a Collect for Output snares:

- The QuarkXPress layout

- Graphics linked to the document

- Screen and printer fonts used in the document (be sure to check those options in the Collect for Output dialog)

- Fonts used in placed vector artwork, even though they're not listed under Utilities > Usage > Fonts

But, while the Collect for Output dialog in QuarkXPress versions up through 6.5 offers a check box for embedded pictures—content that has been pasted from the Clipboard into a picture box—it doesn't actually collect those images as externally available files in the Pictures folder created by Collect for Output. Let this be another inspiration to not paste content into QuarkXPress. While it does output correctly, there's no way to edit the content if it requires color correction or retouching. This has been remedied in

QuarkXPress 7.0, but it's preferable to import graphics the old fashioned way, by selecting a picture box and choosing File > Get Picture.

There's no reason to manually gather your job files since Collect for Output does all the work for you. There's no excuse for submitting a job with missing fonts or images. Don't try to tell me the dog ate your fonts…

QuarkXPress 7.0

With the release of version 7.0, it's likely that many QuarkXPress users who have been comfortably entrenched in older versions will be inspired to upgrade. QuarkXPress 7.0 provides major enhancements to many features, and adds new capabilities that have the potential to change the way designers work.

New Features

Many of the cautions in the preceding sections still apply, although QuarkXPress 7.0 does collect pasted image content, which is a great improvement. Pasted images are described as PICT files in the Picture Usage dialog, but a Collect for Output will do the right thing by collecting the actual image content, and will provide an external image file.

The changes most likely to affect you are some radically new additions to the QuarkXPress arsenal of features:

- **Single Layout Mode** allows you to create projects that more closely resemble documents created in QuarkXPress 4.0 and 5.0, since they lack the tabbed interface used by the multilayout projects that debuted in QuarkXPress 6.0. For users who are leapfrogging from version 4.0 or 5.0, this may ease the transition.

- **Shared Layouts** allow a *layout* to belong to multiple *projects*. For example, a business card layout could belong to multiple projects for business collateral. Change the content of that business card layout, and all the instances of that layout within other projects will change, in much the same way that a color-corrected image could be updated in multiple pages. This has potential to streamline workflow—but also to cause problems if you fail to note that alterations within a layout will have repercussions in a totally separate project. Oops.

- **Composition Zones** enable multiple users to share an area within a layout. For example, multiple designers can be simultaneously creating ads for an advertising section of a magazine. The originator of the document can earmark areas of the document as shared Composition Zones. Each collaborator works on a designated Composition Zone, and the content of that zone is updated in the finished document when they're finished, without old-fashioned cut and paste. Since the relationship between a project and externally-stored Composition Zones is much like the relationship with imported images, you must remember to update edited Composition Zone content. However, QuarkXPress 7.0 does not warn you that externally-stored Composition Zone content has been modified when you open a project, nor does it squawk when you export or print the project. You must remember to check the status of Composition Zone content by choosing Utilities > Usage, and then selecting the Composition Zone option. You can then update content by selecting a modified Composition Zone in the list and clicking the Update button. Since there is no automatic warning about Composition Zone content, you should make it a habit to check the Usage listing before exporting or printing a project containing Composition Zones, unless you have set the collaboration preferences for the project to automatically update content.

- **Quark Job Jackets** can ensure that a group is basing its work on the same set of colors, style sheets, fonts—even color profiles. The information governing a job jacket is stored in a *job ticket* based on Job Definition Format (JDF) standards, an open and increasingly supported standard to facilitate job requirement tracking. In addition to providing information about job requirements to guide content creators, job tickets can be used to validate that a layout or project is playing by the rules. This is especially helpful in template-driven workflows.

- **PDF/X-1a and PDF/X-3** support is built in, allowing you to create PDF files that are in compliance with those industry standards. QuarkXPress 7.0 adds the option to export Acrobat 5.0-compatible PDF files but does not allow live transparency in exported PDFs even though Acrobat 5.0 supports unflattened transparency.

- **OpenType** support allows you to enjoy the full wonderland of typographic features offered by OpenType fonts, including cross-platform compatibility, discretionary ligatures, swashes, and contextual alternate characters. See Chapter 6, "Fonts," for more information on OpenType features.

- **Transparency** can now be applied to any element in a QuarkXPress 7.0 layout. QuarkXPress 7.0 allows you to apply separate transparency settings to a box, the text inside the box, and a border on the box. You can even apply different transparency settings to individual letters in a text box. Drop shadows can be applied as live effects to any object. While transparency effects greatly expand your creative possibilities, they can be challenging to image, especially if spot colors are involved. Be prepared for a bit of a learning curve and some friendly conversations with your print service provider. Transparency options in QuarkXPress 7.0 are confined to opacity settings. There are no Photoshop-like blending mode attributes, with the exception of drop shadows, which can be set to multiply with underlying objects for realistic darkening. When you export PDF files from QuarkXPress 7.0, note that the Transparency Flattener Resolution value governs the resolution of drop shadows you've created in your layout. The default setting of 300 works for most situations, so you should be fine leaving it as it is.

- **Drop Shadows** can be attached to any object. Since drop shadows are live effects, the position, color and softness of a shadow can be edited at any time. The resolution of drop shadows is governed by the Transparency option setting which is invoked during print or export. The default setting is 300 ppi, which is appropriate for most circumstances.

Improved Support for Photoshop Native Images

QuarkXPress 7.0 offers enhanced support for native, layered Adobe Photoshop files (PSD). Opacity settings in a PSD are honored by QuarkXPress 7.0, allowing you to place layered images with soft-edged layer masks and achieve interesting effects in your page layout. However, Photoshop blending modes such as Multiply are not honored by QuarkXPress. Consequently, any drop shadow effects created in Photoshop will not image correctly from QuarkXPress. Photoshop shadows will knock out underlying objects in your page layout, rather than darkening those objects. For correct shadows, you should create the shadow with the Drop Shadow feature in QuarkXPress 7.0 (Item > Drop Shadow).

While Photoshop will allow vector and text content, such content will be rasterized (rendered as pixels rather than vectors) when imported into a QuarkXPress page, softening the crisp edges. But you still have the advantages offered by maintaining a layered image file. There's no need to flatten a PSD before placing it in a page layout, which means that you no longer have to maintain separate flattened and layered files. But perhaps the most important aspect of layered Photoshop files is the ability to silhouette images with soft, realistic edges rather than the hard, artificial knockout effect of a clipping path.

Exporting PDF Files from QuarkXPress 7.0

The PDF export features of QuarkXPress 7.0 improve on the capabilities of previous versions. The Jaws PDF creation engine is still used, but adds the ability to modify and save custom presets rather than requiring you to set options each time you export to PDF. Most importantly, there are now preset PDF/X-1a and PDF/X-3 options. If a print service provider requests PDF files, but doesn't give you any specifications for creating PDF files, use the PDF/X-1a preset. Choose File > Export Layout as PDF to select one of the PDF/X presets, or to create your own PDF style for future use (**Figure 13.18**).

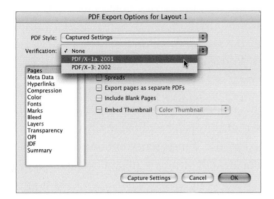

Figure 13.18 The PDF Export options in QuarkXPress 7.0 include presets for PDF/X-1a and PDF/X-3. You can also create and save your own PDF styles.

The default setting for exported PDF files is Acrobat 5.0 compatibility, and there are no visible options for controlling the compatibility setting. If you choose one of the PDF/X presets, compatibility is appropriately set to Acrobat 4.0 in keeping with the PDF/X specification. The choices in the Color options are fairly obvious, although it's worth explaining the difference between *As Is* and *Composite CMYK and Spot*. *As Is* keeps any RGB content as RGB, whereas *Composite CMYK and Spot* converts RGB content to CMYK while maintaining any spot color content (**Figure 13.19**).

Figure 13.19 Your Color Setup choice depends on the type of content in your QuarkXPress document. The *As Is* option prevents the conversion of RGB content to CMYK.

TROUBLESHOOTING

Files that are frequently reopened, reworked, and resaved are susceptible to corruption. Symptoms of corruption include refusal to print or frequent crashes.

If you can't even *open* the QuarkXPress file, things are indeed dire. If you're using QuarkXPress 5.0 or earlier, invest in MarkzTools from Markzware, which can often resurrect seemingly doomed files. Unfortunately, it's not compatible with later versions of QuarkXPress. You may be able to extract some of the text if you open the damaged file in a text editor such as TextWrangler or BBEdit on the Mac, or TextPad on Windows, but remaining layout information will be lost.

What a Drag

If you *can* open the problem file, transplanting its pages into a new, healthy document with Thumbnail Drag *may* cheer it up, although there's no guarantee. To perform a Thumbnail Drag, create a new document of the same dimensions as the problem file. Position the documents side-by-side on your monitor, then place each document in Thumbnail view (View > Thumbnails). Select the pages you wish to move from the bad document (shift-click for multiple pages), then hold down your mouse button and drag the thumbnails on top of the new document (**Figure 13.20**). The first page of the destination document can then be deleted, leaving your old pages in a new environment. In version 6.0 and later, try creating a new project and then using the Append Layout feature (File > Append). Append the layouts from the damaged project. This process may clear up the problem.

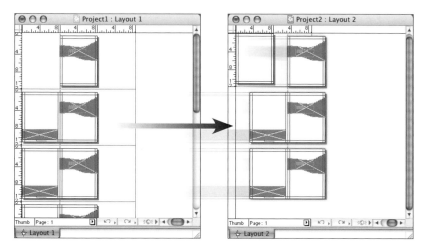

Figure 13.20 Select pages in Thumbnail view, and then drag to a new document of the same dimensions. This may cure a sick document.

Divide and Conquer

If a thumbnail drag doesn't cure the problem file, you'll need to isolate the content that's causing the crashing or failure to print or export. The culprit could be a corrupt font, a corrupt image—or even a corrupt preview proxy for an image.

First, try a simple File > Save As under a new name for the file. Sometimes that's enough to shuffle things back into place. If that fails (hey, it was worth a shot!), tackle the two most likely villains—fonts and graphics.

Try to isolate the problem: Can you print up through page six, but then it caves? Suspect something on page seven. Try to print page seven. If it crashes, you're on the trail. Make a copy of the file, then start doing exploratory surgery.

Delete all the text boxes on the problem page. If it still won't print, delete half the picture boxes. If it prints, you know the problem is somewhere in the bunch of picture boxes you deleted. Revert to the saved copy of the file, and then delete just one quarter of the picture boxes. Won't print? Then you know the culprit is still on the page. Keep winnowing until you identify the bad boy.

Once you've isolated the graphic, open it in the originating application, select all its contents, and copy and paste it into a fresh new file. Save that file under a new name and import it into QuarkXPress. Test to see if it behaves. If so, go back to your original document, and replace that graphic with the new, improved version. Test to see if it's cured.

If deleting the text boxes enabled you to print, it's likely that the problem is a corrupt font. Try changing the text to another font. If this works, you've found the problem. Either substitute a font that's similar to the problem font, or reinstall the font from the vendor's original disk that's buried somewhere in the archaeological site that is your Old Disk burial ground.

CHAPTER FOURTEEN

Acrobat Production Tips

In 1991, Dr. John Warnock, one of the cofounders of Adobe Systems, proposed Project Camelot, in which he suggested using the graphics and imaging operators of PostScript to create portable documents that could be displayed and printed on any computer, regardless of the originating application. These documents would contain all the resources necessary to represent the original document for display and printing. Images and vector art would be crisp. Regardless of operating system or computer platform, fonts would be embedded, ensuring that text would be readable and line breaks would be preserved—even if recipients didn't have the same fonts as the document's creator. Sound familiar?

Thus, what came to be known as Adobe Acrobat was intended to create what might be called digital carbon copies for office document interchange and storage. But a funny thing happened in the graphic arts world. We discovered that converting stubborn documents to Portable Document Format (PDF) files often enabled us to salvage nightmare jobs. For example, while Microsoft Word allows you to add festive clip art and other decorative bits such as Word Art to documents, it's really intended for word processing. Turning a Word file into something suitable for printing in two spot colors might require that you generate a PDF, then open that PDF in Adobe Acrobat Professional and use the PitStop plug-in from Enfocus to deconstruct the artwork, fix the things that fell apart during the conversion, and then assign the correct printing colors. It may seem like the long way around, but at least you'd have something that could be printed as intended.

Fast-forward to current day. Many publications and print service providers request that you submit your jobs as PDF files to eliminate the need to send a combination of page-layout files, support artwork files, and the necessary fonts. While this simplifies job submission, it also shifts the responsibility for more of the job's quality control to the shoulders of the person making the PDF file. That would be *you*.

ACROBAT PRODUCT LINE

Currently the Acrobat family consists of five products, each having a specific target audience:

- **Acrobat 7.0 Professional** provides extensive tools for creating PDF files from images, text files, Microsoft Office files, and Web pages. When you install Acrobat 7.0 Professional, it adds PDF export functionality to Microsoft Office applications, so you can create PDF files from within an open Microsoft Word file, for example, Acrobat 7.0 Professional also offers dedicated tools for modifying PDF files for a wide range of industries from graphics to architecture. Acrobat 7.0 Professional offers a set of print-production tools that make it worth upgrading from previous versions of Acrobat. It's the most popular and widely used version of Acrobat. The product consists of two applications: Acrobat itself, which displays and manipulates PDFs, and Acrobat Distiller, which converts PostScript to PDFs.

- **Acrobat 7.0 Standard** is focused on creating PDFs from office applications. Consequently, it lacks the print-oriented preflighting and repair tools found in the professional product, although it does allow users to participate in comment and review processes. Acrobat Standard also consists of the Acrobat application (Standard version) and Acrobat Distiller.

- **Acrobat 3D** (available for Windows only) is the newest Acrobat offering, intended for engineering users. It provides specialized tools for creating PDF files from CAD programs as well as the editing and commenting tools available in the professional version. When you install Acrobat 3D, it adds PDF export functionality to 3D applications such as SolidWorks. Even if you don't own a CAD program, Acrobat 3D supports drag-and-drop PDF creation for many CAD files. If you already have Acrobat 3D and need the print-production features of Acrobat 7.0 Professional, you don't need to also purchase a copy of the professional product: Acrobat 3D has all the features of Acrobat 7.0 Professional, including Distiller, plus the whiz-bang, 3D functionality.

- **Acrobat 7.0 Elements** (Windows only) is for use in enterprise office environments. Elements enables the creation of PDFs from office applications but has no ability to modify PDFs. Elements is not a shrink-wrapped product. It's sold only in multiseat increments, with a minimum of 100 seats.

- **Adobe Reader 7.0** is the free PDF viewer. Previously, Reader users could do only what the name implies—read (and print) PDFs. But now they can participate in comment–and–review processes if a PDF has been rights enabled from within Acrobat 7.0 Professional.

Don't be confused by the growing Acrobat family. For those of us in the graphic arts who need to manipulate PDF files, the appropriate version to use is Acrobat 7.0 Professional.

WHERE DO PDFS COME FROM?

Acrobat isn't like drawing or page-layout applications. There are no paint brushes or pen tools, and there's no command for creating a new, blank PDF file. PDF files usually begin life somewhere else, outside of Acrobat. While Acrobat enables you to create PDFs from a scanner, an existing image, or a Web page, they're often exported from other applications such as Adobe InDesign or Illustrator. They may be the result of generating a PostScript file and feeding that to Distiller, or they may be created by some other proprietary process, such as the Global Graphics Jaws interpreter used by QuarkXPress 6.0 and later to process PostScript.

Although Adobe Systems originated the PDF concept and its specifications, *anyone* is allowed to use the information in the publicly available PDF Reference to write software that creates, reads, or edits PDF files. Given that the PDF Reference is in excess of 1000 pages, it's clearly not a trivial undertaking.

All PDF-creation solutions are not the same. Some third-party implementations of the PDF specifications, such as those used to generate PDF files from non-Adobe applications, may not fully utilize all the features possible in a PDF file. This is *not* to imply that non-Adobe methods of creating PDFs are inferior. On the contrary, some commonly used PDF creation tools, such as the Global Graphics Jaws Interpreter built into QuarkXPress 6.0 and later, create perfectly good PDF files. But non-Adobe applications may have slightly different controls or options, which makes it challenging to generalize about how, exactly, to go about making a PDF file. For that matter, not all Adobe applications use the same approach when making PDFs.

CREATING PDF FILES

The chapters on Illustrator, InDesign, QuarkXPress, FreeHand, and Adobe Photoshop have offered some suggested PDF-creation settings, but it may be helpful to consider what's important regardless of the tool you're using to create PDF files.

Determining Which Type of PDF You Should Create

A document consists of images, text, lines, and color areas on a page of a certain size. The purpose of creating a PDF is to retain all of these components of the document across multiple operating systems and to ensure that it can be printed as intended. It all sounds so simple, doesn't it? However, there isn't a single, one-size-fits-all recipe for creating PDF files. Broadly speaking, there are several types of PDF files you're likely to create.

- PDF files to be submitted to a print service provider should be generated from page–layout or drawing applications after carefully checking content and job requirements. Images need to be high resolution, which can result in large file sizes. Fonts must be embedded correctly, and it's important to properly define your colors as CMYK, color-managed RGB, or spot color. Think of this as a hermetically sealed, final job file, and don't count on editing it to perfection later.

- PDFs for e-mail (for example, for commenting and review) will require that you sacrifice image quality in the interest of smaller files, but font embedding must still be handled correctly to ensure accurate display and printing.

- PDF files that will be posted online need to be small enough for downloading, but documents such as product brochures or instructional manuals should contain enough image detail to make them satisfactory resources. You'll have to reach a compromise between desired image quality and reasonable file size. You might consider breaking larger documents into smaller files such as those that are chapter or topic based, and then hyperlink the files together to aid the end user in finding their way.

- PDF files intended for distribution on CD/DVD can be larger files since downloading isn't an issue, so you don't have to compromise image quality. You might even consider adding multimedia content and extensive hyperlinking to enrich the files. While such features take you beyond a purely print environment, you can easily start with print-ready PDF files, and bring them to life with Acrobat's built-in multimedia capabilities. For more on the lively possibilities of adding movies, sounds, and interactivity to PDFs, check out *Creating Rich Internet Media Publications* by Bob Connolly (Peachpit Press, 2006).

PDF Settings and Some Important Standards

The default PDF-creation settings that are part of Acrobat Distiller include a wide spectrum of starting points for generating PDF files (Table 14.1). Settings such as Standard, Smallest File Size, and Press Quality give some hint of what kind of PDF file they're intended to create. But what about settings such as PDF/X-1a and PDF/X-3? The names don't tell you much. Well, actually, they don't tell you anything. But the oddly named settings are based on standards intended to ensure that a PDF behaves as expected. The X in PDF/X-1a represents the x in exchange, signifying that a PDF complying with one of the PDF/X standards can be exchanged between the PDF's originating application and its recipient with some assurance the recipient will get a usable file.

Table 14.1 Acrobat comes with an assortment of PDF-creation settings available through Acrobat Distiller. Think of them as starting points.

Setting	PDF Version	Downsample/ Threshold[1]	Compression Image Quality	Color Policy	Font Policy[2]	Description
Smallest File Size	5.0	100/150	Low	Convert to sRGB	Subset: Warn & Continue	For on-screen display and e-mail: Converts all images to sRGB.
Standard	5.0	150/225	Med	Convert to sRGB	Embed+Subset: Warn & Continue	For viewing and printing business documents: Converts ALL images to sRGB.
High Quality Print	5.0	300/450	Max	Leave Unchanged	Embed+Subset: Warn & Continue	For viewing and printing design documents (RGB *not* converted to CMYK).
Press Quality	5.0	300/450	Max	Convert to CMYK	Embed+Subset: Cancel Job	For prepress: Converts RGB images to CMYK.
PDF/X-1a:2001	4.0	300/450	Max	Convert to CMYK	Embed+Subset: Cancel Job	For prepress. Converts RGB images to CMYK, defines TrimBox[3], BleedBox.[4]
PDF/X-3:2002	4.0	300/450	Max	Leave Unchanged	Embed+Subset: Cancel Job	Standards-based: For use in fully color-managed workflows.
PDF/A-1b:2005 (RGB)	5.0	300/450	Max	Convert to sRGB	Embed+Subset: Cancel Job	For archive: Standards-based. Converts all RGB & CMYK images to sRGB.
PDF/A-1b:2005 (CMYK)	5.0	300/450	Max	Convert to CMYK	Embed+Subset: Cancel Job	For archive: Standards-based. Converts all RGB images to CMYK.

[1]Downsampling reduces image resolution. Threshold is the resolution above which Distiller will downsample image content.
[2]Font Policy specifies what Distiller should do if it cannot embed a font.
[3]TrimBox is the trim edge of the document, based on the originating file.
[4]BleedBox is the limits of defined bleed, based on information in the originating file.

The Digital Distribution of Advertising for Publications (DDAP) association established requirements for print-ready PDFs for advertisement submission, which were then implemented by the Committee for Graphic Arts Technologies Standards (CGATS) as the basis of the PDF/X standards. (Was that enough acronyms for you?) With the constant increase in the numbers of PDF files submitted for advertising, the PDF/X standards are intended to streamline file submission.

The most commonly requested PDF format for print is PDF/X-1a. (The *2001* appellation you see in Acrobat 7.0 Professional is added because PDF/X is an evolving standard and this marks the 2001 definition of PDF/X-1a.) To comply with the PDF/X-1a specification, a PDF file must meet the following requirements:

- Images must be CMYK or spot color (no RGB or LAB images).

- Fonts must be embedded and subset. Subsetting embeds only the characters needed in the PDF file and assigns a special name to the font content so that an output device will not substitute another font for it.

- The trim edges of pages must be explicitly defined. Internally, a PDF file refers to this information as *TrimBox*.

- The bleed limits must be explicitly defined. Internally, this is called *BleedBox*.

The PDF/X-3 is a specification intended for use in a color-managed workflow. The stipulations are similar to those for PDF/X-1a, with the exception that image content can be RGB tagged with color profiles. Unless you and your print service provider are using color management, you're unlikely to be asked to submit PDF/X-3 files. And PDF/A-1b indicates an emerging PDF standard for archiving documents for reference long into the future. The *A* represents *archive*.

Cross-Platform Parity (or the Lack Thereof): An Acrobat Fact of Life

Acrobat implementations on Macintosh and Windows are not identical, and there is not complete feature parity between the platforms. The Windows version of Acrobat has much better integration with Microsoft products and also includes LiveCycle™ Designer for creating forms, which isn't available on Macintosh. PDF files themselves are platform-independent, however. There are even versions of Reader for Linux and mobile platforms such as Palm® OS, Pocket PC, and the Symbian OS.

Acrobat Distiller

Distiller isn't very flashy. When you launch the application, all that appears is a floating window that looks like a disembodied dialog box (**Figure 14.1**). There are no tool palettes or other obvious controls. But there's much more than meets the eye. Some of the menu commands are way up at the top of the monitor on the Macintosh in the standard location for menu commands in Macintosh applications, but they are seemingly completely separate from the floating window that you see. Distiller's presentation on Windows is a bit more sensible—the menu commands are right on the top rim of the Distiller window.

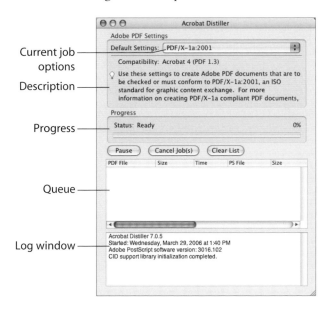

Current job options

Description

Progress

Queue

Log window

Figure 14.1 Acrobat Distiller may not look complicated when you open it, but there's a powerful PDF-generating engine under the hood. Select a preset PDF recipe from the Default Settings list, or create your own job options by choosing Settings > Edit Adobe PDF Settings from the menu at the top of your computer screen on the Macintosh (not shown here) or the top edge of the Distiller window (PC).

So what does Distiller do? Distiller's job in life is to convert PostScript to PDF. Period. To convert a PostScript file to a PDF file, you can just drag and drop the PostScript file onto the Distiller window. Distiller uses the settings currently selected in the application. You can also open a PostScript file through File > Open on the Distiller menu. Distiller will process EPS files as well, provided you have the necessary fonts on your computer (or they're embedded in the EPS file), although PostScript itself is its preferred and intended diet. If you've fed a healthy PostScript file to Distiller and chosen the correct job option, you'll watch the progress bar fill up, and soon you'll have a PDF file. If you've dragged multiple PostScript files into Distiller, they'll be listed in the queue box at the bottom of the Distiller window, in which you can reorder, cancel, or pause queued jobs.

As each PDF is created, a small PDF icon appears next to its name in the list. Double-click the entry in the queue window, and the PDF file opens in Acrobat (great if you're not sure where you saved the file). If Distiller can't create a PDF file, the log at the bottom of the Distiller window will contain an explanation of the problem, although it doesn't contain any suggestions to help you.

There are two other doorways into Distiller....

If you need to convert more than the occasional PostScript file, you may wish to create what's called a *watched folder*, which allows you to batch-distill multiple PostScript files. This is especially useful if you need to convert many PostScript files with the same Distiller settings. Note that the software license for Distiller dictates that you are to use it to process PostScript files only for yourself or for others who also own a license for Distiller.

To create a watched folder, first create a folder to be used as the target folder. Then, choose Settings > Watched Folders from the Distiller menu (remember, it's way up at the top of your monitor on the Mac). In the watched folder window (**Figure 14.2**), click Add Folder, and then navigate to the folder you created to earmark the folder to be watched by Distiller.

Figure 14.2 The Watched Folder window includes controls for designating folders for Distiller processing as well as options for editing the settings that are used.

By default, the PostScript files will be processed using the current settings in Distiller. However, you can modify these settings by clicking the Edit Settings button and then modifying the settings options. You can choose to delete the PostScript files once they're converted to PDF files or have Distiller move the PostScript files into another folder after processing. When you click the OK button, Distiller will create two folders inside your watched folder. One is the *In* folder, where you'll drop the PostScript files to be processed. The other folder created is the *Out* folder, where Distiller will place the finished PDF files (and the processed PostScript files, if you choose that option).

The other doorway to Distiller is the Acrobat "printer" named Adobe PDF 7.0 that's added to your system during Acrobat installation. (Depending on the version of Acrobat installed, the name you see may be slightly different, but you should be able to recognize it easily.) Printing to this target printer generates PostScript and immediately awakens Distiller to process it using the last settings that were selected in Distiller. However, depending on the application from which you are printing, the Print dialog may allow you to select other job options without opening Distiller first.

Note that the list of job options in Table 14.1 is taken from Acrobat Distiller. You'll see the same options across all of the Adobe CS2 products, but you won't necessarily see the names for PDF options in non-Adobe products. How do you select the right settings for a print-ready PDF? It's helpful if your print service provider gives you definite specifications for creating a PDF that fits their workflow. Lacking such guidance, you're almost always safe choosing PDF/X-1a as a start, and then making one minor modification: Amid all the strictures of the PDF/X-1a specification, there's no stipulation about the resolution of image content. You should remedy that oversight by choosing an appropriate image resolution in the image-compression settings. As a reminder, PDF/X-1a and PDF/X-3 formats are not the same. PDF/X-3 is for color-managed workflows. Choose PDF/X-3 only if your print service provider instructs you to do so. It's more likely that PDF/X-1a is what they want.

While QuarkXPress versions up through 6.5 don't offer a named PDF/X-1a option for creating PDFs, the upcoming QuarkXPress 7.0 includes settings for PDF/X-1a and PDF/X-3. If the PDF-export function in the application you're using doesn't offer named versions of PDF settings, such as those available in Distiller, how can you create something resembling a PDF/X-1a-compliant file? It's not difficult, but you need to stick to some basics:

- Set compatibility to Acrobat 4.0. While this may seem old-fashioned given that Acrobat (at this writing) is at version 7.0, it's dictated by the capabilities of most RIPs, many of which prefer Acrobat 4.0-flavored PDF files. At some point, we'll no doubt have PDF-native RIPs that handle more current PDF formats, but for now you should go for the safe choice. Global Graphics and Artwork Systems already market PDF-native RIPs, but most vendors' offerings convert PDF files to PostScript or a proprietary internal format at some point in the process, which means that content is not maintained in the PDF format throughout the workflow. Since Acrobat 4.0-compatible PDF files don't contain live transparency, there's less chance that a RIP that is not PDF based will incorrectly process the file.

- Set image resolution to 300 ppi for typical 150-line screen work, and to 200 ppi for 133-line screen jobs (more about image handling in a moment). Consult with your print service provider to find out the line screen that will used on your job. If you don't know, you're safe using 300 ppi.

- Set image compression to Automatic (JPEG).

- Ensure that all image content is CMYK or spot or some combination thereof. Convert any RGB content to CMYK.

- Set font embedding to embed fonts. Enable subsetting, and set the subsetting threshold to 100 percent.

Handling Image Content

The primary cause of a PDF file's size is image content, so if you want to make a smaller PDF, that's where you have to squeeze. It's a bit of a juggling act. You have to balance the size of the PDF with the results of compressing and resampling images and decide whether to compromise image appearance to create a more petite file. When making decisions about image compression and resampling, you have to consider the nature of image content as well as the intended use for the PDF file. If the document's text is the most important content, and images are just incidental accents (such as gauzy, out-of-focus photographs of soft clouds), then you can be more liberal when compressing images. However, when the images are key elements—for example, in a technical manual wherein it's crucial to differentiate between small details—you'll have to be willing to accept a larger PDF so you can maintain important detail.

Image compression and resampling options can look overwhelming in Distiller and other applications' PDF creation dialogs. There are so many fields and menu choices. But in most cases, you're just being asked the same question about different types of image content. What should happen to color images? How should it handle grayscale images? And what about bitmap images (also called bilevel—black and white with no shades of gray)? This gives you some flexibility. For example, you might want to maintain higher resolution in color images, but not mind reducing the resolution of less-important grayscale images. Separate controls allow you to do that.

Resolution Settings

If you want to more aggressively reduce the file size of a PDF, you can set the base resolution and downsampling threshold to the same value (**Figure 14.3**). *Downsampling* is the process of reducing the number of pixels in an image. An image downsampled from 300 ppi to 72 ppi is much smaller, because it's constituted of smaller, coarser pixels. The downsampling threshold is the resolution above which Distiller will downsample image content. A setting that downsamples images to 300 ppi if they're above 450 ppi ignores images whose resolution falls between 300 and 450 ppi, leaving their resolution unchanged. Setting both downsampling and the threshold to the same value forces images between 300–450 ppi to also be downsampled. You're discarding pixels, but at this level, it shouldn't result in an obvious loss of detail.

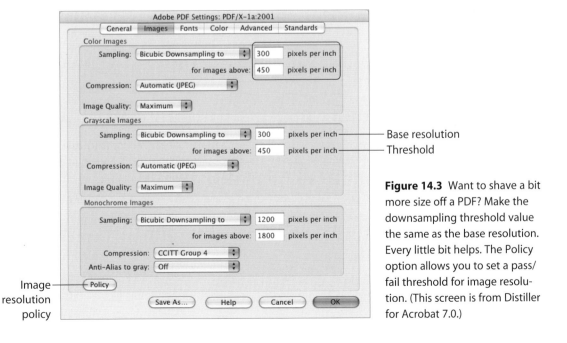

Figure 14.3 Want to shave a bit more size off a PDF? Make the downsampling threshold value the same as the base resolution. Every little bit helps. The Policy option allows you to set a pass/fail threshold for image resolution. (This screen is from Distiller for Acrobat 7.0.)

Compression Settings

Besides allowing you to resample image content to economize PDF size, Distiller and some other PDF-creation processes provide options for compression. Compression involves methods of re-expressing the image content in a more economical way, usually by eliminating redundant information. Overly aggressive JPEG compression, however, can cause a noticeable erosion of an image, resulting in effects such as rectangular artifacts. But don't be terrified of the JPEG compression option in Distiller. Careful compression levels can reduce image size without visibly degrading the image.

Acrobat Distiller and most other PDF-creation applications use both ZIP and JPEG methods of compression. ZIP compression is *lossless*, meaning that it does not discard image information—it just describes the image in a more compact way. ZIP can reduce the size of flat-color image content such as cartoons or maps. JPEG compression achieves better file-size reduction with photographic image content, because photographs can contain a wide range of colors with smooth transitions. The correct choice of a compression method seeks to reduce the size of the resulting PDF file without unnecessarily impairing its appearance.

What do you do if you have both kinds of content? Good news—choose the Automatic (JPEG) option in Distiller or the Automatic ZIP/JPEG option in QuarkXPress, and each type of content is handled appropriately (**Figure 14.4**). It's worth noting that, since ZIP compression is lossless, it's also perfectly appropriate for photographic images, but it will not produce as small a file as JPEG compression can.

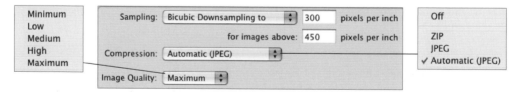

Figure 14.4 ZIP compression is a lossless compression method that can reduce the size of flat-color images such as cartoons; JPEG compression can achieve better results with photographic content. Automatic (JPEG) allows Distiller to choose the right method for individual image content. The Image Quality settings allow you to choose the amount of compression, with Minimum quality being the most aggressive compression setting.

Font Embedding

The purpose of embedding fonts is to ensure that the PDF file looks and prints like the original document. Keep in mind that you're allowed to embed fonts only if the font vendor's End User License Agreement (EULA) allows you to do so—see the Chapter 6, "Fonts," for more on font licensing EULAs.

If you embed a font in a PDF, things can still go awry once the file leaves your hands. If you just embed a font (without subsetting), font substitution can still take place if the RIP is already using a font of the same name. Imagine a RIP thinking, "Why should I bother to pry open this PDF to get its Helvetica Bold, when I already have one warmed up?" It sounds harmless, just substituting one Helvetica Bold for another. But not all Helvetica Bold versions are the same. There may be subtle differences in font metrics that can result in loss of fidelity to the original file. Additionally, fully embedding larger fonts such as OpenType fonts (which can have over 65,000 glyphs) can add to the size of the PDF file.

One solution to these issues is to *subset* font information. Subsetting embeds only the characters used in the document, which reduces file size. If your PDF consists of one line of text reading "ABC123," only the characters A, B, C, 1, 2, and 3 are embedded, rather than packing up the entire font. Beyond the file-slimming aspects, subsetting gives each font a unique name. For example, a PDF file containing an *embedded* version of the font, Skia, describes the font as *Skia-Regular.* But a PDF file containing a *subset* version of Skia refers internally to the font by a unique name such as *AMIIKI+Skia-Regular*, eliminating any chance that a RIP will be tempted to use a font named *Skia-Regular* instead.

There are disadvantages to subsetting, however. If multiple PDF files containing subset versions of a font are combined (whether by Acrobat or some other process such as imposition), conflicts can arise, resulting in dropped characters or odd spacing. Consult with your print service provider to see if they'd prefer that you simply embed rather than subset fonts, and supply the fonts themselves along with the job. This may allow some flexibility during later parts of the workflow.

EDITING PDF FILES

Since one of the primary purposes of the Portable Document Format is to maintain document integrity, you shouldn't be surprised that the ability to edit PDF files in Acrobat is rather limited—that's not an accident. We're not supposed to pick at PDF files once they're created. They're supposed to be finished files, ready to ship.

Of course, little things happen—a missing comma, a blemish in an image, the wrong spot color—and desperation drives you to start prying at the corners of a PDF file. That's when you find the limitations.

Acrobat offers three editing tools in the TouchUp toolbar (**Figure 14.5**). Choose Tools > Advanced Editing > Show TouchUp Toolbar to display the tools. Use the TouchUp Text tool for selecting and editing text. Use the TouchUp Object tool to select images and vector objects to edit content in imaging applications such as Photoshop and vector–editing applications such as Illustrator. You may never use the TouchUp Reading Order tool, which allows you to modify object attributes to create more accessible files for visually impaired users. *Accessible* PDF files have specialized underlying structure enabling them to be displayed in a way that makes them more easily read by visually impaired readers. Text in such a PDF file reflows as the reader zooms in, and line breaks are altered so that the reader is not forced to move the file onscreen to see a complete line of text. This reflow is a display effect: The PDF file cannot be saved or printed in the reflowed state. Accessible PDF files are also more easily read aloud by applications called *screen readers*. Screen readers are specialized utilities that read onscreen content so that sight-impaired users can hear what they cannot otherwise read. Acrobat 7.0 Professional and Standard, as well as the free Reader product, contain a rudimentary built-in screen reader. If you want to experiment with it, choose Read Aloud from the View menu in one of the Acrobat products.

Figure 14.5 TouchUp tools: TouchUp Text (left), TouchUp Reading Order (center), TouchUp Object (right).

Editing Text

To edit text (or attempt to), use the TouchUp Text tool to highlight text and change it. It's important to note that the purpose of font embedding is to ensure that a PDF file displays correctly and prints as intended. The fonts themselves are not available for you to use in any other way—and that includes editing text. Consequently, you do need to have the necessary fonts active on your system to add or delete text in a PDF file. If you attempt to edit text in an unavailable font, you'll receive a warning alert (**Figure 14.6**).

Figure 14.6 You can't edit text in a PDF if you don't have the necessary fonts active on your system. Font embedding is for display and printing purposes only—it doesn't make the font available to you for any other use.

If you do have the necessary fonts active on your system, you can edit text, although you may find that Acrobat refuses to embed some fonts after editing. It's honoring the limitations of the font's licensing, which in some cases allows embedding for the purposes of display and print, but forbids editing. It can be frustrating when you encounter these roadblocks, but Acrobat offers no way around it in some cases. You may be forced to go back to the originating application to make the changes, and then export a new PDF file. Of course, if you don't have the original file, this option isn't available.

Even if you have the correct font, you can only edit one line of text at a time. Text won't wrap as it would in a page–layout program. To make extensive text edits, go back to the original application if possible, or use the PitStop PDF-editing plug-in from Enfocus that greatly extends Acrobat's editing capabilities.

Even without PitStop, you may be surprised to discover that although you may be prevented from adding or deleting text, you can still change attributes such as size, fill color, stroke attributes, and baseline position of existing text. To change attributes of the text, select it with the TouchUp Text tool and then right-click (PC) or Control-click (Macintosh) and choose Properties from the context menu. Don't get too excited: You can't assign spot colors, and while you can create a CMYK color on the Macintosh, you're limited to choosing RGB values on Windows.

Are you starting to take all this bad news as a sign that you're not supposed to tinker with text in PDF files? Good. Hold that thought. It will keep you out of all kinds of trouble.

Editing Graphics

Surprisingly, you can alter graphic content in a PDF file more extensively than you can edit text. Using the TouchUp Object tool on the TouchUp toolbar, you can select graphic content for manipulation in Photoshop or Illustrator. When you install Acrobat, it searches for the locations of the newest versions of Photoshop and Illustrator on your computer and opens them when you embark on a TouchUp edit.

> **TOUCHUP TIP #1:** Although Acrobat will allow you to designate external editors other than Photoshop and Illustrator, the lines of communication don't work both ways. You'll be able to extract the content, but you can't write the corrected content back into the PDF file.

Choose the TouchUp Object tool, select the desired graphic content in the PDF, and then right-click (PC) or Control-click (Mac) to view the context menu, and then select Edit Image or Edit Object, depending on the type of content you've selected (**Figure 14.7**). The appropriate external application will launch and open a temporary file of the graphic for editing. For example, if you've selected vector content, Illustrator is opened. If you've selected an image, Photoshop is opened. The title bar of a TouchUp image in Photoshop or Illustrator displays a name such as *Acro1143710152.pdf*, indicating that it's a TouchUp file.

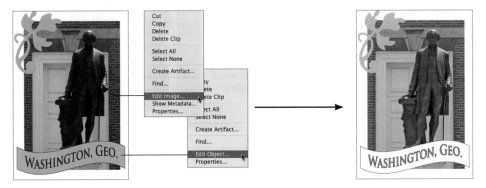

Figure 14.7 Select an image (left) with the TouchUp Object tool, and then right-click (PC) or Control–click (Macintosh) to select Edit Image. Then the image is available to modify in Photoshop. Make your changes, and then choose File > Save, and the corrected image is saved back into the PDF (right). Select vector content, and then right-click (PC) or Control–click (Macintosh) to select Edit Object from the context menu to open the vector content in Illustrator. Make your changes, choose File > Save to send the modified content back to Acrobat, and then save your corrected PDF file.

TouchUp Bug in Photoshop CS2

When you save a finished TouchUp image in Photoshop, it's supposed to slip back into the PDF neatly, replacing the original content. Unfortunately, there's a bug in Photoshop CS2 that causes TouchUp images to fall to the lower lefthand corner of the PDF page when saved back into the PDF. Adobe recommends using the TouchUp tool to nudge the image into an approximation of its original position. This is no way to live. The closest to a real fix is to keep an earlier version of Photoshop on your computer for moments like this. Photoshop 7.0 and CS behave correctly when communicating back to the PDF file. By default, Acrobat looks for the most recent version of Photoshop installed, so you'll have to manually hook it up to the earlier version. Choose Acrobat > Preferences (Macintosh) or Edit > Preferences (Windows), and then select TouchUp from the options. Change the Image Editor to Photoshop 7.0 or CS. This is also the place to designate the default vector and object editing application that Acrobat should use when you select vector elements on the PDF page for TouchUp.

The goal in using the TouchUp Object tool is to sneak into the PDF file, extract the graphic content (whether vector or raster) for the external editing application, make the necessary edits in Photoshop or Illustrator, and then slip the corrected image or vector art back into the PDF. To pull this off, you have to play by the rules that limit the extent to which you can change TouchUp content, especially in Photoshop. Note that you can't add layers in Photoshop and sneak an image back into the PDF. You can create layers as necessary to accomplish the corrections, but you'll have to flatten before returning the image to Acrobat. But you can still do more than you might think. You can fix blemishes, scale, change color modes — even convert to a duotone. You can't add transparency or blending modes, however. When you're done, choose File > Save in Photoshop, and the corrected image is saved back into the PDF file.

Using the TouchUp Object tool to select vector content takes you to Illustrator to modify the selected content. As with images, you can make your edits, and then choose File > Save to write the vector content back into the PDF file. There are fewer limitations when editing vector content. For example, you can add layers and even rotate and scale content in Illustrator. When you choose File > Save, Illustrator communicates the changes back to Acrobat and modifies the PDF file accordingly.

> **TOUCHUP TIP #3:** *Need to extract an image or vector component from a PDF file for use in another job? Has the client lost the original artwork for their company logo? If they have a PDF file containing the logo, you can use the TouchUp tool to extract the content so you can use it outside of Acrobat. When you have a TouchUp image or vector object open in Photoshop or Illustrator, you can choose File > Save As and select another format (such as PSD or TIFF for images; EPS or AI for vector objects) to save as a file on disk rather than saving it back into the PDF file. This is a great way to extract artwork from a PDF file if you've lost the original artwork. Understandably, it wouldn't be polite to extract artwork you have no rights to use.*

While the TouchUp tools may bail you out of problems as deadlines loom, it's often safer to go back to the original file to make corrections, if you can. Sometimes PDF files just fall apart during editing (nature's way of saying don't mess with them). You should watch carefully for shifted content or unwanted changes. If you're required to frequently edit PDF files because your customers send you PDFs with problems, you should consider adding some third-party PDF-editing tools to your Acrobat arsenal. Here are some of the handiest:

- PitStop (Enfocus Software) is a widely used plug-in for Acrobat that allows you to make extensive text edits, global changes to fonts and colors, and other major alterations.

- Quite a Box of Tricks (Quite Software), is a plug-in often referred to as QABOT that can convert a PDF to CMYK (if it's been created with spot-color or RGB content) or grayscale. (Great if you need to submit an ad for the black-and-white pages of a publication.) It can also convert all text to black and perform a number of other helpful operations.

- PDF Enhancer (Apago, Inc.), is a standalone application that can dramatically reduce the file size of PDFs, add page numbering and watermarking, and perform conversion of text to outlines.

PRINT PRODUCTION TOOLBAR

While the graphics and text editing in Acrobat is a bit limited, the introduction of the Print Production toolbar in Acrobat 7.0 gave us some valuable new weapons with which to find problems in PDF files and fix them (**Figure 14.8**). To display the print production tools, choose Tools > Print Production > Show Print Production Toolbar. If it's necessary to perform any major surgery, you'll still need to use third-party add-ons such as those mentioned in the previous section. But you can now accomplish quite a bit just by using Acrobat's built-in tools.

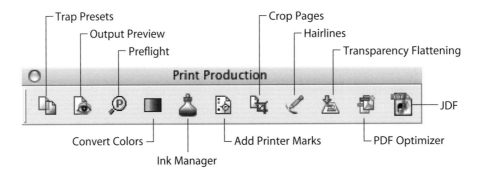

Figure 14.8 The Print Production toolbar in Acrobat 7.0 provides functions that greatly extend your ability to find and fix problems without returning to the original application that created the PDF file.

The Print Production tools fall into two major categories: Forensic tools help you find problem areas in a PDF file, while the repair tools allow you to actually alter content to fix problems. As with other toolbars in Acrobat, this toolbar can float anywhere in the document window, or can be docked in the toolbar area at the top of the application.

Forensic Tools: What's Wrong with this PDF?

Acrobat 7.0 Professional contains two great forensic tools: Output Preview and Preflight. The two tools take different approaches, because they're meant to call attention to different problems.

The Output Preview tool takes a visual approach, selectively displaying content according to parameters you choose so you can find problems. You can easily highlight such elements as RGB images, spot–color content, overprinting elements, and rich black areas.

Some problems aren't so easily found visually, which is where the Preflight tool comes in. The Preflight tool tests a PDF file against set of rules that you choose, called a preflight profile, to determine problems mechanically. The preflight process then generates a report to tell you what's wrong. The Preflight tool can determine if a PDF file complies with the PDF/X-1a standard, and can check for such problems as insufficient image resolution, incorrect page size, or font embedding issues.

Output Preview

Select the Output Preview tool, and then use the controls to show and hide objects in the PDF by various criteria. You'll see a list of inks used in the PDF file, and you can selectively show and hide individual plates to see where the inks are used in the page (**Figure 14.9**).

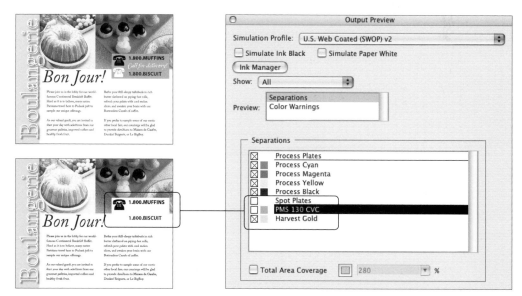

Figure 14.9 Open a PDF (top-left), and then use the Separations controls on the Output Preview dialog to toggle plates on and off. Here, one rectangle uses an ink named PMS 130 CVC (right). But there's another spot color named Harvest Gold. Even if you aren't familiar with the job, there's something suspicious about that.

Select *Show* on the Output Preview dialog to view options for isolating RGB content (**Figure 14.10**) and other types of color space such as grayscale, CMYK, and spot color. As with all the Output Preview options, it's up to you to pay attention and take note of what's displayed. In Figure 14.10, one image is displayed when the Show > RGB option is selected. Now we've discovered that we have one problem image, which must be converted to CMYK for output.

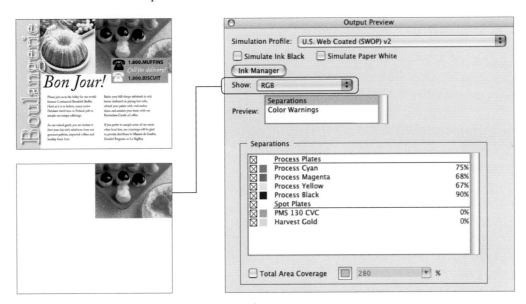

Figure 14.10 From the Show list, choose RGB, and any RGB objects are displayed while everything else is hidden. It's a quick way to isolate images that are using the wrong color space.

The color-warning tools in the Output Preview dialog can highlight various printing ink behaviors, such as overprinting content, rich blacks, and violations of total area coverage, which is the maximum accumulation that can be printed under given press and paper conditions (**Figure 14.11**).

If you have large areas carrying more ink than your print service provider recommends for your job, you'll have to go back upstream and alter image content and other artwork so the job will print acceptably. Your print service provider can give you some guidance regarding the ink limits for your job after decisions have been made on which press and paper to be used. If you're doing your own conversions of RGB images to CMYK, you can factor in this value in your color separation setup.

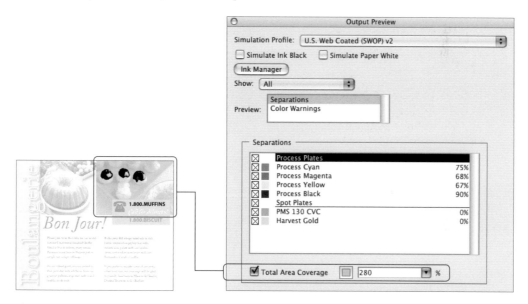

Figure 14.11 There's a practical limit to the total area coverage for a given printing condition (including the press, the type of paper, and so on). If you know the correct value, Acrobat can highlight problem areas. A few little spots here and there aren't a major issue. But larger areas that exceed the limit will have to be fixed in the originating application. Acrobat can't fix this issue for you.

Preflight

Preflight is a mechanical check of a PDF that tests the file against a set of predefined rules to see if it passes (**Figure 14.12**). You can test for problems with issues such as image resolution, spot colors, font embedding, or compliance with a standard such as PDF/X-1a. Depending on the rules that constitute the profile you select (and there's quite a variety of preflight profiles supplied with the program), Acrobat can display an error, provide information, or just ignore the results. Preflight profiles can check for a wide variety of issues beyond compliance with the PDF/X-1a standard.

Figure 14.12 Choose the appropriate Preflight profile, and then click Execute on the Preflight dialog to test the file.

If there's a long list of problems in the preflight report, Acrobat offers a quick way to find the problem visually. Select the item in the preflight report window, and then select the "Show selected page element in Snap view" check box (**Figure 14.13**). The item is displayed in a floating window so you can identify it. Why is it called Snap view? As your mother would say, "Well, it just *is*." Perhaps it's a vestige of the preflight's feature's earlier incarnation as a German product named CheckUp. For now, it will have to remain a mystery, but at least you know what it does.

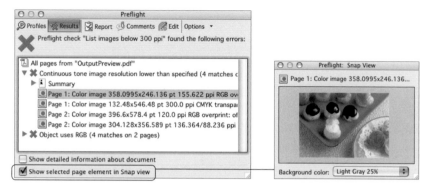

Figure 14.13 To easily locate a problem, highlight the item in the Preflight report, and then select "Show selected page element in Snap view," which will display the selected item in a floating window.

While Acrobat ships with an extensive set of prefabricated preflight profiles, you may still want to create a custom profile for your needs. The easiest way to do this is to select an existing profile, duplicate it, and then modify it to suit your needs (**Figure 14.14**).

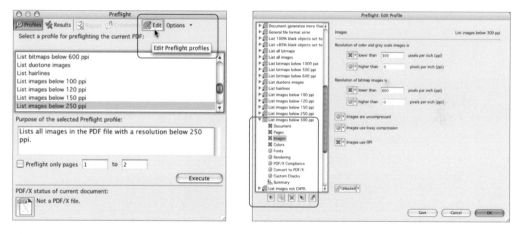

Figure 14.14 Edit Preflight profiles to create custom versions for your workflow. Select a profile that gives you a good start, and then click Edit (top). In the Edit Profile dialog, use the icons at the bottom of the list to add, duplicate, delete, import, and export preflight profiles. Choose a topic out of the profile's list of tests, modify the parameters to fit your needs, and then save as a new profile.

If you need to preflight multiple files with the same profile, you can automate the process by creating a Preflight Droplet. In the main Preflight dialog, click Options, and then choose Create Preflight Droplet from the menu (**Figure 14.15**).

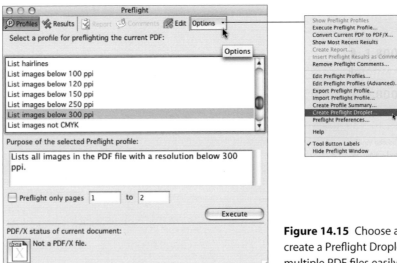

Figure 14.15 Choose a profile, and then create a Preflight Droplet to batch process multiple PDF files easily.

In the Droplet Setup dialog, you can designate Success and Error folders, allowing Acrobat to sort the preflighted PDF files into separate folders so you can quickly determine which ones passed the preflight criteria (**Figure 14.16**). Acrobat creates a Droplet icon to represent the batch process. To start the process, shift-click to select multiple PDF files, and then drag the whole bunch on top of the Droplet. Caution: If you drag a *folder* to the Droplet, it won't process the files inside. You have to drag the PDF files themselves to the Droplet icon.

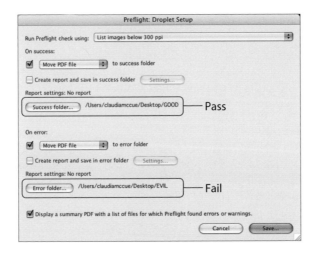

Less than 300

Figure 14.16 To set up a Preflight Droplet, choose a profile, and then tell Acrobat what to do with the PDFs that pass and those that fail (left). Here, the Droplet will move the passing PDFs to the GOOD folder, while the failing PDFs will go in the EVIL folder. Click the Save button, and Acrobat creates a Droplet wherever you specify (above).

The preflight-and-sort process doesn't change the PDF files to Acrobat 7.0 files. It just peeks inside the files and sorts them according to the assigned preflight profile without resaving the PDF.

PDF Optimizer

The PDF Optimizer functions are usually used to alter PDF files, but there's also a handy forensic tool in the PDF Optimizer options: Audit Space Usage can point out what kinds of content are contributing to file bloat.

Repair Tools

Once you've found all the problems with a PDF file, how do you fix them? Some problems—such as missing fonts, text reflow, and low-resolution images—are best fixed in the originating application or by using a third-party, PDF-editing tool such as those described in the section "Editing PDF Files." But you can still fix some common problems without leaving Acrobat by using the built-in repair tools.

Convert Colors

If you've discovered that you have RGB images in a PDF, and you have no access to the original file to generate a PDF, you can select the Convert Colors tool on the Print Production toolbar to convert RGB content to CMYK. You can specify a document profile as well as a destination space to ensure an appropriate conversion (**Figure 14.17**).

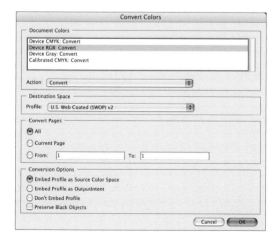

Figure 14.17 Select Convert Colors to make color–space changes such as RGB to CMYK, CMYK to grayscale, and so on.

Ink Manager

Suppose the Output Preview tool has revealed that the PDF file contains multiple spot colors: PMS 130 CVC, Pantone 130 C, and Spot Yellow. You know that it's supposed to be a five-color job: CMYK+Pantone 130 C. Rather than return to the original application, you can repair the problem with the Ink Manager. Choose a spot ink in the list, and then select the correct spot ink from the Ink Alias list at the bottom of the dialog box. This converts all content that is in the wrong spot color so that it will be output on the correct plate (**Figure 14.18**).

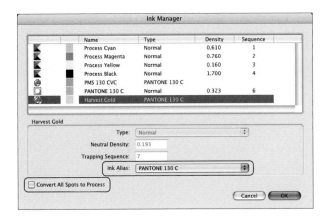

Figure 14.18 Use the Ink Manager to map one spot color to another spot color. Select the errant spot color in the list, and then use the Ink Alias list to choose the target ink. You can also convert all spot colors to process with one click (lower left), or map a spot ink to a process ink.

 ## Add Printer Marks

If you need to add trim and crop marks to a PDF file, you can specify trim and bleed marks, as well as color bars and page information by using the Add Printer Marks tool. You can also select from several styles or printer marks, including those comparable to the ones generated by InDesign and QuarkXPress. For the position of such marks to be correct, the PDF file must contain properly defined TrimBox and BleedBox information from the originating application. But when you add marks, they will initially fall outside the visible edge of the page, which will make you think you've done something wrong. You haven't. You just have to follow up by expanding the document's dimensions so the marks show. For that, you need the Crop Pages tool. Acrobat even politely informs you to follow up with the Crop Pages tool (**Figure 14.19**).

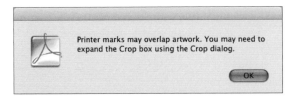

Printer marks may overlap artwork. You may need to expand the Crop box using the Crop dialog.

OK

Figure 14.19 When you add printer marks, Acrobat prompts you to expand the page dimensions with the Crop Pages tool.

Crop Pages

The Crop Pages tool is a multipurpose tool. Think of it as the change-document-dimensions tool, because it can crop as well as increase page size (**Figure 14.20**). While increasing the page size actually changes the dimensions of the PDF page, cropping with the Margin Controls just visually masks out the area outside the margin dimensions. Page content still exists. It just doesn't show. That's why cropped PDF files show no reduction in file size. Everything is still there, lurking. Since cropping isn't final, you may find that some other applications ignore cropping instructions and show the original full content.

If you've used the Printer Marks tool, the Crop Pages tool is your next stop. You'll need to add sufficient new material on the page to allow the marks to be visible. Adding one inch in both directions will usually do the trick. For example, if you've added marks to a page that's currently 8.75 by 11.25 inches, set the new page dimensions to 9.75 by 12.25 inches.

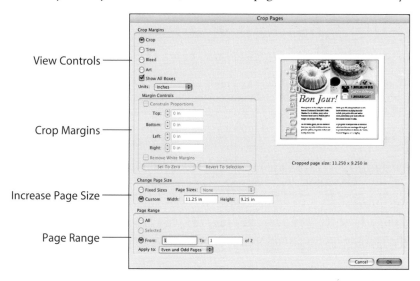

Figure 14.20 In the Crop Pages controls, Margin Controls crop the document. Change Page Size increases the document's page size, but does not scale the content.

Fix Hairlines

Thin lines can come from CAD artwork or from vector art that's been greatly reduced in a page layout. While direct-to-plate imaging and newer press controls provide the ability to image and print small details that might have disappeared in transit 20 years ago, a line of infinitesimal width can benefit from a little fluffing up to ensure imaging (**Figure 14.21**).

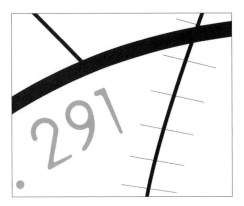 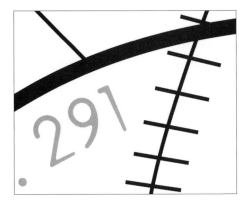

Figure 14.21 Hairline strokes (left) may be challenging to image and print predictably, depending on printing conditions. You can use the Fix Hairline tool to plump them up to a less anemic weight (right).

The Fix Hairlines tool allows you to increase the weight of stroked lines using a threshold value (**Figure 14.22**). It also offers options for padding Type 3 fonts (which can contain patterned or gray components) or pattern fills. Note that exercising these options may add more complexity to the PDF file, since this could result in a large number of elements in the file being modified. A pattern fill could contain hundreds (or thousands) of lines, each of which would have to be modified during the hairline fixing process. But in a typical PDF file, the hairline fixing should just take a few seconds.

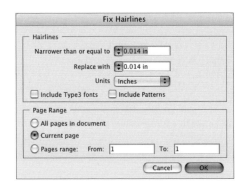

Figure 14.22 The Fix Hairlines tool adds weight to thin strokes.

Transparency Flattening

If your print service provider can't accept PDF files containing live transparency, such as PDF files that are generated by InDesign or Illustrator, you can use Acrobat's Transparency Flattening controls to manage the flattening process (**Figure 14.23**).

Drag the Raster/Vector Balance slider all the way to the right. You should see 100 in the Raster/Vector value. Use the resolution of the print service provider's RIP for the Line Art and Text resolution value, and set the Gradient and Mesh resolution to an appropriate image resolution, such as 300 ppi. Don't select the options for converting text or strokes to outlines, so you can avoid any fattening of text or rules.

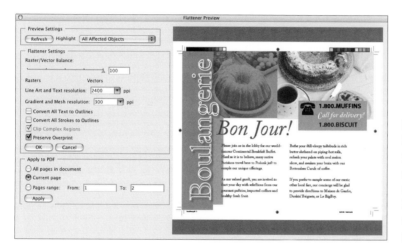

Figure 14.23 The Transparency Flattening options enable you to see what areas will be affected by flattening. You can control the process rather than being at the mercy of a RIP that can't handle live transparency in PDF files.

PDF Optimizer

To make a lower-resolution PDF from an existing PDF file, or to save for a previous version of Acrobat, use PDF Optimizer rather than going all the way back to the originating application and generating a new PDF. The PDF Optimizer also produces better results than the old-fashioned method of printing to PostScript from Acrobat and then using Distiller to process the new PostScript file—a process referred to as *refrying*. That method carries the risk of losing font embedding or introducing color errors. In addition, PDF Optimizer offers much more granular control over file-size reduction than the Reduce File Size option available under the File menu, which just uses a default setting with no visible controls.

Trap Presets

It's unlikely that you'll be required to use the Trap Presets features in Acrobat 7.0, since trapping is a complicated undertaking that's best left to the knowledgeable folks at the print service provider. The Trap Presets feature in Acrobat doesn't actually create traps within the PDF file: It lets you specify trap settings that are subsequently used as instructions by a RIP that uses the Adobe In-RIP Trapping engine. The trap settings you choose only affect the print stream out of Acrobat—no trapping instructions are stored in the PDF. However, the presets you create are available as presets in Acrobat for future use.

 JDF

Job Definition Format (JDF) information may not mean much to you right now, but watch this acronym. The ability to generate an electronic job ticket and store it within a PDF file has the potential to streamline workflows and reduce job errors. JDF information can contain details such as page size, number of colors, binding requirements, and even contact information for people involved in the job. It's an electronic version of the old job information sheet that traveled with a physical job jacket as job materials traveled through a printing plant. The appearance of JDF functionality in Acrobat is a hint that the road is being paved for JDF to be increasingly important in the way we define and track jobs. Unless your print service provider is currently using JDF-based job ticketing, you won't be required to explore this part of Acrobat.

USING EXTERNAL PDF EDITORS

PDFs are more complex than they look. Under the hood, they're a spaghetti-like network of things such as XObjects, Arrays, Page Tree Nodes, and Optional Content Groups. That's why some edits can't be undone in Acrobat (**Figure 14.24**). You'd break the spaghetti.

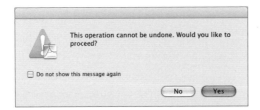

Figure 14.24 There is no Undo command for many operations in Acrobat. This is nature's way of letting you know that PDF files are more complicated than you might think. At least you're warned.

Even if you're using some of the excellent, third-party add-ons for Acrobat to perform edits, it's advisable to work on a copy of your file just in case things fall apart.

As for using Adobe Illustrator to edit PDF files...*don't.* We've all done it in desperation in the olden days before PitStop and other PDF-editing software. There was no viable alternative back then, and deadlines will drive you to do such things. But if it wasn't generated by Illustrator, opening a PDF file in Illustrator without the necessary fonts available will wreck font embedding, and manipulating objects may cause unexpected loss of content. It's OK to edit PDFs saved directly from Illustrator, however. They're special files: The original Illustrator file is contained within the PDF, and that's what you'd actually be editing, provided you use the default option to retain Illustrator editing capabilities. But you're risking the possibility of file damage when you use Illustrator to edit PDF files created by other applications. It's preferable to return to the originating application to make edits. Then create a new PDF file and go on with your life.

APPENDIX

Print Production Resources

When you enjoy what you do for a living, your education never stops. And if your education never stops, there's a good chance that you'll get more enjoyment out of what you do for a living. I once worked with a guy who didn't understand my fondness for learning new software. He once said to me, "If you learn that, they'll just make you do it all the time." Understandably, he couldn't fathom why I'd go to trade shows and conferences for fun. I'm sure he was disturbed by the fact that I referred to the now-defunct Seybold Seminars in Boston as "Spring Break."

If you consider yourself an avid, life-long learner, and you'd like to add to your arsenal of printing knowledge, I hope you'll find the resources in this appendix useful. I've included information about organizations, online resources, books, and publications, and even some print-related tourist destinations. Really.

ORGANIZATIONS

Organizations related to the graphic arts industry vary in structure and offerings. Some are small, loosely knit, informal user groups that meet for snacks and presentations (not necessarily in that order of importance). Some larger organizations are more like corporations with regional chapters, and they often hold annual international conferences that include extensive seminar offerings, exhibit booths, and awards banquets.

Some organizations consist only of a Web presence and perhaps online forums. Regardless of the type of group that appeals to you, it's helpful to join organizations in order to see how other people approach design and print. Meeting other professionals in the industry, and seeing their work, is inspirational as well as educational.

User Groups

Unlike groups geared toward general design or printing industry members, user groups are usually devoted to a single software program or a suite of programs. The Adobe Acrobat and InDesign user groups hold chapter meetings in various cities around the world. While these two groups are supported by Adobe, they are funded and run by the group members themselves. A typical user group meeting might include demonstrations of software features, opportunities to have questions answered and technical issues solved by expert users or guest speakers, and a chance to win software, books, and other door prizes. And don't forget those snacks.

- Adobe Acrobat User Community   *www.acrobatusers.com*

  Started in 2006, the Acrobat user community is growing rapidly. The Web site offers links to the individual chapters, as well as tips, tutorials, and video presentations.

- Adobe InDesign User Group   *www.indesignusergroup.com*

  The InDesign user group Web site is a rich portal to all things InDesign, including chapter information, useful plug-ins, and tutorials. It's also an easy doorway to the Adobe forums and the great InDesign Secrets site. Check out the InDesign Secrets podcast!

Online Communities and Forums

Joining online communities and forums is sort of like raising your hand and having the entire world answer you. Post a question in an online forum, and the answers arrive in your in-box. Strong emotions and priceless information make the online communities like lively little villages, including the inevitable family squabbles.

Some forums (fora? forii?) are sponsored by software vendors, and feature the expected product announcements and sales pitches in addition to useful resources. Some forums are maintained strictly by enthusiasts, and are free of any corporate influence.

- Adobe Forums   *www.adobe.com/support/forums*

  Adobe forums are available for all Adobe products. While the forums are predominantly user-to-user in nature, they are moderated for civility, and Adobe staff are frequent contributors. The topics are a mix of general software issues and printing issues.

- Macromedia Products, including FreeHand MX   *www.communitymx.com*
  CommunityMX includes news about Macromedia products Dreamweaver, FreeHandMX, Fireworks, and ColdFusion, as well as online tutorials.

- National Association of Photoshop Users   *www.photoshopuser.com*
  The National Association of Photoshop Users (NAPP), is a national organization that provides *online* tutorials, publishes a bimonthly magazine, and hosts regional seminar events in addition to its yearly Photoshop World conference. Members are also eligible for discounts on software and hardware.

- PDF Zone   *www.pdfzone.com*
  A service of Ziff Davis Media, PDF Zone contains PDF-related industry news, as well as tips, tricks, and tutorials. Not all of the content is print-related, though.

- Planet PDF   *www.planetpdf.com*
  Planet PDF is a service of BinaryThing, a software development company devoted to Acrobat solutions. The searchable Planet PDF store offers a huge variety of plug-ins and software related to Acrobat. The online content also includes tips, tricks, and PDF-themed articles about a wide spectrum of industry uses for Acrobat.

- PrintPlanet   *www.printplanet.com*
  Created and maintained by Dave Mainwaring, the PrintPlanet forums are some of the most lively and most useful printing resources on the Web. Forums are devoted to individual topics, including prepress, digital printing, printing technology, packaging, and fonts. And there are great training resources available in the associated PrintPlanet University, a service of PrePress Training Solutions.

- QuarkXPress Forums   *www.quark.com/service/forums*
  While most of the Quark forums are unmoderated, the Printing, PDF, and Fonts forums provide a great way for QuarkXPress users to share and solve real-world printing issues with their peers. Have a problem? You're probably not the only one. And someone else probably has the answer.

- Typographica   *www.typographi.com*
  Typographica is home to lively discussions of font designs, readability issues, and tutorials on font creation, which should give you some deep respect for the efforts of font designers.

Printing Industry Organizations

You may consider yourself to be purely a designer, with no interest in pursuing the technical end of the printing trade. But the online educational resources provided by these printing industry organizations can be very helpful when you want to understand more about printing processes.

- Association of Graphic Communications   *www.agcomm.org*
  An affiliate of GAIN, the AGC provides print-oriented training for graphics software in the northeastern U.S.

- IDEAlliance (International Digital Enterprise Alliance)   *www.idealliance.org*
  IDEAlliance offers seminars (including some that are available online) on highly technical topics such as XML.

- International Prepress Association   *www.ipa.org*
  The IPA offers a great variety of online seminars on a wide range of topics ranging from graphics software to PDF creation to print processes.

- Pacific Printing and Imaging Association   *www.pacprinting.org*
  The PPIA offers training and print-oriented seminars in the Pacific Northwest.

Packaging Organizations

Packaging adds another dimension to the printing process, both literally and figuratively. These packaging organizations offer extensive educational resources.

- Flexographic Technical Association   *www.fta-ffta.org*
  The FTA Web site offers industry news, online articles, and information on upcoming flexography-related events and training sessions.

- Institute of Packaging Professionals   *www.iopp.org*
  The IOPP Web site provides access to an extensive bookstore, comprehensive links to industry resources, and information on packaging conferences and training events.

- Paperboard Packaging Council   *www.ppcnet.org*
  Devoted to the folding-carton industry, the PPC Web site provides numerous informational pieces in PDF format, as well as links to publications and industry events. Additional, premium content is available to PPC members.

Technical Education Organizations

The printing industry contains a number of organizations devoted to education and providing reference materials.

- Graphic Arts Educational and Research Foundation   *www.gaerf.org*

  GAERF was created by the National Association for Printing Leadership (NAPL), The Association for Suppliers of Printing, Publishing and Converting Technologies (known as NPES for some ancestral reason), and the Printing Industries of America, Inc. (PIA). These three associations own the Graphic Arts Show Company, (GASC), which is responsible for a number of industry trade shows, including the huge, annual GraphExpo event in Chicago. GAERF finances educational programs and provides information about these programs on its Web site.

- Graphic Arts Information Network   *www.gain.net*

  A joint effort of Print Industries of America and the Graphic Arts Technical Foundation, GAIN sponsors publication of an extensive library of print-related books, available through the GAIN Web site. There is also an online job bank and links to industry events.

- Specialty Graphic Imaging Association   *www.sgia.org*

  The SGIA focus is on printing processes that fall outside of offset printing. It offers coverage of a diverse range of imaging and printing processes, including screen printing, large-format inkjet printing, and textile printing.

- The National Council for Skill Standards in Graphic Communications   *www.ncssgc.org*

  The National Council for Skill Standards offers educational resources and certification programs for printing-industry professionals.

CONFERENCES AND TRADE SHOWS

Perhaps because the Internet has become such a rich source of information, some graphic arts and printing conferences have evaporated. It's no longer necessary to make a pilgrimage to a trade show for the sole purpose of cornering someone in a booth to get answers to questions about equipment or software. Instead, it's easy to go to a vendor Web site and scroll through posted information. The venerable Seybold Seminars became a casualty of this shift in recent years, a victim of declining attendance. However, there's still a market for the large shows such as DRUPA and On Demand Expo, which feature running presses printing live jobs and finishing equipment spewing out pocketfolders.

Printing Industry Events

In addition to featuring fully operational equipment, most printing exhibitions, conferences, and trade shows offer seminars on printing issues. Some exhibitors provide hands-on educational demos. And don't forget to fill up your bag with all those cute tchotchkes such as promotional light-up pens, squeezable software mascots, and company T-shirts.

- Digital Print World   *www.digitalprintworld.co.uk*

  Geared toward digital printing (as opposed to offset or letterpress printing), the annual Digital Print World is a predominantly British show, but it attracts attendees from all over the European Union.

- DRUPA *www.drupa.com* (English-language site); *www.drupa.de* (German-language site)

  Held every even-numbered year, DRUPA is enormous. That's why it's a two-week event. Featuring nearly 2,000 vendors and welcoming nearly 400,000 attendees, DRUPA is truly an international print show. Attendees can see everything from software vendors to bookbinding machines.

- Graphics of the Americas   *www.graphicsoftheamericas.com*

  This Miami-based trade show is oriented toward Latin American printing consumers. While many exhibitors speak Spanish, and many of the educational sessions are presented in Spanish, it is a fully bilingual show.

- IPEX   *www.ipex.org*

  Held in England, IPEX is very much an international print show, with large attendance from the United States and Europe.

- On Demand Conference and Exposition   *www.ondemandexpo.com*

  Focusing on digital, on-demand printing solutions, the On Demand Expo includes exhibits and educational sessions devoted to variable data printing issues.

- Print/GraphEXPO/Converting Expo   *www.graphexpo.org*

  The GraphEXPO shows in Chicago occur annually, but every four years (2001, 2005, 2009, and so on), they kick it up a notch and present the even larger PRINT show. The PRINT shows include actual operating printing and finishing equipment and occupy the massive McCormick Place Convention Center from the floors to the rafters. Wear comfortable shoes.

Design Conferences

Many design-oriented conferences are worth attending for the hands-on training sessions that are presented by software sponsors or training consultants. Don't forget to leave extra space in your suitcase for those tempting paper samples too.

- AIGA National Conference   *www.aiga.org*

  Because the AIGA partners closely with Adobe and Aquent, conferences often include training sessions.

- HOW Design Conference   *www.howconference.com*

  Software companies such as Adobe, Quark, and Extensis are sponsors and exhibitors at the HOW Design Conference. Take advantage of their hands-on training sessions as well as the software demonstrations in exhibit booths.

- InDesign and Creative Suite Conferences   *www.barrycon.com*

  Both the InDesign Conference and the Creative Suite Conference are well attended by designers and printers. The informal atmosphere encourages real-world questions and the opportunity to network.

Acrobat/PDF Conferences

Entire conferences devoted to a file format? Why, you never hear anyone gushing about a weekend spent at the annual *TIFF Festival*. There is not a theme park named *EPS World*. The fact that there are *two* PDF-themed annual conferences is evidence of the importance of Acrobat and the PDF file format across a wide range of industries.

While you may not be interested in some of the developer-level sessions, there are always sessions devoted to the use of PDF in print. Both conferences are sponsored in part by industry vendors such as Adobe, Enfocus, Global Graphics, and Logitech. Both conferences, held annually, feature training sessions, seminars, and vendor exhibits. Many industry speakers and sponsors participate in both events. How can you choose which conference to attend? Consider the session listings and the location.

- Adobe Acrobat PDF Conference   *www.agitraining.com*
  Presented by the American Graphics Institute, this conference is usually held in Orlando, Florida.

- The PDF Conference   *www.pdfconference.com*
  Presented by Carl Young Training Associates, the PDF Conference is usually held in the fall in the Washington, D.C., area.

DESIGN AND PRINTING BOOKS

I know. We can read PDF files onscreen. But there is still no substitute for the tactile joys of ink on paper. Maybe I'm just old-fashioned, but I still feel that books are the most portable, shareable, tangible way to store information. Besides, how could you fill all those bookshelves with the impressive, leather-bound spines of ... PDFs?

Desktop Publishing

- *Inside the Publishing Revolution: The Adobe Story* by Pam Pfiffner (Adobe Press, 2002)
  This book is a rousing account of the huge upheavals in design and printing that have sprung from Adobe Systems. It introduces you to Adobe co-founders John Warnock and Charles Geschke and many of the inspired Adobe minds, and provides a fascinating timeline for the developments in software and technology that made desktop publishing possible.

- *The Non-Designer's Scan and Print Book* by Sandee Cohen and Robin Williams (Peachpit Press, 1999)

  This concise and very readable book is not just about scanning. It's full of tips about prepress and print production, with many examples to explain the concepts.

General Design

While there are hundreds of books on all aspects of design from color to type to visual concepts, three books stand out for capturing important basics. No fluff, just concise and illuminating concepts to make you think differently about aspects of design that are easily taken for granted.

- *Before and After* by John McWade (Peachpit Press, 2003)

  John McWade makes design and production look so easy. Along with his examples of great design solutions, he explains printing requirements and suggests design approaches that allow you to deal with printing limitations.

- *Before and After Graphics for Business* by John McWade (Peachpit Press, 2005)

- *The Mac is Not a Typewriter,* Second Edition by Robin Williams (Peachpit Press, 2003)

  One of the classic guides for desktop publishing, this book helps you learn the rules for creating professional-looking type. Topics range from avoiding amateur mistakes such as double spaces and straight quotes, to typographic niceties such as kerning and hanging punctuation.

General Printing

Some of these printing tomes are encyclopedic and can be measured by the pound as well as page count. Some are more instructional in nature. It's difficult to single out any of the books in this list—they're all quite good. But I've earmarked several as being essential guides for designers wanting to deepen their understanding of printing.

- *The Basics of Print Production* by Mary Hardesty (Graphic Arts Technical Foundation, 2002)

- *The Complete Guide to Digital Color: Creative Use of Color in the Digital Arts* by Chris Linford (Collins Design, 2004)

- *Desktop Publishing Primer* by Hal Hinderliter (Graphic Arts Technical Foundation, 2004)

- *Forms, Folds, and Sizes: All the Details Graphic Designers Need to Know But Can Never Find* by Poppy Evans (Rockport Press, 2004)

  The title says it all: This is a great guide to important printing issues, and an essential reference for designers.

- *The GATF Guide to Desktop Publishing* by Hal Hinderliter and Jim Cavuoto (Graphic Arts Technical Foundation, 2000)

- *Getting It Printed,* Fourth Edition by Eric Kenly, Mark Beach (HOW Design Books, 2004)

- *Getting it Right in Print: Digital Prepress for Graphic Designers* by Mark Gatter (Harry N. Abrams, 2005)

- *A Guide to Graphic Print Production* by Kaj Johansson, Peter Lundberg, Robert Ryberg (John Wiley and Sons, 2002)

- *Handbook of Digital Publishing, Volume I and II* by Michael L. Kleper (Prentice Hall, 2001)

- *Makeready: A Prepress Resource* by Dan Margulis (Henry Holt and Company, 1996). This book is out of print, but it is worth searching for on used-book sites.

- *Official Adobe Print Publishing Guide,* Second Edition by Brian P. Lawler (Adobe Press, 2005)

  This book covers print processes from offset to digital, with excellent examples explaining such concepts as duotones, trapping, and proofing.

- *PocketPal,* 19th Edition by Michael Bruno, Frank Romano, Michael Riordan (Signet, 2003)

  The *PocketPal* was first published by International Paper Company, and it is updated every few years. It's small but mighty and includes a glossary and great, short explanations of printing processes. You should have a copy in your backpack at all times.

- *Printing Technology* by J. Michael Adams, Penny Ann Dolin (Thomson Delmar Learning, 2001)

Typography

Desktop publishing put typesetting into the hands of many eager typists who often lacked the instincts or training for typographic finesse. But enhancements to design software and the enticing possibilities afforded by OpenType fonts have inspired a return to the art and craft of typography. If you love beautiful typography, or you want to learn more about how typography works as part of designing and printing, here are some books that are part reference, part inspiration.

- *The Complete Manual of Typography* by James Felici (Adobe Press, 2002)

- *The Elements of Typographic Style* by Robert Bringhurst (Hartley and Marks Publishers, 2004)

- *Thinking with Type: A Critical Guide for Designers, Writers, Editors, and Students* by Ellen Lupton (Princeton Arch, 2004)

- *U&lc: Influencing Design and Typography* by John D. Berry, editor (Mark Batty, 2005)

SOFTWARE-SPECIFIC BOOKS

Somehow, the original software manuals are never enough, are they? They're either arcane, or a bit skimpy. And some of them appear to be written by engineers who are proud of the features, but who may have no idea how their software is used in the real world.

Acrobat

- *Adobe Acrobat 7 Tips and Tricks: The 150 Best* by Donna Baker (Adobe Press, 2005)

- *Adobe Acrobat 7 PDF Bible* by Ted Padova (John Wiley and Sons, 2005)

- *Adobe Acrobat 7 for Windows and Macintosh: Visual QuickStart Guide* by Jennifer Alspach (Peachpit Press, 2005)

- *Adobe Reader 7 Revealed: Working Effectively with Acrobat PDF Files* by Ted Padova (Adobe Press, 2005)

- *Reviewing PDF Documents in Acrobat: Visual QuickProject Guide* by Donna Baker (Peachpit Press, 2005)

Adobe Creative Suite

- *Adobe Creative Suite 2 How-Tos: 100 Essential Techniques* by George Penston (Adobe Press, 2005)
- *Real World Adobe Creative Suite 2* by Sandee Cohen, Steve Werner (Peachpit Press, 2006)

Freehand

- *Macromedia FreeHand MX: Training from the Source* by Patti Schulze (Macromedia Press, 2003)
- *Macromedia FreeHand MX for Windows and Macintosh: Visual QuickStart Guide* by Sandee Cohen (Peachpit Press, 2003)

Illustrator

- *Adobe Illustrator CS2 Revealed* by Chris Botello (Course Technology, 2005)
- *Real World Adobe Illustrator CS2* by Mordy Golding (Peachpit Press, 2005)

InDesign

- *Exploring InDesign CS2* by Terry Rydberg (Thomson Delmar Learning, 2005)
- *InDesign Type: Professional Typography with Adobe InDesign CS2* by Nigel French (Adobe Press, 2006)
- *Real World InDesign CS2* by David Blatner, Olav Martin Kvern (Peachpit Press, 2006)

Photoshop

- *Adobe Photoshop CS/CS2 Breakthroughs* by David Blatner, Conrad Chavez (Peachpit Press, 2005)
- *The Photoshop CS2 Help Desk Book* by Dave Cross (Peachpit Press, 2005)
- *Photoshop CS2: Up To Speed* by Ben Willmore (Peachpit Press, 2005)

Photoshop Specialty Topics

You would need to build an addition to your house to hold all of the books written about all the versions and the many aspects of Photoshop. But there are a few indispensable resources that can greatly improve your mastery of Photoshop in production. *Real World Color Management, Second Edition*, for example, is not devoted solely to Photoshop, but it's a classic on the topic of color management.

- *Adobe Photoshop Restoration and Retouching,* Third Edition by Katrin Eismann, Wayne Palmer (New Riders Press, 2005)

- *Photoshop LAB Color: The Canyon Conundrum and Other Adventures in the Most Powerful Colorspace* by Dan Margulis (Peachpit Press, 2005)

- *Photoshop Masking and Compositing* by Katrin Eismann (New Riders Press, 2004)

- *Professional Photoshop: The Classic Guide to Color Correction* by Dan Margulis (John Wiley and Sons, 2002)

- *Real World Color Management,* Second Edition by Bruce Fraser, Chris Murphy, Fred Bunting (Peachpit Press, 2004)

QuarkXPress

At this writing, there are no QuarkXPress 7.0 books to be found. Rest assured, they will start hatching soon.

- *QuarkXPress 6 Bible* by Galen Gruman, Barbara Assadi (John Wiley and Sons, 2003)

- *Real World QuarkXPress 6* by David Blatner (Peachpit Press, 2003)

PUBLICATIONS

If you agonize over using trees to print magazines, note that some of these publications are available electronically. Highly recommended electronic versions include *Before and After Magazine*, *Design Tools Monthly*, *Graphic Exchange Magazine* (which includes QuickTime movies), and *InDesign Magazine*.

Desktop Publishing

- *Design Tools Monthly*   *www.design-tools.com*

  Great tips, bug alerts, and industry news condensed into one great resource. In addition to the monthly newsletter, you receive shareware and freeware software and fonts. Available in both print and downloadable PDF versions.

- *InDesign Magazine*   *www.indesignmag.com*

  Despite the name, InDesign Magazine is about more than just a single program. Published six times a year as an electronic magazine (there is no printed version), this engaging publication includes great tips and tricks, information about bug work-arounds, and articles about printing issues, plug-ins, and design in general.

Design

- *CMYK Magazine*   *www.cmykmag.com*

- *Dynamic Graphics Magazine*   *www.dynamicgraphics.com*

- *Graphic Exchange Magazine*   *www.gxo.com*

- *HOW Magazine*   *www.howdesign.com*

- *I.D. Magazine*   *www.idonline.com*

- *Print Magazine*   *www.printmag.com*

- *STEP Inside Design*   *www.stepinsidedesign.com*

Printing Technology

- *American Printer   www.americanprinter.com*
- *Electronic Publishing Magazine   ep.pennnet.com/home.cfm*
- *Graphic Arts Monthly   www.gammag.com*
- *Package Design Magazine   www.packagedesignmag.com*
- *Printing Impressions Magazine   www.piworld.com*

Tutorials

- *Before and After Magazine   www.bamagazine.com*
- *Layers Magazine   www.layersmagazine.com*
- *X-Ray Magazine   www.xraymag.com*

DESTINATIONS

Maybe I'm the only person who would go to a printing-themed museum on vacation.

Oh, I'm not? Good! I'll see you there!

- Robert C. Willliams Paper Museum   *www.ipst.edu/amp*
  Institute of Paper Science and Technology
  Georgia Institute of Technology
  500 10th Street NW
  Atlanta, GA 30332-0620

- Ben Franklin's Courtyard and Print Shop   *www.ushistory.org/tour/tour_fcourt.htm*
  318 Market Street
  Philadelphia, PA 19106

- Crane Museum of Papermaking   *www.crane.com/about/museum*
  30 South Street
  Dalton, MA 01226

- Hamilton Wood Type and Printing Museum   *www.woodtype.org*
  1619 Jefferson Street
  Two Rivers, Wisconsin 54241

- International Printing Museum   *www.printmuseum.org*
  315 Torrance Boulevard
  Carson, CA 90745

- Museum of Printing History   *www.printingmuseum.org*
  1324 West Clay Street
  Houston, Texas 77019

- Museum of Printing   *www.museumofprinting.org*
  800 Massachusetts Avenue
  North Andover, MA 01845

INDEX

4-Color Process Guide, Pantone, 34
3D artwork, Adobe Illustrator, 179-180

A

a lowly apprentice production, inc. (ALAP), 102
AAs (artist alterations), 12
Acrobat. *See* Adobe Acrobat
activating fonts in operating system, 113-114
Adobe Acrobat, 287-317
    7.0 Professional, 8, 133, 288-317
    Acrobat Distiller, 293-296
    cross-platform issues, 287, 292
    font embedding, 299
    graphics editing, 301-304
    image content, 296-298
    PDF files, 289-299
        external PDF editors, 316-317
        table of PDF-creation settings, 291
        see also PDF (Portable Document Format)
        files
    print production toolbar, 304-316
    product line, 288
    production tips, 287-317
    settings and standards, 290-292
    text editing, 300-301
    types of files, 289-290
Adobe Bridge, 218, 232
Adobe FreeHand, 189-215
    binding and finishing considerations, 54, 57-58
    bleed considerations, 210-211
    creating multiple pages, 106
    EPS, 87, 98
    exporting PDF files, 212-215
    exporting raster formats, 208
    exporting vector formats, 208-211
    fills and strokes, 199-205
    fonts and graphics, 189-195
    incorporating images into vector files, 103
    lens effects, 198
    live raster effects, 196-197
    live vector effects, 196
    native file formats, 99

    production tips, 189-215
    simplifying complex artwork, 206-207
    text in vector artwork, 101
Adobe Gamma, 48
Adobe Garamond Pro, 109
Adobe Illustrator, 165-187
    blended objects, 185
    Clean Up function, 172
    creating multiple pages, 106
    Creative Suite (CS)
        importance of version, 165-169
        vector graphics, 99
    3D artwork, 179-180
    EPS, 98-99
    filters and effects, 174-179
    guidelines, 57
    images
        incorporating into vector files, 103
        linked and embedded, 184
    importance of version, 165-169
    incorporating images into vector files, 103
    native file formats, 99, 227, 230
    OpenType fonts, 110, 166
    Pantone recipes, 186-187
    PDF files, 10, 100
    planning for bleed, 54
    production tips, 165-187
    saving for earlier versions, 170-171
    saving for other applications, 187
    Simplify function, 172
    simplifying complex artwork, 172-173
    Transform palette, 58
    transparency, 149-150, 180-183
    trapping, 11
    vector-based EPSs, 87
Adobe InDesign, 217-262
    color palette, 231-232
    control palette, 58
    converting QuarkXPress and PageMaker files, 238-242
    copying and pasting into, 221
    document issues, 243-246
    fonts, 108, 110

graphics, 217-226
guidelines, 57
libraries, 246
native files, 99, 227-230
OPI/APR workflows, 83
page size, 52
PDF creation methods and settings, 260-262
PDF files, 10
planning for bleed, 54, 244-245
preflight considerations, 8
problems, 256-259
production tips, 217-262
silhouettes, 153-154
swatches, 231-238
swatches palette, 231-232
TIFF, 83
transparency, 149-150, 247-255
variable data, 44
vector graphics, 98-99
Adobe Lightroom™, 79
Adobe-Microsoft collaboration, 112
Adobe Multiple Master Fonts, 112
Adobe Myriad Pro, 110
Adobe PageMaker
    converting files to InDesign documents, 238-241
    TIFF, 87
    variable data, 44
Adobe PDF. See PDF (Portable Document Format) files
Adobe Photoshop
    album, 79
    color considerations, 145, 148
    color management, 47-48
    converting RGB to CMYK, 146
    creating duotones, 156-157
    desktop publishing, 3
    elements, 79
    EPS, 87
    gradients, prepress production, 9
    image resolution, 145
    image size considerations, 143-144
    layered files, 146-148
    multilayered files as part of job submission, 134
    native files, 88-89, 148, 160, 227-230, 265, 283
    native PSD files. See native files
    OpenType fonts, 110
    Photoshop Album, 79
    production tips, 143-163
    saving files, 161-163
    scaling up, 81
    scanners, 78
    silhouettes and masking, 150-156
    spot color, 158
    transparency, 149-150
    vector elements, 159-163
Adobe Photoshop Album, 79
Adobe Photoshop Elements, 79
Adobe PostScript
    convert to PDF, Acrobat Distiller, 293-295, 315
    description, 23
    desktop publishing, 3
    EPS, 72, 74, 86-89, 97-99
    fonts (Type 1), 107-108
    RIPs, 10
    transparency, limitations, 181-182
Adobe Reader, 288
ALAP (a lowly apprentice production, inc.), 102
Aldus PageMaker, 3
Alsoft, MasterJuggler, 114
alterations. See corrections
alternative silhouetting methods, 154-156
Apago, Inc., 8, 304
Aperture, Apple, 79
Apple, 3
    see also Macintosh
Apple Aperture, 79
Apple Font Book, 113
Apple iPhoto, 79
Apple LaserWriter, 3
Apple-Microsoft collaboration, 108
APR (automatic picture replacement), 83
aqueous coatings, 17, 42
Art Files, 101
artist alterations (AAs), 12
Artwork Systems, 10, 296
automatic font activation, 115
automatic picture replacement (APR), 83
automatic recovery, 243

B
baseline, 17
BBEdit, 285
Bézier shapes, 104
binding and finishing, 14-15, 20, 51-75
    basic rules, 52-55
    bindery, 17

binding methods, 65-68
folding, 55-58
imposition, 58-64
multidimensional considerations, 69-75
black
black-and-white printing, 27-29
rich black, 39-40, 45
blanket, 17
Blatner, David, 264
bleed
checking for job submission, 131
common problem, 8
die cut pieces, 72
exporting FreeHand files, 210-211
importance of planning, 54
InDesign document, 244-245
blended objects, 185
blind embossing, 74
bluelines, 2, 11, 17, 139
BMP, Windows, 95
Bridge, Adobe, 218, 232
bump plate, 158
Bunting, Fred, 47

C

calibration of monitors, 48
camera-ready art, 3, 17
cameramen, 2, 17
case binding, 65-66
Caslon Pro, 109
CEPS (color electronic prepress systems), 2-3, 17
CGATS (Committee for Graphic Arts Technologies Standards), 292
characters and glyphs, 109, 111
chase, 17
choke, 37-38
clipping paths, 151-154, 270-271
CMYK (cyan, magenta, yellow, black)
adding spot color, 158
Adobe Illustrator, 171
checking raster images, 129
converting RGB to, 146, 311
converting screen captures to, 92-93
description, 30
imaging software that does not support, 79-80, 100-101
inDesign, 219, 231-232
limitations, 33-34

PDF files, 292
QuarkXPress, 273
versus RGB, 94
TIFF, 87
see also color
coatings and varnishes, 42-43
Code Line Communications, 101
coil binding, 15, 17, 68
Collect for Output feature, QuarkXPress, 280-281
color, 30-43
approximating spot colors with process, 35-36
black. *See* black
CEPS (color electronic prepress systems), 2-3, 17
CMYK. *See* CMYK (cyan, magenta, yellow, black)
color break, 4, 17
Color Bridge, Pantone, 36
Color Formula Guides from Pantone, 34
Color Key, 2, 18
color management, 47
color mode, 171
color temperature, 18
colorimeter, 48
corrections, 148
HSB (Hue-Saturation-Brightness), 171
ICC (International Color Consortium), 94
inks. *See* inks
mechanical color, 4, 22
moiré, 31-32
multi-ink colors, 273
Photoshop production, 145-146, 148
process colors, 30, 35-36
QuarkXPress, 273-274
Real World Color Management, 2nd ed., 47
RGB. *See* RGB (red-green-blue)
rich black, 39-40, 45
separations, 18, 78, 158, 194
spot color. *See* spot color
swatches. *See* swatches
Toyo, 19, 34, 41, 127, 231, 273
TRUMATCH, 35-36, 231, 273
comb binding, 15, 18, 67
Committee for Graphic Arts Technologies Standards (CGATS), 292
common problems encountered in preflight, 7-8
comp, 18
composition zones, QuarkXPress 7.0, 282

compression
    PDF file settings, 297-298
    recompressing, 95
    WinZip, 133
    Zip disks, 136
computer-to-plate (CTP)
    contract proofs, 50
    creating plates, 12
    definition, 18
    prepress, 8
    stochastic screening, 32
Connolly, Bob, 290
continuous tone, 18
contract proof, 11-13
    definition, 18
    importance, 50
conversions
    CMYK
        converting RGB to, 146, 311
        converting screen captures to, 92-93
    Convert Colors, 311
    PageMaker files, converting to InDesign, 238-241
    PDF (Portable Document Format) files, 293-295, 293-295, 315, 315
    QuarkXPress, converting files to InDesign documents, 238-242
copying and pasting into InDesign, 221
Corel Corporation, 80
corrections, 12
    color, 148
    retouching, 129
    see also editing; proofs
creating PDF files, 289-299
creating plates, 12-13
Creating Rich Internet Media Publications, 290
Cromalin proofs, 2, 19
cropping images, 84
cross-platform issues, 119-124
    file naming. See file naming for cross-platform use
    fonts, 123-124
    graphics applications, 119
    graphics formats, 124
    job submissions, 135
CSR (customer service representative), 6, 126-127

CTP (computer-to-plate)
    contract proofs, 50
    creating plates, 12
    prepress, 8
    stochastic screening, 32
cure, 19
custom binding, 68
custom fills, 204
custom halftone settings, 204
custom mixed inks, 19, 41-42
customer alterations, 12
customer service representative (CSR), 6, 126-127

D
Dainippon Ink and Chemicals, Inc., 34
DCS 2.0 (Desktop Color Separations), 158
DCS (Desktop Color Separation) images, 194
DDAP (Digital Distribution of Advertising for Publications), 292
debossing, 19, 74
definitions, 17-25
    slang terms, 52
Desktop Color Separation (DCS) images, 194
Desktop Color Separations (DCS 2.0), 158
desktop printer considerations, 49
desktop publishing, advent, 3-4
dfonts, 111-112, 265
DIC Guide, 34
die line, 70, 72
diecutting, 2, 15, 19, 71-73
digital cameras, quality, 79
Digital Distribution of Advertising for Publications (DDAP), 292
digital photographs, 84
digital press, 19
digital printing, 13, 43-46
    advantages, 43-44
    challenges, 44-46
    Pantone colors for, 45-46
Distiller, Acrobat, 293-296
DocuColor™, 46
document color mode, 171
document construction, 105-106
Document Raster Effects Settings, 178-179
dot etchers, 2, 19
dot gain, 19, 28
dots per inch (dpi), 29

double hit, 39
Douma, Mark, 111, 265
downsampling, 297
dpi (dots per inch), 29
drag and drop in InDesign, advantages and disadvantages, 218-220
drawing programs, 53
drop shadows, 88, 99
  Adobe Illustrator, 175-179
  InDesign, 230, 255
  QuarkXPress, 268, 283
  transparency, 149-150
dummy
  folding, 62
  importance of creating, 69
duotone images, 87, 146, 156-157

E

edges, 55
editing
  EPS files, 98
  external PDF editors, 316
  PDF files, 299-304
effects and filters, Adobe Illustrator, 174-179
embedded path, 271
embedding fonts, 101-102, 133, 299
embedding images, 221-222
  FreeHand, 191
  Illustrator, 184
  InDesign, 221-222
  vector files, 103, 130
embossing, 2, 19, 73-74
encapsulated PostScript. *See* EPS
End User License Agreements (EULAs), 116-118, 134, 299
  see also licensing issues
Enfocus PitStop, 8, 287, 301, 303
EPS (encapsulated PostScript)
  diecutting and embossing, 72, 74
  editing of files, 98
  exporting FreeHand files, 207-210
  placement of files, 98
  raster images, formats for print, 86-89
  saving Illustrator files, 170, 184, 187
  vector graphics, 97-99
estimators, 7, 19

EULAs (End User License Agreements), 116-118, 134, 299
  see also licensing issues
exporting files
  Adobe FreeHand, 208-215
  bleed, 210-211
  PDF (Portable Document Format) files
    FreeHand, 195, 212-215
    QuarkXPress, 276-278, 284
  QuarkXPress, 276-278, 284
  raster formats, 101, 208
  vector formats, 208-211
Extensis FontReserve, 114
Extensis™ Suitcase, 108, 114-115
Extensis™ Suitcase Fusion, 108, 114-115
extrude, 205
Eye-One Display 2, 48

F

files
  compression. *See* compression
  cross-platform use, file naming for
    file extensions, 122-123
    forbidden names, 122
    path designation, 120
    punctuation, 121
    submitting files for print, 130
  extensions, 122-123
  file path designation, 120
  hybrid, 159-162
  multilayered, 134, 146-148
  native, 99
  page layout, 131-132
  submitting, 132-136
  see also EPS, PDF, TIFF, vector, raster
film strippers, 2, 20
filters and effects, Adobe Illustrator, 174-179
finishing. *See* binding and finishing
FireWire, 136
flatness value, 152
flats, 2, 12, 20
flattening layered files, 148
flattening transparency, 181-183, 247-255, 315
flexography, 13, 20
FlightCheck Designer, 132-133, 259
FlightCheck Professional, 8, 132-133
FlightCheck Studio, 132, 259

fluorescent inks, 41
FM (frequency modulation) screening, 32
foil stamping, 2, 20, 41, 75
folding, 14, 56-58
folding dummy, 20, 62
fonts, 107-118
   activating in operating system, 113-114
   activation applications, 108, 115
   automatic font activation, 115
   checking vector artwork for job submission,
      130
   conflicts, 115
   cross-platform issues, 123-124
   embedding, 101-102, 101-102, 133, 133, 299,
      299
   font handling, FreeHand, 190
   FontAgent Pro, 108, 114-115
   FontDoctor™, Morrison SoftDesign, 115
   FontReserve, Extensis, 114
   licensing issues, 116-118
   major formats, 107-113
   management programs, 114-115
   OpenType, 109-111, 115, 282
   .pfb, 107
   .pfn, 107
   PostScript (Type 1), 107-108, 123
   printer fonts, 107
   QuarkXPress, 265, 282
   screen fonts, 107
   subsetting, 117, 299
   substituting, 113
   TrueType, 108
FontAgent Pro, 108, 114-115
FontDoctor™, Morrison SoftDesign, 115
FontReserve, Extensis, 114
FPO (for position only) scans
   definition, 20
   preparing raster images, 82-84
   prepress, 8
Fraser, Bruce, 47
FreeHand. See Adobe FreeHand
frequency modulation (FM) screening, 32
Fujifilm/Enovation, 94
fulfillment, 16

G
Gamma, Adobe, 48
ganged, 20
Garamond Pro, Adobe, 109
Genuine Fractals, 84
ghosted replica, 168
GIF (Graphics Interchange Format), 95
glazed embossing, 74
Global Graphics, 10, 274, 289, 296
glossary of printing terms, 17-25
   slang terms, 52
glue flap, 71
gluing, 15
Gluon's Pro Grids & Guides, 57
glyphs and characters, 109, 111
gradient fills, 199
gradients, 9
graphics
   cross-platform issues, 119, 124
   editing, PDF files, 301-304
   Graphics Interchange Format (GIF), 95
   InDesign
      editing, 224-225
      embedding and unembedding, 221-222
      placing, 217-221
      transforming, 225-226
      updating missing or modified, 222-224
   PNG (Portable Network Graphics), 95
   QuarkXPress, 269-272
      clipping paths, 270-271
      PDFs as artwork, 272
   vector graphics. See vector graphics
Graphics Interchange Format (GIF), 95
gravure, 13, 20
GretagMacbeth, 48, 50
guidelines, folding, 57

H
hairlines, 314
halftone, 20, 28
halftone dots, 28
hinting, 102, 130
history of print production, 1-4
hot type, 2, 20
HP ElectroInk, 45
HP Indigo, 43, 45
HSB (Hue-Saturation-Brightness), 171
hybrid files, 159-162

I

ICC (International Color Consortium), 94
IDLK files, 243
iGen3™, 46
Illustrator. *See* Adobe Illustrator
images, 9
  embedded images
    FreeHand, 191
    Illustrator, 184
    InDesign, 221-222
    vector files, 103, 130
  formats for print
    appropriate, 86-94, 194
    inappropriate, 95-96, 100-101
  image swap, 83
  imagesetters, 21, 46, 130, 181
  imaging software, 79-80
  importing, 193
  incorporating images into vector files, 103-104
  linked images
    FreeHand, 191-193
    Illustrator, 184
    vector files, 103, 130
  PDF files, handling image content, 296-298
  proofs, checking, 136-137
  raster images. *See* raster images and raster
    image processor (RIP)
  rotating, 85, 130-131, 144
  ultimate use issues, 143-145
  vector graphics. *See* vector graphics
  see also Adobe Illustrator; Adobe Photoshop
importing files
  Adobe Illustrator, Creative Suite (CS), 165-169
  FreeHand, 194-195
  images, importing, 193
  PDF, 195, 276-278
  QuarkXPress, 276-278
  raster images, 194-195
  scaling, 194-195
  version, importance of, 165-169
imposition, 8, 11
  basic imposition, 59-60
  definition, 21, 58
  multipage imposition, 60-64
InDesign. *See* Adobe InDesign
Ink Manager, 180, 235-237, 312

inks, 27-50
  custom mixed, 41-42
  large coverage areas, 38-39
  metallic and fluorescent, 41
  multi-ink colors, 273
  problem, 40-41
  rich black, 39-40
  specialty, 41
  spot colors, 34-35
  see also CMYK, RGB
Insider Software, 108, 114
International Color Consortium (ICC), 94
interpolation, 81
Iomega JAZ, 136
iPhoto, Apple, 79

J

Jaws, Global Graphics, 274, 284, 289
JDF (Job Definition Format), 282, 316
job jacket, 6, 21, 282
job submission, 125-141
  checklists, planning for print, 128-132
    page layout files, 131-132
    raster images, 129-130
    vector artwork, 130-131
  communication with print service provider,
    126-127
  press check, 140-141
  proofing cycles
    corrections, 139
    image proofs, 136-137
    imposed bluelines, 139
    page proofs, 138-139
    signing off on proofs, 140
  sending job files, 132-136
    application files, 133-136
    InDesign's Package function, 259
    PDF files, 133
    QuarkXPress, Collect for Output feature,
    280-281
job ticket, 6-7, 21, 282
JPEG compression, 298
JPEG (Joint Photographic Experts Group), 95-96

K

kiss plate, 158
knock out, 21
Kodak, 43, 94

L

aminate, 21
LaserWriter, Apple, 3
layered files, 134, 146-148, 163, 229-230
layout adjustment, 246
layout spaces, 264
leading, 21
lens effects, 198
letterpress printing, 13, 21
licensing issues, 116-118, 134, 299
    Acrobat Distiller, 294
    fonts, 116-118, 299
lighting considerations, 48
Lightroom™, Adobe, 79
line shots, 21
linen tester, 21
lines per inch, 28
linking images
    FreeHand, 191-193
    Illustrator, 184
    vector files, 103, 130
Linux, 292
lithography, 21
live raster effects, 196-197
live vector effects, 196
LiveCycle™ Designer, 292
lossless compression, 298
lossy, 95
loupe, 21
lower case, 21
lpi (lines per inch), 29

M

Macintosh, 48, 99, 101
    Acrobat Distiller, 293
    cross-platform issues, 119-124, 292
    QuarkXPress, 264-265, 268, 279
    see also Apple
Macintosh OS X System Fonts, 111-112, 123

Macromedia FreeHand. See Adobe FreeHand
makeready, 7, 13, 21
management programs, fonts, 114-115
"marching ants," 147, 151
Markzware, 8, 132, 238, 259, 285
masking and silhouettes, 150-154
MasterJuggler, Alsoft, 114
Matching System, Pantone, 34
matchprint proofs, 2, 22
mechanical, 1, 22
mechanical color, 4, 22
metallic inks, 41
metamerism, 50
Microsoft, 80
    Adobe collaboration, 112
    Apple collaboration, 108
    Office applications, 87, 288
    Windows, 48, 95, 100-101, 110, 112, 114
    Word, 87
mock up, 22
moiré
    black-and-white printing, 29
    color printing, 31-32
MonacoOPTIX, 48
monitor considerations, 47-48
Morrison SoftDesign, FontDoctor™, 115
multi-ink colors, 273
multidimensional pieces, 69-75
multilingual support from OpenType fonts, 110
multiple images, importing, 193
Multiple Master Fonts, Adobe, 112
multiple pages, creating in Illustrator and
        FreeHand, 106
Murphy, Chris, 47
Myriad Pro, Adobe, 110

N

native files
    Illustrator native files (AI), 99, 227, 230
    InDesign CS2, 229-230
    Photoshop native files (PSD)
        advantages, 148, 160
        description, 88-89
        InDesign, 227-230
        QuarkXPress, 265, 283

O

Office applications, 87, 288
offset printing, 13, 22
on-press imaging, 13
onOne Software, 84
open prepress interface (OPI), 9, 22, 83
OpenType Fonts, 109-111
operating systems
    activating fonts in, 113-114
    Linux, 292
    Macintosh. *See* Macintosh
    platform issues. *See* cross-platform issues
    Unix, 121
    Windows. *See* Windows, Microsoft
OPI (open prepress interface), 9, 22, 83
outlining text, 102-103, 118, 130, 268
oxidation of metallic inks, 41

P

age creep, 63
page-layout applications, 3
page layout files
    checking for print, 131-132
    final package components, 134
page proofs. *See* proofs
PageMaker, Adobe. *See* Adobe PageMaker
PageMaker, Aldus, 3
Paint Shop Pro, 80
Painter™, 80
Palm OS, 292
Pantone
    4-Color Process Guide, 34, 187
    changes in recipes, 186-187
    Color Bridge, 36
    colors for digital presses, 45-46
    Matching System, 34
paths
    file path designation, 120
    images, 151-154, 270-271
    see also silhouettes
pattern fills, 199-200
PDF (Portable Document Format) files
    Acrobat Distiller, 293-296
    bleed information, 312
    compression settings, 297-298
    conversions, 293-295, 315
    creating PDF files, 289-299

    creation methods, 260-261
    creation settings, 261-262, 291
    editing PDF files, 299-304
    exports and imports
        FreeHand, 195, 212-215
        QuarkXPress, 276-278, 284
    external PDF editors, 316-317
    files as artwork, 231
    font embedding, 299
    graphics, editing, 301-304
    image content, 296-298
    PDF Enhancer, Apago, Inc., 304
    PDF Optimizer, 311, 315
    PDF Print Engine, 10
    PDF Reference, 289
    PDF/X-1a and PDF/X-3 and PDF/A-1b, 282, 292
    print engine, 10
    print production toolbar, Acrobat 7.0, 311, 315
    print to Distiller/PDF printer, 278
    print to PostScript, Distill manually, 279
    QuarkXPress, 274-279
    raster images, 88-89
    resolution settings, 297
    saving hybrid files, 161-162
    settings and standards, 290-292
    submitting PDF files to print service provider, 133
    table of PDF-creation settings, 291
    text editing, 300-301
    trim information, 312
    types of files, 289-290
    vector graphics, 100
Pen tool, 150, 152, 271
percentage opacity, 149-150
perfect binding, 15, 22, 65-66
personalization, 22
.pfb (printer font binary), 107
.pfm (printer font metrics), 107
Photoshop. *See* Adobe Photoshop
pica, 22
PitStop, Enfocus, 8, 195, 287, 301, 303
PitStop Professional, 195
pixels
    definition, 77
    generating, 175-177
    hiding, 147
    pixels per inch (ppi), 29, 80

placement of EPS files, 98

planners, 7, 22

plates

bump plate, 158

creating, 12-13

CTP. *See* CTP (computer-to-plate)

kiss plate, 158

platesetters, 23, 46, 130, 181

touch plate, 158

platforms. *See* operating systems

PNG (Portable Network Graphics), 95

pocket folder, 69

Pocket PC, 292

point, 23

point text, 98-99, 169

Portable Document Format. *See* PDF (Portable Document Format) files

Portable Network Graphics (PNG), 95

post binding, 68

PostScript. *See* Adobe PostScript

PostScript emulation, 201

PostScript fills, 200-201

PostScript (Type 1) fonts, 107-108, 123

ppi (pixels per inch), 29, 80

preflight, 4, 7-8

Adobe Acrobat, 308-311

checking files for submission, 132-133

definition, 23

InDesign's preflight and Package functions, 259

prepress, 8-12, 23

open prepress interface (OPI), 9, 22, 83

press check, 2, 14, 23, 140-141

press issues, 36-43

press proof, 23

press room, 13-14

print job, steps in, 4-16

print production toolbar, Acrobat 7.0, 304-316

Add Printer Marks, 312

Convert Colors, 311

Crop Pages, 313

Fix Hairlines, 314

Ink Manager, 312

JDF (Job Definition Format), 316

Output Preview, 305-307

PDF Optimizer, 311, 315

Preflight, 308-311

Transparency Flattening, 315

Trap Presets, 316

print service provider

communication, 126-127

fonts, 118

guidelines and specifications, 55, 132-133, 135

settings for print-ready PDF, 295

submitting files to, 132-136, 191

printers

alterations, 12

desktop printers, 49

fonts. *See* fonts

printer's spreads, 23, 60-61, 132

printing, black-and-white, 27-29

printing, color. *See* color

printing plant, job flow diagram, 5

printing terms, glossary, 17-25

Pro Grids & Guides, Gluon's, 57

problem inks, 40-41

problem-solving, InDesign

Info palette, 258

preflight and Package, 259

tools, 256-258

problem-solving, QuarkXPress, 285-286

process, approximating spot colors with, 35-36

process color guides, 35

process colors, 30

production, 4, 8

production tips

Acrobat, 287-317

FreeHand, 189-215

Illustrator, 165-187

InDesign, 217-262

Photoshop, 143-163

QuarkXPress, 263-286

profiling, 47

Project Camelot, 287

projects, QuarkXPress, 264-265

proofs, 2, 22

contract, 11-13, 50

definition, 23

image, 136-137

page, 138-139

signing off, 140

PSD (Photoshop native files)

advantages, 148, 160

description, 88-89

InDesign, 227-230

QuarkXPress, 265, 283

Q

Quark Job Jackets, 282
Quark XPert Guides, 57
QuarkVista™ Picture Effects, 266-267
QuarkXPress, 263-286
    cautions, 267-281
        Collect for Output feature, 280-281
        colors, 273-274
        graphics, 269-272
        PDF files, 274-279
        text styling, 267-269
    converting files to InDesign documents, 238-242
    fonts, 265
        see also OpenType fonts
    gradients, 9
    Measurements Palette, 9
    OpenType fonts, 110, 282
    page size, 52
    Photoshop native files, 88, 265, 283
    planning for bleed, 54
    preflight, 8
    problem solving, 285-286
    production tips, 263-286
    projects, 264-265
    saving files to earlier versions, 264-266
    silhouettes, 153-154
    TIFF, 87
    transparency, 149-150, 283
    trapping, 11
    vector graphics, 98-99
    version 7.0, 281-284
        exporting PDF files, 284
        native images, 283
        new features, 281-283
    versions, 263-267
QuarkXPress 4 Book, 264
Quite a Box of Tricks, Quite Software, 304

R

random proofs, 136
raster images and raster image processor (RIP)
    appropriate image formats, 86-94
    black-and-white printing, 29
    checklist, planning for print, 129-130
    contract proofs, 50
    definition, 23
    description, 8-10
    equipment, 78-80
    imaging software, 79-80
    inappropriate image formats, 95-96
    live raster effects, 196-197
    raster formats, exporting, 101, 208
    raster images, preparing, 77-96
    rasterizing, 88
    resolution and image fidelity, 80-86
    TrueType fonts, 108
rasterizing, 88
reader's spreads, 60, 132
Ready, Set, Go!, 3
Real World Color Management, 2nd ed., 47
Real World QuarkXPress 5.0, 264
Real World QuarkXPress 6.0, 264
recompressing, 95
Reflex Blue, 40-41
registered embossing, 74
registration
    definition, 23
    digital printing, 45
    printing inks, 36-37
resolution
    checking raster images, 129
    DCS images, 194
    fonts, 107
    Illustrator considerations, 174-179, 184
    image fidelity, 80-86
    importing images into FreeHand, 193
    InDesign considerations, 234, 250
    monitor, 90-91
    Photoshop considerations, 145
    QuarkXPress considerations, 275-276
    screen ruling, 46
    settings, PDF file, 295-297
    stochastic screening, 32
    transparency flattening, 315
    vector artwork, 97, 130, 159-160

retouching, 129
reversing out, 39
RGB (red-green-blue)
    Adobe Illustrator, 171
    checking raster images, 129
    versus CMYK, 94
    computer monitor, 33
    converting to CMYK, 146, 311
    image format features, 89
    inappropriate image formats for print, 95-96
    InDesign, 219, 231-232
    PDF files, 292
    QuarkXPress, 273
    screen captures, 92
    TIFF, 87
    see also color
rich black, 39-40, 45
RIP. *See* raster images and raster image processor
ROOM (RIP Once, Output Many), 24
rotating images, 85, 130-131, 144

S
saddle stitching, 14-15, 24, 65
salesperson, 6, 126
save dialogs, Adobe Illustrator, issues, 170-171
saving QuarkXPress files to earlier versions, 264-266
scaling
    checking page layout files, 131
    raster images, 81-82, 130
    raster images imported into FreeHand, 194-195
    vector graphics, 97
scaling down, 82
scaling up, 81
scanners and scanning, 2, 9, 24, 78
    FPO. *See* FPO (for position only) scans
scatter proofs, 136
schedulers, 7, 24
scoring, 24, 71
screen angle, 31
screen captures, 90-93
    converting to CMYK, 92-93
screen fonts, 107
screen frequency, 28
screen printing, 13, 24

screen readers, 300
screen ruling, 28
service bureau license, 117
ShadowCaster, 150
shadows, 205
    drop shadows. *See* drop shadows
shared layouts, QuarkXPress 7.0, 281
sharp, 38
sheetfed press, 24
shingling, 64
shipping, 16
short runs and digital printing, 43-44
signature, 14, 24, 60
signing off on proofs, 140
silhouettes
    alternative methods, 154-156
    definition, 24
    masking, 150-154
    prepress, 8
simplifying complex artwork
    FreeHand, 206-207
    Illustrator, 172-173
single layout mode, QuarkXPress 7.0, 281
size
    images, 143-144
    trim size, 52
slang terms, 52
    see also glossary of printing terms
smudge, 205
Snap view, 308
software versions, issue with print provider, 134-135
specialty finishing, 2
specialty inks, 41
spiral binding. *See* coil binding
spot application of coatings and varnishes, 43
spot colors
    adding to CMYK image, 158
    approximating with process, 35-36
    description, 34-35
    designations, 35
    digital printing, 45-46
    Pantone recipes, 186-187
    transparency and overprinting, 254
spread, 37-38
stitching, 14

stochastic screening, 32
StuffIt, 133
submitting job files to print service provider, 132-136, 191
    application files, 133-136
    PDF files, 133
subsetting fonts, 117, 299
substituting fonts, 113
Suitcase, Extensis, 108, 114-115
Suitcase Fusion, Extensis, 108, 114-115
swatches, 231-238
    colorizing images, 237-238
    InDesign Color palette and Swatches palette, 231-232
    Ink Manager, 235-237
    problems, 233-235
    see also color
Symbian OS, 292

T
tagged image file format (TIFF), 87-89, 96
text
    fonts. *See* fonts
    lower case, 21
    PDF files, 300-301
    styling buttons, 267
    synchronized, 264
    TextPad, 285
    TextWrangler, 285
    Unicode, 109
    uppercase, 25
    vector files, handling text
        checking for job submission, 131
        embedding fonts, 101-102
        outlining text, 102-103
TextPad, 285
textured fills, 202
TextWrangler, 285
three dimensional pieces, 69-75
thumbnail drag, 285
TIFF (tagged image file format), 87-89, 96, 265
tiled fills, 202-203
toolbars. *See* print production toolbar, Acrobat 7.0
touch plate, 158
TouchUp Bug in Photoshop CS2, 302

Toyo, 19, 34, 41, 127, 231, 273
trade shops, 2, 24
transparency
    blend space, 248
    definition, 24
    flattener presets, 249-252
    flattening, Acrobat, 315
    flattening, Illustrator, 181-183
    flattening, InDesign, 247-255
    Illustrator, 180-183
    InDesign, 247-255
    Photoshop, 149-150
    PostScript, limitations, 181-182
    QuarkXPress, 283
trapping
    definition, 24
    description, 37-38
    prepress, 8, 11
    trap presets, Acrobat, 316
trim
    PDF files
        trim information, 312
    trim size, 52
trimming, 14, 54
TrueType Fonts, 108, 123
TRUMATCH, 35-36, 231, 273
Type 1 fonts (PostScript), 107-108, 123
typesetters and typesetting, 2, 25

U
ultraviolet (UV) coatings, 42
Unicode, 109
Unix and file names, 121
UPC (universal product code), 25
uppercase, 25

V

variable data, 13
    digital printing, 43-44
    variable data printing (VDP), 25
varnishes and coatings, 42-43
VDP (variable data printing), 25
vector graphics, 97-106
    avoiding unnecessary complexity, 104-106
    checklist, planning for print, 130-131
    file formats
        EPS (encapsulated PostScript), 97-99
        exporting vector formats, 208-211
        formats not appropriate for print, 100-101
        native file formats, 99
        PDF (Adobe Portable Document Format), 100
    filter *versus* effect, Adobe Illustrator, 174
    incorporating images, 103-104
    live vector effects, 196
    Photoshop, 159-163
    resolution, 97, 130, 159-160
    text, 101-103
    vector file formats, 97-101
viewing booth, 25

W

Warnock, Dr. John, 287
watched folder, 294
web press, 25
Windows, Microsoft, 48, 95
    Acrobat Distiller, 293
    Control Panel, 110, 114
    cross-platform issues, 119-124, 292
    Enhanced Metafile Format (EMF), 101
    system fonts, 112
    Windows Metafile Format (WMF), 100
WinZip, 133
wire binding, 15, 25, 68

X

X-Rite, 48
Xeikon, 43, 45-46
Xerox, 43, 46
XPert Guides, Quark, 57
XPert Print, 102
XTensions, 57, 150, 263

Z

ZIP compression, 298
Zip disks, 136